Mediation and Crim

Mediation
and Criminal Justice

Victims, Offenders and Community

Edited by
Martin Wright and Burt Galaway

Ⓢ SAGE Publications
London ● Newbury Park ● New Delhi

Editorial matter and arrangement © Martin Wright and Burt Galaway 1989
Introduction and Chapter 18 © Martin Wright 1989
Chapter 1 © Dean E. Peachey 1989
Chapter 2 © John Harding 1989
Chapter 3 © Helen Reeves 1989
Chapter 4 © Mark Chupp 1989
Chapter 5 © June Veevers 1989
Chapter 6 © Rose Ruddick 1989
Chapter 7 © Mark S. Umbreit 1989
Chapter 8 © Gilles Launay and Peter Murray 1989
Chapter 9 © Margaret Shaw 1989
Chapter 10 © Martti Grönfors 1989
Chapter 11 © Frieder Dünkel and Dieter Rössner 1989
Chapter 12 © Jean-Pierre Bonafé-Schmitt 1989
Chapter 13 © John O. Haley 1989
Chapter 14 © David Watson, Jacky Boucherat and Gwynn Davis 1989
Chapter 15 © Maria R. Volpe 1989
Chapter 16 © Sally Engle Merry 1989
Chapter 17 © Robert B. Coates and John Gehm 1989
Prospects © Burt Galaway 1989

First published 1989

SAGE Publications Ltd
28 Banner Street
London EC1Y 8QE

SAGE Publications Inc
2111 West Hillcrest Drive
Newbury Park, California 91320

SAGE Publications India Pvt Ltd
32, M-Block Market
Greater Kailash - I
New Delhi 110 048

British Library Cataloguing in Publication data

Wright, Martin, *1930–*
    Mediation and criminal justice: victims,
    offenders and community.
    1. Criminal law. Justice. Administration.
    Mediation
    I. Title   II. Galaway, Burt
    342.5'5

    ISBN 0–8039–8063–9
    ISBN 0–8039–8064–7 Pbk

Library of Congress catalog card number 88–61785

Typeset by Photoprint, Torquay, Devon
Printed in Great Britain by J.W. Arrowsmith Ltd, Bristol

Contents

The Contributors

Jean-Pierre Bonafé-Schmitt is a researcher at the Lyon Group of Industrial Sociology, CNRS (Centre National de la Recherche Scientifique), University of Lyon II, France. He has undertaken research in France and the USA on labour relations and tribunals. His most recent book is *Les justices du quotidien: les modes formels et informels de règlement des petits litiges: étude comparative France/USA*.

Jacky Boucherat conducted studies of mediation as research assistant in the Department of Social Administration, University of Bristol, UK.

Mark Chupp, previously director of the Victim-Offender Reconciliation Program in Elkhart, Indiana, is now serving with the Mennonite Central Committee in Costa Rica.

Robert B. Coates is professor, School of Social Work, University of Utah, USA. He was previously research director for the PACT Institute of Justice, and has taught at the University of Chicago and the Harvard Research Institute, where he participated in studies of the Massachusetts deinstitutionalization programme.

Gwynn Davis is a research fellow in the Faculty of Law, University of Bristol, UK. He has conducted several studies of third-party mediation in divorce and is author of three books on this and other forms of dispute resolution. Since October 1985 he has been monitoring experiments in victim/offender mediation and reparation.

Frieder Dünkel is at the Criminological Research Unit, Max Planck Institute for Foreign and International Penal Law, Freiburg, Federal Republic of Germany. He is the author of several books on comparative penology, with particular reference to non-custodial sanctions.

Burt Galaway is professor, School of Social Work, University of Minnesota, Minneapolis, USA. He has done extensive research on restitution, community service sentencing, and victim/offender mediation, including public opinion studies in New Zealand.

John Gehm is program director, PACT Institute of Justice, Valparaiso, Indiana, USA. He manages a national VORP resource centre.

Martti Grönfors is docent, Department of the Sociology of Law, University of Helsinki, Finland, and director of the mediation project in Vantaa, Helsinki.

John O. Haley is professor of law and East Asian studies and director of the Jackson School of International Studies, University of Washington, Seattle, Washington, USA. A specialist on Japanese law, he has taught frequently in Japan and has published on Japanese law and legal systems.

John Harding is chief probation officer for Hampshire, UK. He has extensive experience in the probation service and is author of *Victims and Offenders: Needs and Responsibilities* and editor of *Probation and the Community: A Practice and Policy Reader*.

Gilles Launay is psychologist at Maidstone Prison, Kent, UK. He has been a psychologist in the prison service since 1977 and received a fellowship from the Institute of Criminology, Cambridge in 1985 to study victim/offender reconciliation.

Sally Engle Merry is an associate professor of Anthropology, Wellesley College, Massachusetts, USA. She has conducted studies of mediation, especially mediation of conflicts between parents and adolescents.

Peter Murray is research officer, Kent Probation Service, UK. He has conducted studies of innovations in the probation services, including day centres, computerized information systems, and victim/offender meetings.

Dean E. Peachey is coordinator, Network for Community Justice and Conflict Resolution, Kitchener, Ontario, and serves as lecturer at Conrad Grebel College, University of Waterloo, Ontario, Canada.

Helen Reeves has been director of Victim Support (the National Association of Victims Support Schemes), UK, since its foundation in 1979. Previously, as a probation officer, she worked in courts and in an experimental day training centre in inner London.

Dieter Rössner is professor of Criminal Law and Criminology, University of Göttingen, Federal Republic of Germany. He previously served as a judge and prosecutor and as an adviser on prisons.

Rose Ruddick, formerly a probation officer, is on the Executive Committee of the Forum for Initiatives on Reparation and Mediation (FIRM), UK. Between 1985 and 1988 she was project leader of the Coventry Reparation Scheme, one of the pilot projects funded by the UK Home Office.

Margaret Shaw is director of the Institute of Judicial Administration, New York, USA. She was previously vice-president of Conflict Management Resources Inc. and founding director of the Persons in Need of Supervision Mediation Project for the New York Children's Aid Society.

Mark S. Umbreit is vice-president for research and programs, Minnesota Citizens' Council on Crime and Justice, Minneapolis, USA. He is past president (and founder) of the PACT Institute of Justice in Valparaiso, Indiana. He serves as a consultant to the US Department of Justice and has worked with more than 30 local groups on the development of VORP projects in the USA.

June Veevers is a retired police sergeant, Devon and Cornwall Constabulary, UK. She has extensive experience as a juvenile liaison officer, worked with the Exeter Joint Services Support Team, and served as reparation coordinator.

Maria R. Volpe is coordinator, Dispute Resolution Program, and associate professor, Department of Sociology, John Jay College of Criminal Justice, City University of New York, USA.

David Watson is a lecturer, Social Administration Department, University of Bristol, UK. He has published in the fields of jurisprudence and social policy, including work on Scottish children's hearings and on data protection.

Martin Wright is information officer of Victim Support (the National Association of Victims Support Schemes), and vice-chair of the Forum for Initiatives in Reparation and Mediation (FIRM), both in the UK. After being librarian of the Cambridge Institute of Criminology, he became director of the Howard League for Penal Reform. He is author of *Making Good: Prisons, Punishment and Beyond.*

Introduction

Martin Wright

To belabour criminal justice is not hard. The complaints are all too familiar. Some of its flaws could in theory be put right: court delays could be reduced with more resources and better methods of timetabling, more information could be given to victims and more consideration paid to their feelings when attending court or giving evidence.

Other problems are more fundamental. In those cases where the complainant and the accused are known or related to each other, court procedure is concerned more with reaching a 'result' by determining the 'facts' of the incident than with the background which gave rise to it; witnesses, including the parties themselves, may actually be prevented by the rules of evidence from telling 'the whole truth' as they see it. They leave court, as they arrived, as disputants; the process does not reconcile them.

With crimes by strangers, the procedure offers little opportunity for personal contact. Victims often would like to see what their offender looks like, to express their feelings to him or her, and to ask questions: 'Why did you pick on me? Can any of what you stole be recovered?' Victims may feel that offenders are protected by lawyers and procedural safeguards such as the right to remain silent, to challenge jurors, and to claim a higher standard of proof ('beyond reasonable doubt') than that used in civil cases ('on the balance of probabilities'). It is not always appreciated that the reason for these safeguards is that the accused, if convicted, is liable to punishment, particularly in the United Kingdom and the United States, where courts impose imprisonment more liberally (or illiberally) than in mainland Europe. This is what makes it necessary to go to such lengths to minimize the risk of convicting an innocent person.

Attempts to reform the system are frequently made. Improved protection for defendants has been introduced, such as the right to a defending lawyer; but this has produced a reaction in some quarters, people suggesting that the safeguards were allowing some offenders to escape conviction altogether, and pressing for some of them to be taken away again. As the damaging effects of punishment on many offenders began to be recognized, there was a move towards rehabilitative measures; then surveys of research suggested that rehabilitation did not 'work' and led, illogically, to a return to punishment, under the euphemism 'just deserts', which has not been shown to work any better.

Reforms are also beginning to be introduced from the victim's point of view, such as assistance and information for victims attending court, and the provision of separate waiting rooms for prosecution and defence witnesses – a development which testifies to the failure of the adversarial system to reconcile.

In the last three decades, however, more radical ideas have been taking shape. Some have been concerned with the *outcome*. Schafer (1960) showed how many jurisdictions already provide for compensation by offenders to their victims – though he regarded compensation as a form of punishment. Eglash (1958) suggested 'creative restitution': the aim should be not to punish the offender but to restore the victim's situation as far as possible to what it was before, or even to a better state. Another proposal, by Barnett (1977), was to make restitution to the victim the primary aim of the system.

A second strand of thinking at about the same time was concerned with the *processes* of justice. Based on the idea of giving justice back to the community and the participants themselves, it drew part of its inspiration from anthropological studies of justice in primitive societies (for example Gibbs, 1963; Nader, 1969; Nader and Todd, 1978). Some critics argued that this method of handling disputes was not suited to complex urban societies; advocates of community-based conflict resolution replied that, on the contrary, it could be one way of re-creating some of the community responsibility which is often lost in modern cities. Instead of keeping the parties separate, until the formal proceedings in which one of them is convicted, they are invited to come together, in an atmosphere of structured informality, in the hope that both can be reconciled.

Most of the first projects putting these ideas into practice were in America: for example the Columbus (Ohio) Night Prosecutor Program (Palmer, 1975), the Neighborhood Justice Centers (McGillis and Mullen, 1977), and the Community Boards of San Francisco (McGillis and Mullen, 1977: 163–72; Alper and Nichols, 1981: 149–54). One feature was that the line between civil and criminal disputes was blurred: a criminal act such as an assault might often prove to be the culmination of a dispute with a long history. Project leaders became convinced that in such cases mediation was actually superior to criminal prosecution as a means of restoring peace to the disputants and to the neighbourhood. Some schemes, like the Boston Municipal Court mediation programme of the Crime and Justice Foundation, concentrate on offences (including serious ones) between disputing people with a relationship to each other (Crime and Justice Foundation, 1980).

The next major development was the use of the same principle of mediation in cases where the victim and the offender were not neighbours or workmates, but strangers. This is a primary theme of the present book. What these projects have in common is 'bringing people together' to resolve conflict, to use the title of a British survey of mediation projects (Marshall and Walpole, 1985). The techniques for doing so have evolved differently in different countries, as will be seen. Mediation is a flexible technique, which can be applied in many different situations, and at different stages of the criminal justice process. We have not attempted to survey the whole field, nor to include all the countries where similar ideas are unfolding, but we believe that the examples we have selected are interesting in themselves and each throws some light on the issues which are raised by the introduction of mediation.

The book is arranged in three parts. The first describes the origins, and some of the difficulties, of victim/offender mediation in North America and Britain, as seen by two of those who were personally involved (Dean Peachey and John Harding). Also at first hand, Helen Reeves outlines the emergence of Victims Support in Britain; the newly formed National Association of Victims Support Schemes, although sympathetic to mediation, decided that at that stage of its development it should concentrate on the needs of all victims, rather than become involved with a project which can only benefit those whose offenders are caught. She stresses that victims should benefit in reality, not just in rhetoric; or if they are being asked to take part mainly for the benefit of the offender, this should be made clear. Traditionally, criminal justice does something to the offender (punishment or rehabilitation). Reparation goes beyond this, by requiring the offender to do something to make amends to the victim or the community. Victims support completes the picture: it embodies the principle that society (both the state and individual citizens) should take care of victims, whether or not their offenders are caught, as an integral part of its response to crime.

The second part, 'Mediation in Practice', begins with a description of what actually takes place in mediation (Mark Chupp), although victim/offender meetings are not always as structured as this; then two schemes are described, operating at different stages of the criminal justice process, and one which concentrates on violent offenders (June Veevers, Rose Ruddick, Mark Umbreit). Another method is to bring together groups of victims and offenders who have committed offences against different people. This enables victims whose offenders have not been caught, and offenders whose victims refuse to take part, to meet each other; its authors (Gilles Launay and Peter Murray) would claim that it may also have advantages over one-to-one meetings. Although adolescent/parent conflicts do not normally involve crime, Margaret Shaw's chapter has been included because such disputes can be a precursor of delinquency. They can lead to 'status offences' – conduct such as truanting or running away which, in the USA, are offences only when committed by juveniles; but it may be more helpful to deal with these 'offences' through mediation than through the courts. Part II concludes with reviews of mediation projects in European countries: Finland (Martti Grönfors), West Germany, Austria and Switzerland (Frieder Dünkel and Dieter Rössner), and France (Jean-Pierre Bonafé-Schmitt). These countries have come to mediation in different ways: to relieve the courts, to create an alternative to the courts, to encourage the use of reparation by the courts. They have come upon different problems in doing so: obtaining the necessary support from the criminal justice system (France), securing continued funding from (national or local) government sources without losing the spirit of community empowerment (Finland), and establishing a new process when it has not been possible to create posts with sole responsibility for making the project succeed (West Germany).

Part III, 'Problems and Potential', begins with an account by John Haley of the Japanese approach; this combines traditional cultural attitudes with a legal system influenced by those of both Europe and America, but Haley suggests that the Japanese values could in turn have a beneficial influence in the high-crime societies of the West. Instead of agonizing over whether it is right for punishment to be reduced when an offender has made a reparative gesture, the Japanese welcome the opportunity to mitigate punishment; this could be part of the explanation of their relatively low rates of crime. In contrast David Watson and his colleagues consider whether reparation and mediation could be accommodated within a retributive concept; it might be easier to gain judicial and political acceptance for this, because it would require less of an imaginative leap, but it seems to retain many of the drawbacks of the retributive approach. It also excludes the concept of reparation by the offender to the community, through community service, to complement reparation to the individual victim. There are advantages in regarding reparation and mediation not as a *form of* punishment but as an *alternative* to it.

Mediation also has possibilities in other contexts; the police, for example, often attempt to act as mediators, but in conditions which lack most of the features on which mediation projects rely: trained mediators accepted by both parties, a relaxed setting on neutral territory, a structured though informal procedure, and so on. They might be glad, therefore, to be able to refer disputes involving children and families for possible mediation (Maria Volpe). A critical approach to mediation balances this part of the book: Sally Merry assesses a project for young people in conflict with their parents which is derived from the Scottish children's panels but has the advantage of not being part of the formal system.

The final chapters move on to evaluation. Robert Coates and John Gehm outline the first evaluation of a Victim/Offender Reconciliation Program. They show that there is still some way to go before the 'reconciliation' of its name is accepted by all the participants as the primary aim, and identify possible goals and their implications. (Evaluation of the four Home Office funded projects in England will be published shortly.) One question often raised is whether reparation, rather than punitive measures, is acceptable to public opinion, and Martin Wright reviews some public opinion surveys that have addressed this topic, suggesting that it is. Burt Galaway concludes with an assessment of future prospects for mediation.

Our aim in compiling this book has been to combine descriptions of the development of victim/offender mediation, and of selected individual projects, with responses to some of the questions legitimately asked of a new method. The traditional adversarial technique has been tried and tested – and in many ways found wanting. There is a growing literature about the possibilities offered by a new *outcome* of criminal justice, in the form of reparation, and our contributors have something to say about that; but our main concern is with the value of a different *process*, mediation, as a way of dealing with the conflicts which may lead, or have led, to one of the legally prescribed forms of harm inflicted by one citizen on another, commonly lumped under the label 'crime'. Some of the questions the book addresses are as follows.

What does mediation do for victims?

Taking part in mediation, like giving evidence in court, asks a great deal of the victim. Its advocates claim that at the end it is more likely to resolve their conflict, rather than close the case without giving victim and offender any chance to be reconciled. Some of our contributors state the theoretical advantages (for example the empowerment of victims, mentioned by Mark Chupp), and victims' willingness to take part in the hope of helping the offender rather than themselves (identified by Helen Reeves, and borne out by John Harding and Rose Ruddick). We also asked the authors of the first major empirical study of victim/offender mediation, Robert Coates and John Gehm, to summarize their findings, which show that most victims were glad to have taken part and would do so again.

But there are also warnings. Helen Reeves is concerned that victims may be 'used' by the system and feel under pressure to take part, for example through having guilt feelings at sharing responsibility for the offender's fate; Coates and Gehm found no evidence of this, though one victim in ten expressed some dissatisfaction, but Chupp concedes that it may happen. Another concern, expressed by Mark Chupp and Sally Merry, is whether mediators can compensate for a power imbalance between the parties.

What does it do for offenders?

The first reaction of the lay person or lawyer, accustomed to think only in terms of severity and leniency, is often that mediation allows offenders to avoid punishment. Others reply that facing one's victim is a more demanding experience than undergoing punishment. But this is really irrelevant, since mediation and reparation operate on a different dimension. It is interesting, though, that the Japanese think also of the rest of society, the punishers; mediation and reparation make it possible for them to inflict less punishment, as John Haley shows. Coates and Gehm show that the great majority of the offenders in their sample are satisfied with the process; this does not necessarily mean that they have 'got off lightly', but that they have felt fairly dealt with – an important criterion if offenders are to have respect, rather than resentment, for the law, and one not always met by the traditional criminal justice system.

We did not want our contributors to be uncritical advocates for mediation, and they have raised question marks for offenders as well as for victims. Although many supporters of mediation and reparation see it as an alternative to punishment, and argue that participation should be voluntary, the offenders studied by Coates and Gehm saw it as punishment and felt they had to take part. This may of course be due to the way mediation was incorporated into the justice system and the way it was presented to them. It would be interesting to know whether more of them would recognize reparation as distinct from punishment if it were so presented to them by courts and probation officers. Their feeling that they are being punished, rather than being given an opportunity to make amends, may also be fed by coerced participation; would it be different either if the mediation, and possible reparation, were an alternative to prosecution, and possible punishment, or if they were not invited to take part in mediation until after criminal justice officers had either imposed a sanction, or decided not to?

Other problems that need to be addressed are whether a mediated agreement should affect the sentence (discussed by David Watson and his colleagues); whether there could be an unfair bias in the selection of offenders, favouring those with a good prognosis (Frieder Dünkel and Dieter Rössner); and whether reparation would in practice be an alternative to a traditional sentence or added on (Coates and Gehm; Dünkel and Rössner).

What other advantages are claimed for mediation?

In addition to its uses in civil dispute resolution, which is not a central theme of this book, mediation can be used in ways which may directly contribute to crime prevention. With children, for example, it could help to resolve some of those intractable disputes where the child and the family or the school are at odds; apart from reducing distress, this could be a preventive measure, because young people in such conflicts are at risk and a proportion of them are liable to get into trouble, as Margaret Shaw indicates. We also asked Sally Merry to warn of any pitfalls; she shows that, while mediation can be effective with children, for example in the Children's Hearings Project in Cambridge, Massachusetts (inspired by the Scottish juvenile panels), it can also be manipulative and controlling.

Mediation could also be in the interests of the police, particularly when they are called upon to intervene in domestic disputes, as we have seen. Maria Volpe shows that they already often attempt to use informal mediation, but they are working against the odds; what might help the police, as well as the troubled family, would be the existence of mediation centres to which they could refer the family instead of being faced with only a stark choice: to charge or not to charge.

There is potential benefit for the community at large in a non-adversarial method of reducing conflict. When mediation was first used with what the public regards as typical offenders, however, that is with 'street crimes' committed by strangers, early projects attracted some hostile and uninformed press comment, as Harding and Reeves point out. The idea will need to prove itself and to explain the fundamental difference between mediation and other methods, which is that mediators have no power to impose a settlement: they enable participants to find their own. Such at least is the principle; but the mediation process contains opportunities for covert coercion. Mediators must either renounce this, or must be conscious of it and use it only to the minimum extent necessary to enable participants to move towards agreement.

Involvement of the community is often regarded as an important feature of mediation, and several of our contributors reflect this. It is claimed that not only do trained volunteers bring everyday experience to mediation sessions, but their involvement empowers the community to handle its own conflicts rather than abdicate responsibility to professionals. They take their understanding of mediation out to relatives and colleagues, so that more people will understand the value of mediation in settling conflicts. Not all mediation schemes, however, succeed in drawing on a cross-section of the community for their volunteers; these often have, in Merry's experience, for example, a higher level of education than the participants.

Is its ethical and philosophical base sound and acceptable?

There has long been ambiguity about the purpose of sanctions for wrongdoing. They are conveniently assumed to fulfil more than one purpose; different theorists and different actors in the system give priority to different aims. It used to be believed that punishment could be combined with reformation through hard work, or penitential reflection, or therapy. Community service orders are variously regarded as a form of punishment, or as rehabilitation, although in many ways the most secure base is to regard them as reparation by the offender to the community. There is a danger that mediation, with or without reparation, will fall into the same trap. This becomes more obvious with the present-day emphasis on evaluation. It is impossible to assess a project's performance without a clear definition of what it is trying to do; simply to let it develop and see what happens is a recipe for confusion. Statements beginning 'mediation is . . .' or 'mediation results in . . .' need to be closely examined: the word 'mediation' could refer to a concept, or to the actual practice of a project, which may not be the same.

It is also possible that the objective most justifiable in theory is not the one most acceptable to practitioners. Thus if the criminal justice system is seen as intended primarily to prevent crime, there is a temptation to claim that mediation and reparation will have such an effect. But that could lead to disillusionment, because the primary aim, as originally conceived in the Victim/Offender Reconciliation Programmes, was reconciliation, as the name implies;

they do not measure their effectiveness by crime figures – although a reduction would be a welcome side-effect. Again, if the system is seen as basically retributive, and unlikely to change, it may be easier to gain acceptance for mediation and reparation within a retributive attitude to justice. Watson and his colleagues present a case on these lines. This is a case that could be argued if 'retribution' were taken in its etymological sense of 'paying back'; the offender would repay the harm by doing something constructive. The trouble is that most people use it as being synonymous with punishment. This would also bring confusion: the distinguishing feature of punishment is that it is unpleasant, or even painful, but with mediation and reparation it makes no difference if the offender actually enjoys them, so long as their primary objective is achieved. Moreover, equal pain should be imposed on offenders of equal culpability (both are in practice unquantifiable, but that is by the way); mediation, however, can only take place if the victim is willing, and any reparation agreed between them will vary in every instance. With punishment, moreover, we are back to the traditional concern for what happens to the offender, while ignoring the victim; one of the strongest parts of the case for mediation is that it breaks free from this. Similar considerations apply to such goals as rehabilitating the offender, reducing cost, or easing the pressure on the grinding machinery of criminal justice. It appears that the most consistent case for mediation and reparation is based on regarding them as ends in themselves. The traditional ends of criminal justice might occur as desirable side-effects, but in the main would be treated separately: the decision whether to restrain physically those whose behaviour is so dangerous that they cannot be left at liberty would be made independently, and crime prevention policy would be based on a problem-solving strategy and social education rather than on the threat of fearful consequences (Wright, 1982: ch. 9).

How does it relate to the criminal justice system?

When an offender has come to notice, mediation can be introduced either instead of the criminal justice system, or subject to it. Only in the former case (or if the criminal justice agencies have discharged the case, for example by a police caution or a court sentence, by dropping the prosecution or by an absolute discharge) is the mediation free from any coercion. It is maintained by some that true mediation cannot take place if there is any prospect of further action by the courts: offenders will hope that by agreeing they will escape a more severe punishment, and victims may feel constrained by the knowledge that, if they refuse to agree, the offender may be condemned to something worse. The Forum for Initiatives in Reparation and Mediation, for example, in its response to the Home Office discussion document on reparation (FIRM, 1986), maintains that 'participation must be felt by both parties to be voluntary and non-coercive', and has 'reservations about any method which could be felt to put pressure on victims and offenders to take part in mediation; [FIRM] would like to see mediation separated from the criminal justice process, so that the opportunity for reconciliation between victim and offender would be entirely unconstrained'. FIRM goes on to express concern 'that the victim should not feel coerced into taking part by the fear that if he refuses, he may risk retaliation by having forced the offender into the criminal justice system. Similarly the offender should not feel constrained into admitting guilt and taking part reluctantly in mediation by the prospect of risking a custodial sentence otherwise.' It may be noted that fear of intimidation is also present in the existing system, as a common reason for not reporting certain crimes; another reason is not wanting to harm the offender (US President's Commission, 1967: 18). It is also possible that some victims, though they agreed reluctantly, were glad afterwards. As Reeves has commented elsewhere, there is a danger that if inaccurate assumptions are made about victim's feelings, 'more harm *may* be done than good' (her emphasis), so people with first-hand experience of victims should be involved in planning (Reeves, 1984). In France, as Bonafé-Schmitt mentions, some mediation projects grew out of victims support work.

The advocates of mediation are, however, under pressure to compromise in order to persuade the system to refer cases to them; otherwise victims and offenders in all but the most minor offences will be denied the opportunity. Referral may take place at various stages, as shown in Launay and Murray's Table 8.1. First, it can be after a police caution, as described by June Veevers in Exeter; in this case the offences will be only minor ones. Secondly, the prosecutor could defer the decision whether to prosecute, or the court at a preliminary hearing could adjourn in contemplation of dismissal; in either case, if mediation was completed to the victim's satisfaction, the case would not proceed. This could lead to 'net-widening', and there is a risk that such decisions would be less favourable to disadvantaged offenders, who do not make such a good impression on decision-makers; and the offender and victim would be under some pressure in making their choice, unless they were asked *after* the decision to discontinue the case. Thirdly, referral to consider mediation can take place after conviction and before sentence, as in Rose Ruddick's Coventry scheme, although

Coates and Gehm found that victims did not like the delay. It could be argued that there would be no coercion in this situation if the court let it be known that it would take no account of any mediated agreement; but as this could make the offender feel that he has paid twice for his offence, Watson and colleagues are against it, and so are Dünkel and Rössner; and the Valence project, described by Bonafé-Schmitt, has an understanding with the prosecutor that in the event of conciliation there will be no prosecution. In Japan, as Haley suggests, mediation and reparation are built into the system in such a way that the victim is not given the role of prosecutor, nor enabled to use the process for revenge. A fourth possibility would be for the court to let it be known that if successful mediation did not take place, the sentence would be an order for compensation or community service; thus the outcome of mediation would only make the difference between one reparative sanction and another, not between reparation and punishment. The fifth possibility (with the greatest built-in delay) is that mediation takes place after a punitive sentence has been carried out, as in Mark Umbreit's account of the project at Genesee; while current attitudes prevail, this is probably the only way in which the most serious cases can be referred to mediation.

On the basis of experience, research, and reflections so far, can any model be recommended?

The time is not yet ripe for a clear recommendation of any one model of mediation. At this stage it is only possible to suggest, tentatively, what seem to be desirable directions for its development. The case for these preferences will not be argued here, but simply stated; the arguments for and against will be found in the following chapters. First and most important is the point that there should be agreement on which of several desirable aims should take precedence. Reduction of crime, denunciation of harmful acts, and several others are all valuable; but in many ways the original ideal of the Victim/Offender Reconciliation Programme has most to commend it. This may determine the way it is put into effect. If it operates within the criminal justice framework, it may influence the latter, but may never break free from it; the surer way, perhaps, would be to start with an independent project for dispute resolution, and as confidence builds up, to be asked to mediate cases of increasing seriousness. In those cases where the offender is identified quickly, this enables the case to be disposed of without waiting for the delays of the courts. Acceptance of the concept will be slow, however, and progress will depend on winning support for the idea; this may be more readily forthcoming, in the early stages, if the project concentrates on cases where there is a relationship between the parties.

Secondly, mediation shows the importance of process, as distinct from outcome. There will need to be further study of the relative merits of different styles of mediation; at present it appears that there are advantages in using more than one mediator, and, on occasion, resorting to private sessions with the parties separately – provided that 'shuttle diplomacy' does not take over the proceedings. It will be an advantage also to state some principles to be followed, as Rose Ruddick does. Thirdly, the management structure should, as Harding suggests, be independent of the criminal justice system. It needs representatives of the relevant agencies such as the court, police, probation and victims support, but should be separate from them. If mediation is to develop, it needs staff who have no other responsibilities; they in turn need to be supported by, and responsible to, independent management.

Fourthly, there are practical matters to attend to. Some of our contributors show the importance of consultation before establishing a project; of working within the existing law; and of finding ways of 'institutionalizing' the project, when it has established itself, without compromising its independence.

Lastly, provision must be made for those cases in which mediation cannot take place, for whatever reason. This may mean bringing victims and 'unrelated' offenders together in groups, as described by Launay and Murray; or rape offenders and female non-professional therapists, as in the Hameln prison project noted by Dünkel and Rössner; but since participation must remain voluntary, the most optimistic proponent of mediation has to accept that the criminal justice system will continue to operate for those who choose not to participate, or those for whom it is apparent that mediation would serve no useful purpose. What mediators will hope, however, is that the justice system will increasingly use restorative, rather than retributive, principles.

Note

The views expressed by Martin Wright are his own, and do not necessarily represent those of Victim Support (the National Association of Victims Support Schemes).

References

Alper, Benedict S. and L.T. Nichols (1981) *Beyond the Courtroom: Programs in Community Justice and Conflict Resolution*. Lexington, Mass.: Lexington Books.

Barnett, Randy (1977) 'Restitution: a new paradigm of criminal justice', *Ethics: An International Journal of Social, Political and Legal Philosophy*, 87 (4): 297–301. Reprinted in B. Galaway and J. Hudson (eds) (1981) *Perspectives on Crime Victims*. St Louis: C.V. Mosby.

Crime and Justice Foundation (1980) *Mediation Training Manual*. Crime and Justice Foundation, 20 West Street, Boston MA 02111.

Eglash, Albert (1958) 'Creative restitution', *Journal of Criminal Law, Criminology and Police Science*, 48 (6): 619–22.

FIRM (Forum for Initiatives in Reparation and Mediation) (1986) *An Interim Response to 'Reparation: A Discussion Document'* (Home Office 1986). FIRM, 19 London End, Beaconsfield, Bucks HP9 2HN.

Gibbs, James L. jr (1963) 'The Kpelle moot', *Africa*, 33 (1): 1–10. Reprinted in P. Bohannan (ed.) (1967) *Law and Warfare: Studies in the Anthropology of Conflict*. Garden City, NY: Natural History Press.

Marshall, Tony and Martin Walpole (1985) *Bringing People Together: Mediation and Reparation Projects in Great Britain*, Home Office Research and Planning Unit Paper 33. London: HMSO.

McGillis, Daniel and Joan Mullen (1977) *Neighborhood Justice Centers: An Analysis of Potential Models*. Washington, DC: National Institute of Law Enforcement and Criminal Justice.

Nader, Laura (ed.) (1969) *Law in Culture and Society*. Chicago: Aldine.

Nader, Laura and H. Todd (eds) (1978) *The Disputing Process: Law in Ten Societies*. New York: Columbia University Press.

Palmer, John W. (1975) 'The night prosecutor', *Judicature*, 59 (1): 23–7. Reprinted in B. Galaway and J. Hudson (eds) (1981) *Perspectives on Crime Victims*. St Louis: C.V. Mosby.

Reeves, Helen (1984) *The Victim and Reparation*. London: National Association of Victims Support Schemes, 39 Brixton Road, London SW9 6DZ.

Schafer, Stephen (1960) *Restitution to Victims of Crime*. London: Stevens.

US President's Commission on Law Enforcement and Administration of Justice (1967) *Task Force Report: Crime and its Impact – An Assessment*. Washington, DC: US Government Printing Office.

Wright, Martin (1982) *Making Good: Prisons, Punishment and Beyond*. London: Burnett Books (Hutchinson).

1

The Kitchener Experiment

Dean E. Peachey

The Victim/Offender Reconciliation Program in Kitchener, Ontario, is frequently recognized as the forerunner of programmes that bring convicted offenders into face-to-face meetings with their victims to explore interpersonal reconciliation and build a plan for reparation (Alper and Nichols, 1981: 69–70; Umbreit, this volume).

Ideas and innovations sometimes have humble, and even un-planned beginnings. A Saturday night vandalism spree by a couple of intoxicated teenagers resentful of the local police in a small town called Elmira was hardly the making of headlines or criminal justice history. And when the two young men were subsequently appre-hended and pleaded guilty on 28 May 1974 to twenty-two counts of wilful damage, they had no idea that their experiences would be told and retold as the 'Elmira Case' in countless articles, speeches, and conference presentations. They were simply instructed to return to court in July to receive their sentences, and they spent the next couple of months in their homes in Elmira, a few miles north of Kitchener, Ontario.

The probation officer who was assigned to prepare their pre-sentence reports was hardly a crusading reformer. But he was prone to dreaming about new ways of doing things. Mark Yantzi had worked in the probation office in Kitchener for five years, after being a full-time volunteer under a programme sponsored by the Mennonite Central Committee (MCC). To be so directly tied to a part of the criminal justice system was itself an experiment for him as a Mennonite: the church had traditionally maintained a separa-tion from governmental affairs, and particularly from the legal system with its reliance on coercive power.

At a meeting of a committee that MCC had just convened to explore other forms of involvement with the criminal justice system, the recent vandalism case from Elmira was discussed. 'Wouldn't it be neat for these offenders to meet the victims?', Yantzi said to the group (Bender, 1985). As a member of the Mennonite church, which has maintained a strong pacifist tradition since its beginnings in the Protestant Reformation in the sixteenth century, Yantzi liked the practical peace-making implications of offenders and victims meeting each other. He then dismissed the idea, assuming that the judge would not even entertain such a notion.

Dave Worth, another participant in the meeting who worked for MCC, challenged Yantzi to give it a try. After struggling over whether to risk his reputation as a probation officer by suggesting something that had no basis in law, Yantzi accepted Worth's challenge. When he submitted his pre-sentence report to the judge, Yantzi enclosed a letter suggesting that 'there could be some therapeutic value in these two young men having to personally face up to the victims of their numerous offences.'

On the day the case was scheduled for sentencing, Worth and Yantzi met in chambers with Judge Gordon McConnell of Provincial Court to present their plan to him. The judge replied that he did not think it was possible for him to ask the offenders to meet the victims. Worth and Yantzi resigned themselves to the inevitable, and went into the courtroom to await the case. When the case was called, the judge ordered a one-month remand to allow time for the convicted pair to meet the victims and assess their losses, 'with the assistance of Dave Worth and Mark Yantzi'. As Worth recounts the scene:

> I don't know who was more surprised. I remember that Bill Morrison, the Crown Attorney, turned to look at us with a quizzical expression on his face (as if to say, what is this all about?) The two offenders certainly looked confused. The judge had a smile on his face. Mark and I looked at each other. Now what were we going to do? (Worth, 1986)

Accompanied by Worth and Yantzi, the two offenders (aged 18 and 19) retraced their steps from the night of vandalism. They visited each of the places where they had damaged property, slashed tyres, or broken windows. The circuit took them to private homes, two churches, and a beer store. The probation officer and the MCC representative simply stood by with their notepads while the two youths knocked on doors, explained who they were, and why they were there. In all they spoke to twenty-one victims (an additional victim had moved and could not be contacted) whose damages totalled $2189.04. Approximately half of that amount had already been covered by the victims' insurance policies, leaving $1065.12 in actual losses to the victims.

On 26 August the youths appeared in court and Yantzi reported to the judge what had happened. The judge ordered a $200 fine for each, and placed them on probation for eighteen months. Drawing on the information that was presented to him, the judge included as a term of the probation order that each youth should make restitution in an amount up to $550 to be paid to the victims as the probation officer arranged. Both the fine and the restitution were to be paid within three months.

Three months later the youths had visited all the victims and handed each a certified cheque for the amount of his or her loss. The experience of personally confronting the victims had been a difficult one for the two teenagers, but one that also had its rewards. One of them commented afterwards, 'I didn't quit because of my self-respect, and I didn't want to have to look over my shoulder all the time' (Yantzi and Worth, 1977).

On receiving the restitution payments, the victims expressed a wide variety of reactions, as reflected by the following comments:

> Thanks, I never expected to see that money. I think I'll spend it in a very special way to help somebody else.

> Thanks a lot. I was young too, only some of us didn't get caught.

> Aren't you ashamed of yourself? You know this really isn't going to cover it all. Who is going to pay for all those trips to Guelph for parts? Who is going to pay when they raise my insurance premiums? I don't want anybody to go to jail, but you know I hope we don't ever have this problem with you again, or anybody else. (Yantzi and Worth, 1977)

This first experimental case identified issues that were to continue to haunt the concept throughout succeeding years: multiple victims with a range of personal responses, the involvement of insurance companies in restitution,[1] and the considerable time lapse between the occurrence of an offence and the completion of the restitution process. But the experiment was also successful beyond everyone's expectations.

Buoyed by their results, Worth, Yantzi, and the MCC committee continued to brainstorm ideas and refine the process upon which they had stumbled. Although they were unaware of anyone else who was conducting victim/offender meetings of this type, they were operating in a milieu that encouraged experimentation. The Elmira case occurred at a time when the Canadian Law Reform Commission was issuing a series of working papers on alternative ways of dealing with offenders, and the Ontario probation service was just beginning to promote community involvement in corrections.[2] Elsewhere a few groups were starting to promote restitution as a primary response to crime (e.g. Hudson and Galaway, 1977). Only a few years earlier the Columbus (Ohio) Night Prosecutor Program began operating as the widely publicized forerunner of numerous programmes in the United States to mediate minor disputes out of court.

The intuitive and experiential orientation of the Kitchener group distinguished them from some of these other initiatives. Yantzi and his colleagues did not work toward a defined set of objectives. Instead, they continued to experiment with a handful of cases, while they tried to understand what it was that they were attempting to do. When they eventually formulated a programme proposal in the summer of 1975, they used the name Victim/Offender Reconciliation Project. The name was awkward, but it deliberately reflected their emerging perspective on the work. *Reconciliation* between victims and offenders was becoming an important goal. The use of the term 'project' as compared to 'programme' also indicated a deliberate effort to remain fluid and avoid becoming settled into any particular mode of operation:

> We see ourselves as being continually involved in a process of refining our purpose and function. The project was not begun with a definitive plan, and it is still exploring new avenues of application. We are learning by our mistakes and successes and are moving slowly but steadily, making every effort to consult with and keep informed those persons affected directly or indirectly by our project. (Yantzi and Worth, 1977: 1)

The evolutionary nature of the project complicates the current task of chronicling its development. The Kitchener VORP has operated under three distinctly different organizational structures. Office forms and statistics kept by the project have moved through successive transformations, and the earliest information categories do not necessarily match current ones. For example, the probation base of the initiative in its early years meant that despite the avowed emphasis on meeting the needs of both victims and offenders, early records pertained almost entirely to offenders. Aside from some short-term research efforts, little is known about the victims in the first few years of the programme.

In late 1975 two people were hired as 'researchers' for seven months through a government employment programme. They worked under Yantzi's supervision, their principal methodology being participant observation, as they conducted and reflected on victim/offender meetings. During this phase VORP dealt with 61 offenders and 128 victims, mostly involving property-related offences. Forty-eight offenders met their victims and 46 of these reached an agreement and followed through on it.

Eventually some structures developed for the project. By 1977 one-half of Yantzi's workload as a probation officer was devoted to VORP. He was supervised in this work by a steering committee composed of representatives from probation, the MCC, and community volunteers. Although the project name highlighted reconciliation, the organizers increasingly saw VORP as a testing ground for several ideas. Meeting the victim face to face and repaying the losses were viewed as ways of encouraging offenders to take greater responsibility for their actions. Although victims received the concrete benefits of restitution, the VORP process was also a way of challenging victims' stereotypes about 'offenders' through personal contact.

Beyond these readily apparent notions, however, the organizers developed a distinctive emphasis on empowering lay participation in the justice-making process. The goals of restitution and personal encounter could have been met through court-ordered restitution or apologies. But as it evolved, the programme developed a stronger view that the victim and the offender should be the ones to decide how much would be paid, and according to what timetable. Influenced by Christie (1977), Yantzi and Worth began to talk about how the state had 'stolen' conflicts away from individuals and developed a monopoly on the criminal justice process. The innovators became reformers as they began to envision a fundamentally different approach to justice – one that placed the disputing parties at centre stage and defined justice primarily as psychological and material restoration rather than as retribution.

This concern for deprofessionalizing the criminal justice process and enhancing citizen participation was extended to the project's staffing. Volunteers played an increasingly important role as case workers who visited victims, explained the project, and then set up and facilitated the victim/offender meetings. Yantzi's role became one of coordinating and supervising the volunteers. Initially volunteers received only a half-day of orientation to VORP. By 1980 this had grown to a twenty-hour curriculum including information about the criminal justice process and training in mediation skills.

Undoubtedly because of its probation base, the project functioned as a post-conviction sentencing alternative. The usual procedure was for a judge to place the offender on probation, with participation in VORP being a term of the probation order. (Probation in Canada does not require the offender's consent, as it does in England.) Judges began to exercise this option in an increasing variety of cases, sometimes with less than satisfactory results. In November 1975, a memorandum to judges and prosecutors indicated that VORP had been most successful when the victims were individuals or small businesses. The same report attempted to suggest some uniform wording for the probation order that would instruct the person being sentenced to 'come to mutual agreement with the victim regarding restitution, with the assistance of the Probation Officer or a person designated by the Probation Officer. If no agreement can be reached, the matter will be referred back to court.' The brief report concluded on a visionary note: 'It is our hope that the process of bringing victims and offenders together to reach a mutual agreement regarding restitution will become the norm.'

Yantzi interviewed each offender referred by the judge to explain the reconciliation process. Although VORP was prescribed in the probation order, Yantzi stressed to offenders that they could choose not to meet the victim and allow the court to determine the amount of restitution. Not surprisingly, about 90 per cent of the offenders opted to deal with the victim rather than take their chances with the judge.

No longer did the mediator simply follow an offender to the victim's door and observe as the anxious individual explained the purpose of the visit. After the offender agreed to participate in the project, a volunteer visited the victim to explain VORP and respond to the victim's questions about the process. Approximately 80 per cent of the victims opted to participate subsequently in victim/offender meetings that were arranged at the convenience of both parties.

The most common place for the reconciliation meeting was the home or business where the crime had occurred. Sometimes, however, the probation office was used, and the mediators even experimented with a park bench and a hamburger restaurant as meeting places.

The project dealt primarily with breaking and entering, theft, vandalism, and other property offences. Although most situations involved fairly small amounts of money, it was not uncommon to handle cases involving several thousands of dollars. If an offender failed to live up to the terms of the agreement, the project would attempt to renegotiate a more workable payment schedule, or otherwise salvage the case. Rarely did offenders default entirely on the agreement. When this happened, however, they were charged with a breach of probation, and returned to court.

The project's novel, yet common-sense approach of 'making right the wrong', soon began to attract considerable attention beyond Kitchener. Presentations by Yantzi and Worth at criminal justice conferences led to requests for training and consultation in a number of Ontario communities. VORP was cited in books and articles on criminal justice innovations (e.g. PREAP, 1976). The interest spilled over into the popular media as well, and the project received coverage in periodicals such as *Reader's Digest* as well as news and feature programmes on national television.

Despite its widespread publicity, the Kitchener programme was never subjected to a formal evaluation. Although numerous undergraduate and graduate students at local universities have studied the programme as a part of course projects,[3] a more rigorous evaluation has not been attempted. In part, the programme's sponsors have discouraged an evaluation, fearing that attempts to measure programme outcomes would focus too heavily on restitution or monetary results. 'How do you measure reconciliation?' has been an oft-repeated question whenever the possibility of an evaluation has been discussed. The difficulty and expense of developing measures that would assess the reconciliation process were generally deemed prohibitive for so small a programme. The lack of a readily available control group also contributed to the low interest in rigorous research.

Despite this lack of empirical documentation, the Ontario probation service actively promoted the development of similar programmes throughout the province. Although approximately twenty VORPs were initiated in Ontario by the early 1980s, the province never undertook a comprehensive research programme on VORP.[4]

Through all this activity, the Kitchener VORP remained relatively small. By 1980, the annual case-load had grown to 144 offenders and 149 victims, and Yantzi was relieved of his remaining probation case-load to work full time for VORP and other innovations.

The Kitchener group remained true to their innovative intentions. They began to think that in some cases – most notably those where the victim and offender already knew each other – it would be best if mediation could take place *before* the case went to court or even entered the criminal justice system. The adversary nature of the legal system with its emphasis on determining guilt or innocence seemed particularly unsuited for handling cases between acquaintances, where both may have contributed to a disagreement leading to an assault or property damage. By handling such conflicts through mediation it might be possible to resolve the dispute to the satisfaction of both parties, and prevent it from escalating to the point where a more serious offence might take place.

Thus, in 1980, they created the Community Mediation Service to deal with neighbourhood and interpersonal disputes outside the legal system.[5] Since it worked with cases before they went to court, or even before charges were laid, it was deemed to be outside the mandate of probation. Community Mediation Service came to be sponsored by the MCC, and within a few months VORP moved from being a joint Probation–MCC project to exclusive MCC sponsorship. However, Probation continued to fund VORP through a contract with MCC, as a part of their increasing emphasis on privatizing services in the community.

Within a year, Yantzi and others involved in VORP also began formulating ideas for providing additional services to victims of crime. For a while the programme became known as Victim/Offender Services, as they conducted a victims' needs assessment. This led to the creation of a separate Victim Services programme under MCC in 1982.[6] After seven years of involvement with VORP, Yantzi left the project to work full-time with the new victims' programme.

Victim Services gradually developed an extensive programme of self-help groups for victims of rape and incest. Once again, concern for dealing with both parties to a crime and a readiness to experiment took the victims' programme in new directions. In December 1982, Yantzi and his associates also began to work with sexual offenders, and especially with families where incest had occurred. Self-help groups were set up not only for victims, but also for offenders, and the mothers and siblings in the families.

The quest for new understandings of reconciliation has also been applied to this area. Although in some cases incest spells the dissolution of the family unit, there are other times when the family decided to stay together or to re-integrate upon the offender's release from prison. In such situations the programme has provided an on-going peer support group for couples who are dealing with similar situations. The programme has also sponsored weekend retreats on sexuality that bring together sexual offenders and victims of sexual abuse.

A further organizational metamorphosis occurred in 1982 as the growing cluster of programmes formed their own structure independent of MCC. This move was in accord with an MCC objective of establishing new programmes, and then allowing them to develop an independent status in the community. The new 'umbrella' organization was called 'Community Justice Initiatives', to demonstrate a concern for working toward the goal of justice in the community through an evolving pattern of methods.

VORP continued to operate as a distinct service, but around this time the letterhead was changed to read 'Victim Offender Reconciliation *Program*'. Perhaps some forms of institutionalization were inevitable. In any event, the individuals operating VORP were responding to concerns that VORP should be seen as an enduring operation rather than of a limited duration, as implied by the term 'project'.

In 1981 VORP achieved its highest case-load, with 163 offenders participating in the programme. The next year began a decline in activity that has continued to the present. A prominent factor in this change was a decision by the Ontario Court of Appeal that the VORP process went beyond the provisions of the law (*R. v. Hudson*, 1982). In December 1981 a sentence that included VORP was appealed. The case was an unusual one for VORP; it involved a misappropriation of funds in the range of $100,000. The judge sentenced the offender to approximately two years in prison, followed by three years of probation. The judge also wanted to order the offender to pay restitution, but the defence and the prosecution were unable to agree whether the victims' losses amounted to $76,000 or $127,000. The judge therefore decided that the amount of restitution should be determined through VORP.

The convicted man appealed the prison sentence, as well as the restitution order. The Ontario Court of Appeal upheld the prison term, but set aside the restitution order because a variety of circumstances made it impracticable for the man to repay such a large amount. Then the appeal judges went on to declare what some persons had privately thought over the years: the manner in which the amount of restitution had been determined was an improper delegation of the judge's sentencing authority. 'A trial judge has no power to delegate the issue of the amount of loss or losses relevant to the question of restitution nor can he delegate the determination of the amount of restitution to be made' (*R. v. Hudson*, 1982: 4).

In sum, the appeal court had ruled that a judge cannot delegate to a probation officer, a volunteer, the victim and offender, or anyone else, the sentencing powers of the court. Although this was not the original basis for the appeal, it was a by-product that would have serious implications for the VORP programme in Kitchener.

Several months after the appeal decision, an offender who had failed to complete his restitution was charged with breach of probation. On the basis of the Hudson case, his lawyer argued that he could not be convicted with violating probation if the probation term (participation in VORP) was improper in the first place. The judge agreed and dismissed the charge. The same happened in a second case, and local judges became understandably reluctant to refer any further cases to VORP.

The appeal court's objection to the VORP process could be met by having the offender return to court following the meeting with the victim to have the judge vary the sentence to incorporate the victim/offender agreement. This was done in some situations, but it had less appeal to the judges, since it meant an extra court date for each case.

An alternative was for the VORP process to take place after conviction, but prior to sentence, with the VORP agreement presented as a part of the pre-sentence report by the probation office. This approach was fine if the judge was inclined to require a pre-sentence report anyway. However, if the judge wanted to pass sentence immediately upon conviction or a guilty plea, there was no time for VORP to work.

The number of offenders referred to VORP dropped from 163 in 1981 to 124 in 1982, and to 64 in 1985. The number of victim/ offender meetings dropped even more dramatically, to an almost negligible level in 1985. Instead there has been a shift in services to monitoring restitution orders on behalf of probation and preparing victim impact statements to be used in pre-sentence submissions.

It is possible that factors other than the Hudson appeal contributed to the diminished case-load, however, as several significant events took place about the same time. The programme moved from official sponsorship by the probation office to operation by a private organization, Mennonite Central Committee, in 1980. Thus, the person coordinating the programme was no longer an officer of the court, but rather a private employee who had less accountability and credibility with the court. In the short term, this was of no real consequence because Yantzi was still identified as the head of the programme, and he was well known to the judges through his years as a probation officer. But when Yantzi left VORP in 1982 to devote his time to Victim Services, he was replaced by an individual who did not have a probation background, and who was relatively unknown to the judges. Although there is no way to determine conclusively whether this transition contributed to the reduced case-load, it seems plausible that it was an important factor. At the time when the programme was being questioned as to its legality, the known and trusted staff person had been replaced by a new face.

In the five years after Yantzi stepped aside as the VORP coordinator, there were three programme coordinators, as individuals left to pursue other job interests. All these persons had social services backgrounds; none had experience in the legal or correctional fields.[7] But with each successive year more and more initiative to maintain the programme had to come from this position, as local judges were making fewer referrals.

In 1984, federal legislation was introduced in parliament that would have amended the Criminal Code to clearly allow for restitution amounts to be determined through negotiations between the victim and the offender. This provision was part of a massive overhaul of the Criminal Code that was never, however, passed.

The reduction in the Kitchener programme has paralleled a general decline of VORP in Ontario. Whether because of the appeal ruling in the Hudson case, or to less promotion by provincial corrections and Probation, the number of active VORP programmes in Ontario has been reduced to six. Elsewhere in Canada, the VORP concept is enjoying renewed interest, however, especially in the wake of 1985 legislation dealing with young offenders that encourages alternative sentencing programmes (Peachey and Skeen, 1986).

If measured by the current case volume, the Kitchener VORP appears to be in a frustrated decline. If, however, the experiment that began in 1974 is viewed not as an attempt to build a fixed programme model, but rather as a continuing effort to apply principles of reconciliation and interpersonal healing to the criminal justice system through a growing number of ways, then indeed the innovations have borne fruit. The principles underlying victim/ offender meetings have been applied in the Kitchener community to situations ranging from minor neighbourhood disputes to more serious cases of sexual abuse. The concern for helping victims deal with the psychological consequences of crime has given rise to a broadened range of services to victims. Efforts to deprofessionalize some of the process have given rise to volunteer involvement in a variety of programmes and a continuing emphasis on self-help responses to problems.

In a larger context, the Kitchener experiment provided the inspiration that led to further innovation in dozens of communities in Canada, the United States, and Europe (of which several examples are given in this volume).

Finally, it must be recognized that unlike a 'demonstration project', which attempts to demonstrate a known process, a true experiment is a risky venture into uncharted waters. Demonstrations may fail, but experiments in themselves do not succeed or fail. They only yield information that can be used to revise or further refine the process under investigation. To quote again from Yantzi and Worth: 'We are learning by our mistakes and successes and moving slowly but steadily, making every effort to consult with and keep informed those persons affected directly and indirectly by our project' (1977: 1). So the factors identified in this chapter that may have contributed to the reduced VORP case-load may also present suggestions for addressing some of the problems encountered in Kitchener and elsewhere. By comparison, they also highlight the significant successes that victim/offender reconciliation programmes have achieved in numerous other communities.

Notes

1 The Crown Prosecutor suggested in this case that restitution should be paid to the insurance companies that had reimbursed some of the victims for a portion of the losses. The judge rejected this proposal, but in subsequent cases the judges did at times require restitution to be paid to insurance companies.

2 The Kitchener programme would not likely never have developed were it not for the receptive attitude of the area probation manager, John Gaskell. A native of England who was familiar with contemporary British probation innovations, he had already championed Yantzi's efforts to develop a volunteer probation programme. Although he was initially dubious about the legality of victim/offender meetings, he released an increasing portion of Yantzi's time for the VORP, and became a staunch proponent of the project who encouraged experimentation while requiring minimal demonstrations of immediate benefits.

3 One of these studies (Dittenhoffer and Ericson, 1983) was published and raised some critical questions about the programme, but its appearance in a law journal did not attract much attention from individuals working in corrections.

4 A small evaluation was conducted of the Ajax-Pickering programme in 1982–3 by the Ministry of Correctional Services, but because of methodological problems, it has not been released to the public.

5 Community Mediation Service was a pioneer project in Ontario, and is currently the longest continuously operated programme of its type in Canada. It has been instrumental in facilitating the development of similar programmes through publications, training courses, and convening two national workshops on mediation.

6 The Victim Services programme has two components. For the first part MCC persuaded the local police to operate a service to victims, using civilian employees of the police department to provide information and emotional support to victims. MCC sponsored a second 'community' component, housed in the same office with VORP and the Community Mediation Service. The purpose of the community component was initially open-ended. It was intended to serve victims who might not fall within the mandate of the police programme, as well as to fulfil an advocacy function for victims. Its primary work gradually developed in self-help responses to sexual abuse. The programme now sponsors over fifteen self-help groups for victims and offenders in sexual abuse.

7 The programme has also had a part-time staff person coordinating cases in nearby Cambridge since 1981. This position has been occupied by three people in those years, all with backgrounds in business or social services.

References

Alper, Benedict S. and Lawrence T. Nichols (1981) *Beyond the Courtroom: Programs in Community Justice and Conflict Resolution*. Lexington, Mass.: Lexington Books.

Bender, John (1985) 'Reconciliation begins in Canada', *Christian Living*, 32 (12): 6–8.

Christie, Nils (1977) 'Conflict as property', *British Journal of Criminology*, 17 (4): 1–15.

Dittenhoffer, Tony and Richard Ericson (1983) 'The victim offender reconciliation program: a message to correctional reformers', *University of Toronto Law Journal*, 33: 315–47.

Hudson, Joe and Burt Galaway (1977) *Restitution in Criminal Justice*. Lexington, Mass.: D.C. Heath.

Peachey, Dean and Cathy Skeen (eds) (1986) *Directory of Canadian Dispute Resolution Programs*. Kitchener, Ont.: Network for Community Justice and Conflict Resolution.

PREAP (1976) *Instead of Prisons: A Handbook for Abolitionists*. Syracuse, NY: Prison Research Education and Action Project.

Regina v. *Hudson* (1982) Ontario Court of Appeal, Oral Judgement, Jan. 7.

Worth, Dave (1986) 'VORP: a look at the past and future', *Community Justice Report*, 5 (1): Supplement.

Yantzi, Mark and Dave Worth (1977) 'The developmental steps of the Victim/Offender Reconciliation Project'. Unpublished paper, Kitchener, Ontario, on file with authors.

2

Reconciling Mediation with Criminal Justice

John Harding

The aim of this chapter is to record in both descriptive and personal terms some of the significant influences which led to the revival of reparative justice in Britain and, in particular, the development of mediation procedures involving victims and their offenders. The revival spans a period of over thirty years, accelerated in both North America and Britain in the last decade. A number of key writers, practitioners and agencies on both sides of the Atlantic became committed to a less retributive and more reconciling criminal justice process, and influenced the principles and shape of practice far outside their immediate location. While the main thrust of the chapter will be devoted to the initiatives of the eighties in Britain, it is appropriate to record the seed-time of the movement, which all too often goes unrecognized.

I was fortunate in the early seventies to be given the responsibility as a senior probation officer in Nottinghamshire for introducing community service as a Home Office sponsored pilot scheme. Part of our thinking at that time was inspired by the 'New Careers' model largely developed in anti-poverty programmes in the USA: that offenders given the right opportunities could gain status and a sense of re-integration with their own community by carrying out acts of service for others whose needs were easily demonstrable. The approach involved staff in seeking out placements with agencies and community groups who could identify with reparative justice, albeit indirect, and were willing to set community service workers alongside the handicapped, housebound, and disadvantaged. No formal attempt was made to link offenders with their victims, although there were many examples of offenders working alongside tenants' association members or community care groups in whose location the offender had committed his crime.

Running parallel to the community service initiative with all its attendant publicity, the search for a more reconciling system of justice was being less conspicuously pursued by Philip Priestley, an ex-probation officer and regional organizer of the National Association for Care and Resettlement of Offenders (NACRO). In 1969,

Priestley, who was later to launch the National Victims Association (now effectively superseded by the National Association of Victims Support Schemes (NAVSS)), set up in Bristol a discussion group with victims and offenders alongside others who were associated with the criminal justice process. The group, over monthly intervals, examined (with remarkable prescience for its time) issues of victim neglect, offender insularity, victim/offender reparations and, in embryo form, victim needs. Priestley felt that the legal/penal system did not allow the victim or the offender any room to explore the beginnings of the reparative wish either generally, or in particular instances:

> There is a clear case for further exploring the question of restitution and reparation in human feeling terms rather than in cash. Although face to face meetings of particular offenders and their victims would not necessarily be appropriate in all or even many cases, the symbolic value of a few offenders relating to a few victims might have profound implications for the public view of the offender. (Priestley, 1970)

Later, in a speech to the Margery Fry centenary proceedings in Birmingham in 1974, Priestley put in a plea for positive justice based on restitution and reparation, rather than negative justice based on retaliation and retribution (Priestley, 1974: 2). Among his proposals he urged the setting up of a victim casualty service offering first-aid help after a crime. The early blueprint emerged by the end of the year as the Bristol Victims Support Scheme, the pioneer model for the steady flow of similar projects that have followed nationwide over the last fourteen years. His hopes of establishing a victim/offender reconciliation movement were to wait a further decade, but he did manage to demonstrate its potential in a documentary for Thames Television in February 1975. He mediated a confrontation between Kevin McDermott, convicted of attempted murder, and his two victims who were badly injured in a knife attack. Priestley claimed after the filmed mediation that preconceived thoughts, anxieties, and pent up bitterness were largely swept away and the victims left with a new appreciation of their attacker as a human being rather than a maniacal would-be killer (Eccles, 1975: 4). McDermott, who served four years in prison for his offence, took part in this historic encounter ten days after being released. Priestley's work, however, had not attracted the attention of the authorities. Even the television programme did little to underscore the needs of victims or the value of a reconciling gesture for young offenders. A more orchestrated and sustained campaign of awareness was being conducted at the same time in Minnesota by Burt Galaway and Joe Hudson, former employees of the Minnesota Department of Corrections and co-organizers of the

first international restitution symposium in Minneapolis in November 1975. As a speaker participant at the conference I was able to
visit the pioneer restitution centre for paroled property offenders in
downtown Minneapolis, and meet those who had long claimed that
reparation should occupy a more prominent position in the
administration of criminal justice.

The centre held up to 25 offenders paroled from the Minnesota
state prison. The programme allowed for property offenders to be
released early from their prison sentences with the consent of the
victim of the offence and the parole board. Once at the centre staff
assisted the offender to find a job and make regular payments to the
victim until restitution was completed. Every attempt was made at
the outset of the programme to enable the offender to meet the
victim and negotiate the terms of the contract. In some instances,
the meetings provided a startling experience for the offender, who
had never had to face one of his or her victims, as well as for the
victim, who generally had never had a conversation with an
offender nor seen the inside of a prison.

Between 1975 and 1980 (when I next visited the United States to
look at the effects of restitution programmes on juvenile and adult
offenders) little progress was made in Britain by way of formally
establishing mediation projects focusing on the experience of crime
for victims and offenders. A handful of British writers continued to
pursue the theme in books and articles, in the wake of Nils
Christie's seminal paper 'Conflicts as property' in the *British Journal
of Criminology* in 1977 (Christie, 1977; Harding, 1976, 1980;
Priestley, 1977; Quaker Social Responsibility and Education, 1979;
Wright, 1977).

The breakthrough occurred in Devon in 1979 when the local
police, the social services and probation departments, led by John
Alderson, John Hanson, and Roy Bailey respectively, jointly
established a youth support team in Exeter to review cases of
delinquency and advise the Chief Constable on their disposition
between prosecution and cautioning. Those of us involved in
planning this venture were influenced by two primary factors: first,
an acknowledgement that crime was not just the concern of criminal
justice agencies but required the cooperation and understanding of
local communities, parents, young offenders and their victims, who
often lived in close proximity to each other; second, the spread of
information about American restitutional experiments through
exchanges and articles. In essence, the Exeter scheme (Veevers,
this volume) involved young offenders in acts of apology and,
sometimes, reparation after the police had made a decision to
caution rather than prosecute an offender. The participation of the

young offenders was entirely voluntary and the offences ranged over theft, criminal damage, burglary, and assaults. Victims have included individuals, shops, firms, schools, and the local authority – nearly all over the intervening years have agreed to assist in the scheme. The direction of the project has significantly changed over the years to the point that reparation is more appropriately focused on second- and third-time juvenile offenders who are more in danger of prosecution (Marshall and Walpole, 1985: 17).

During 1980, before moving to the West Midlands probation service, I had a further chance to study the impact on practice of the reparation movement in the USA. The visit ranged across seven states and included a look at some federally funded restitution projects for juveniles and adult offenders together with some dispute resolution projects in local urban communities outside the jurisdiction of criminal courts. The American experience highlighted a number of issues of relevance to the British scene. First, the contribution that victim surveys make to our understanding of the impact of crime and the frequently unmet needs of victims. Victims require, in particular, not only the availability of local victims support schemes and access to compensation, but also a chance to express their feelings about the criminal incident to the offender and other agencies involved in criminal justice. Second, even though reparation and mediation proceedings are of limited application in the sense that most offences go unreported or undetected, the relevance of such procedures is applicable across a broad spectrum of intervention from the locally managed neighbourhood dispute centre to the pre- and post-court reparative projects run by the probation service and other agencies. Lastly, even though very few restitution programmes in the USA had a mediation component enabling victims to meet offenders, it was evident in those that did that crime victims attached as much, if not more importance to the healing process of mediation than to a compensatory gesture (Harding, 1982).

Three West Midlands projects: key issues

By the early eighties in England there was a small, discernible and increasingly vocal body of interested individuals and organizations who promoted the need for action research programmes in reparation and mediation in both community and court settings. Many knew each other well; a small number had visited programmes in the USA, exchanged ideas prior to their publication in articles and books, shared platforms at conferences, or belonged to a common interest group like the NAVSS reparation working party, later to emerge as a wider coalition of voluntary and statutory involvement known as FIRM, the Forum for Initiatives in Reparation and Mediation. The debate on the relationship between a victim's need and an offender's accountability for his crime was further strengthened at the local level by legislative and social factors, including the 1982 Criminal Justice Act which enabled courts to impose a compensation order for crime victims as a sentence in its own right with primacy over any other financial penalty (although courts have been slow to use this power); the publication of the 1982 British Crime Survey; and the steady growth of local victims support schemes and their national association, the NAVSS, with the consequent spread across towns and cities of information about the needs and perceptions of crime victims.

The influence of outsiders also continued to play a critical part. In Birmingham, Professor Burt Galaway from Minnesota undertook a teaching assignment at the university in the autumn of 1981. Galaway had just completed a national assessment of adult restitution and community service programmes for the US Department of Justice. In six public lectures to various criminal justice/victims support audiences in the Midlands, the South, and the North, Galaway critically looked at the use of restitution as a penal measure, stressing the need for programme designers to be clear about policy goals so that the measurement of outcomes can be effective (Galaway, 1983). As importantly, Galaway introduced audiences to the Mennonite Victim/Offender Reconciliation Programs (VORP), in Canada and Indiana, USA, principally through the use of a tape/slide presentation called 'Crime – the broken community'. Along with others, I later found that the tape/slide was a useful aid to talks with those criminal justice personnel interested in learning more about mediation and reparation. It emphasized the damaging nature of crime to both victim and offender, underscored the need for a personalized process in which both parties could question and express feelings, and stressed the significance of victim and offender taking responsibility for reaching their own agreement with the help of a volunteer mediator. Fortunately, the Mennonite message was conveyed at an early point to the media in England by some of us who felt the principles merited wider circulation. The BBC, early in 1982, filmed programme participants from Elkhart, Indiana at work, providing a model for many English viewers.

That message was further reinforced two years later when Mark Chupp, Director of the VORP in Elkhart, Indiana, attended the first English training programme for probation project staff interested in learning more of the purpose of reparation and skills required in mediation. That conference crystallized the feeling that the probation service had no right of 'ownership' to reparative practices. Crime represents a breach in the social fabric that concerns victims, offenders, the public, and the professionals. Where possible, through the creation of out-of-court community-based mediation centres, one might look to local people as mediators in situations of conflict. The probation service, as it subsequently did in the West Midlands, might have an important role along with other bodies in promoting or supporting the development of a number of pilot models located in identifiable communities. It was also generally acknowledged that reparation was applicable at a number of different points in the criminal justice process from the idea of an apology to the victim, with or without reparation, at the caution stage for a juvenile or adult offender, to a more serious crime where a sentencer might place a reparative agreement between victim and offender alongside some other form of punishment. Possible target areas for experimentation included selection by age group, e.g. 14- to 21-year-olds; by offence, e.g. property crimes and cases of violent crime where the victim and offender had some prior acquaintance; by area, e.g. looking at minor and serious crimes from a housing estate and assessing the practicability of reparation through the mediation process; by seriousness of offence for those on the threshold of custody; and by offender – those in court for the first time – in the hope that an early reparation experience could lead to crime reduction. No preferred model was put forward, but participants generally agreed that reparation, especially if preceded by mediation between victim and offender, was a desirable goal in itself and did not need to be associated with the non-custodial alternatives to gain enhanced credibility. All were agreed on the importance of identifying primary goals for a project while recognizing that other benefits could accrue in the process as well. In outcome terms it was necessary not just to measure the offender's reaction, but to look at other legitimate benefits such as victims' satisfaction, the views of sentencers, and the reduction of community fears.

The Coventry reparation scheme

Early in 1983, the West Midlands probation service obtained a grant from the Cadbury Trust to employ Martin Wright, a leading British advocate of reparation, in carrying out a three-month feasibility study in the city of Coventry. The city has a population of 300,000 and, although formerly prosperous through its car industries, had been in the grip of recession for a decade. It had nearly 30,000 out of work, a third under the age of 25. Wright's detailed study was the first of its kind in England and became an important reference point for other probation areas, parliamentary select committees, the Home Office and the media. Wright consulted a wide range of agencies including the police, the Victims Support Scheme, employers, the trades council, magistrates, clerks to the justices and local probation officers (Wright, 1983). Apart from looking at case eligibility, procedural matters, administration, aims and objectives, Wright set the argument for reparative justice in an historical context and was heavily influenced by the work of the Mennonites, in particular Howard Zehr's account of the fourfold beneficiaries of victim/offender reconciliation – victims, offenders, the community and the criminal justice system (Zehr, 1982: 14–16).

Wright's study focused on a young age group of offenders between 14 and 21 responsible for offences of violence against the person, burglary, theft, and damage. He estimated that a project staff of two, plus ten active volunteer mediators, could handle anything between 150 and 200 referrals a year.

Essentially, the scheme would start with a finding of guilt in court. Before sentencing, the court could order a social inquiry report. At that point, using project eligibility criteria, the court could refer the case to the project to find out whether mediation would be possible. It could do this on its own initiative or on the suggestion of a probation officer, solicitor, or member of project staff. The work of mediation would be carried out by a volunteer whose first task is to see the victim and offender separately and gain consent to a meeting between the parties. If agreement is forthcoming the volunteer would fix a meeting either in the victim's home or on neutral ground. At the post-remand hearing the court, having heard the result of the mediation session, would have a number of options: sentence could be deferred for voluntary completion of the agreement; a probation order with a condition; a conditional discharge; or a community service order. Where possible it was recommended that the courts adhere to the terms of the mediated agreement without adding further penalties.

During the two years that elapsed between the completion of the study and the announcement of the two-year funding by the Home Office for a pilot project in Coventry, a number of significant changes took place in the shape of the proposal. In one section of the report Wright addressed the problem of the impecunious offender unable to pay compensation to his victim. He proposed the adoption of the American 'Earn-it' scheme based on the work of the Quincy probation service and their local judge, Albert Kramer (Klein, 1981). This would have involved the participation of the local business community in finding unemployed offenders temporary work to pay back the victims of their crime, or probation officers assisting them to find places on government-sponsored temporary employment projects. The suggestion aroused the hostility of the National Association of Probation Officers, who opposed the whole notion of probation service involvement with Manpower Service Commission schemes and were anxious that injustice might occur if the better-off offender were penalized less for criminal offences. Locally, the idea was dropped since it also gave concern to magistrates and other professionals given the increasing level of unemployment in the city and the questionable values which would surround the finding of temporary work for offenders just so that they could pay compensation.

More surprisingly, the Coventry scheme decided not to use volunteer mediators, a key component of Wright's staffing policy. A precedent for this rejection was established in the South Yorkshire probation service reparation scheme set up in 1983, where only probation officers acted as mediators in all negotiations between the courts and victims and offenders. The rationale for using the same worker includes consistency, building up trust with each party, developing experience and feeding back information to the courts and others (Coventry Reparation Scheme, 1986). The decision is, perhaps, regrettable since it sets to one side the collective experience of partnership and delegation between paid staff and volunteers as illustrated by the American VORPs and parallel projects in England, notably Wolverhampton and Hampshire, where volunteer mediators not only express a healthy community involvement in criminal justice but are capable of ably sustaining all the procedural links from the point of referral to the submission of a mediated agreement via a court-based worker to the sentencers. Another difference from the original study was the raising of offender eligibility to 17 years or over.

The scheme followed the study by having a structure separate from mainstream probation management. An independent management committee is made up of interested parties in criminal justice, including the victims support scheme, who have endeavoured to find a neutral position for the three workers within the court system so that the service is acceptable to victims, offenders, and the court. Referrals are not confined to a particular target group in terms of age, seriousness, or type of offence. The court is encouraged to look at the circumstances of the case. The criteria include firstly that the offender is showing remorse; secondly, the offence was such that it is felt the victim may gain from knowing who the offender was; thirdly, there appears to be a need for the air to be cleared between victim and offender in order to reduce the risk of future offences occurring between them again; fourthly, the victim and offender are neighbours; fifthly, it appears that the offender may gain from an opportunity of learning what the reality of the consequences of their offence for the victim have been (Coventry Reparation Scheme, 1986: 8).

The primary focus of the scheme is on the mediation process itself and the benefits this experience may bring to individual victims and offenders. The organizers take particular care in preparing offenders and victims for a meeting if both parties are willing to proceed. Emphasis is placed on the learning aspects of the experience – the asking of questions, the expression of feelings, the need for further information, the availability of support services, and developing an understanding of the impact of crime on the other person. In relation to reparation agreements staff act as 'facilitators', encouraging agreements that are simple and short-term in nature, rather than unduly prolonging anxiety and stress on both sides. Finally, project staff prepare an independent report for the court at the end of a 28-day adjournment period; this does not contain recommendations about sentencing but describes the action taken, agreements reached, and the implications for both sides.

During the first year of the operation of the Coventry scheme, 100 cases were referred by the courts. Research has been undertaken by the Home Office, Bristol and Birmingham universities looking separately at the operation of the scheme, the impact of reparation/ mediation upon victims and offenders, and the effect on local criminal justice systems. Early findings by project staff appear encouraging and match some of the experiences of American-based victim/offender reconciliation programmes. About two-thirds of the victims (66) in the first six months accepted some involvement with the scheme, and 38 per cent chose to meet their offender. Most of the 67 offenders had a previous conviction, one third having served a custodial sentence. Crimes included a fair range of all types of offence, with theft and burglary predominating. Practical reparation has been agreed in some cases, apologies in all; victims (where meetings took place) laid greater stress and value on this process than payment of money or an act of service by the offender. The courts appear to have found the information provided by staff to be helpful and relevant to its sentencing decisions, nor has it been necessary in the first 58 cases to impose a custodial sentence. Rose Ruddick, the project leader, commented that from the 39 cases in which mediation/reparation has occurred:

• in 21 cases the defence solicitors felt that the sentence was reduced as a result of the scheme's involvement;

- in 17 cases the magistrates stated that the scheme's involvement had been taken into account;
- in 14 cases defence solicitors felt that the sentence was the same as would have been likely without the scheme's involvement;
- in 4 cases the defence solicitors' view is not known.

(Ruddick, 1986: 4; see also Ruddick, this volume)

Wolverhampton – the victim/offender reparation project

Wolverhampton is the second Home Office funded reparation scheme in the West Midlands, with an operational starting-date in October 1985. The initiative is significantly different from the three other Home Office programmes in that the grant recipient is a local voluntary organization engaged in various community, youth, and employment activities, the Wolverhampton Crypt Association. The project, like that in Coventry, takes its referrals from the court and works closely in association with the police and probation service. The origins of the scheme lay in consultations between the Crypt Association director, Enid Denton, and myself, whom she approached following media publicity over the Coventry proposal. Subsequently a meeting was held at the local police station in Wolverhampton during which I was asked to lead a discussion on the principles and practice of reparation, including showing the VORP tape/slides. The Crypt committee and workers quickly identified with VORP, not least since they ran the town's local victims support scheme within the ambit of the organization. Additionally, the Crypt had gained the esteem of the police and other public bodies in 1981 as a mediating agency during street riots that particularly involved black youths living in the area.

The project steering committee which set up the programme took a similar shape to that of the Coventry scheme, embracing a number of statutory and voluntary agencies involved in criminal justice. One of the identifiable tensions in those early discussions centred around the reluctance of the clerk to the justices to see the courts' control of the criminal process passed to another organization even though both parties may have agreed to a meeting. The tension is, perhaps, still reflected in the first six months' referral figures from the court, when only 21 cases were passed on to the project.

The basic premise behind the programme is as follows: 'The criminal justice system does not require the offender to face up to the consequences of the criminal act and the victim plays a passive role in the judicial process. A system based upon the offender making reparation to the victim faces up to this dilemma.' The project is thus informed both by concern for victims and by the need to re-integrate offenders with the community. It focuses on offenders aged 15 and over with few restrictions placed on the type of offender except that the offence must be punishable with imprisonment and that he/she is willing to take part. The project employs two workers, one of whom was the former police superintendent for the area and had hosted the inaugural gathering in Wolverhampton. The mediators are all volunteers who have been trained in conflict handling skills. They prepare reparative agreements with the paid staff for transmission to the court at the end of the period of pre-sentence remand. The court then passes sentence, and so does retain ultimate control.

Despite the initially slow rate of referrals, the early findings, prior to the full Home Office research reports, indicate that the majority of victims and offenders are prepared to be involved in reparation/mediation proceedings: just under half the participants agree to face-to-face meetings (Image, 1986: 27).

Sandwell mediation and reparation scheme
The initiative for neighbourhood dispute centres more commonly arises from one of two sources: either through a grass roots movement or some inter-agency resolve to handle urban stress and conflict more appropriately at the local level. By contrast, the Sandwell project started as a proposal by a probation ancillary worker who saw the government-sponsored Urban Aid Programme as a vehicle to establish a centre, manned by local volunteers, that focused on interpersonal disputes (especially between neighbours) involving allegations of criminal offences. Sources of referral were seen as including the police and courts as well as agencies outside the criminal justice system. This proposal drew heavily on a National Association of Victims Support Schemes paper providing guidelines for a mediation centre (Freeman, Harding, Reeves and Wright, 1982).

The thinking behind the plan was influenced by neighbourhood dispute centres in the USA and Australia. It envisaged paid staff members, supported by an inter-agency committee, drawing upon the resources of local trained volunteers within a confined public housing area. Unlike a parallel initiative in another West Midlands probation area, Solihull, which ultimately did not attract Urban Aid funding, the proposal was not worked out in any detail with other relevant agencies and community groups until after the funding decision was made. In context, it was not unusual for over a year to elapse before decisions were finalized, and the West Midlands service, like other bodies, was used to many applications being rejected outright. Later on, however, the lack of proper consultation at the time was to cause problems, and significant shifts in the development of the project.

Finally, in 1984 the local authority released to the press news of a three-year funding grant. The *Birmingham Post* ran a feature headed 'Probation Service to set up a citizen's court' together with a disapproving editorial. Local magistrates in one part of Sandwell took exception to the idea of a citizen's court which they saw as undermining their role. After consultations within the service it was decided to switch the siting of the project to the south of the district, where a different court was less anxious about the proposal and after an open meeting with the Deputy Chief Probation Officer endorsed the scheme with some enthusiasm. The project was sited in West Smethwick on a large multi-racial council housing estate, where conditions were poor and neighbourhood disputes frequent.

Two operational aims were identified by the worker from the outset – the establishment of a mediation service for local disputants and a victim/offender reparation scheme taking referrals, in the main, from a local juvenile liaison panel comprising representatives from probation, police, education, and local authority departments. In practice, the police have referred cases to the worker for voluntary mediation after the panel has decided to caution rather than prosecute a young offender. During the first year of operation, the majority of the project's 64 cases were neighbour dispute cases (52), while 12 were concerned with victims and offenders. Referrals of the dispute cases came largely from the Citizens Advice Bureau, but also from schools, housing departments, community groups, the police, probation and social services, with only 10 on a self-referral basis.

In a detailed assessment of the first year's operation, Richard Young, a postgraduate student of the Institute of Judicial Administration at Birmingham University, made several pointed observations on the development of the project and the role of the worker, Deryck Wilson. Without adequate planning for the scheme in the adopted area, the original notion of an inter-agency advisory group never properly took off. The scheme, although supported by an over-stretched local probation staff, lacked structure and a sense of corporate and community ownership. Paradoxically, the absence of structure thrust the worker into a more autonomous role that gave him the opportunity to respond quickly to changing circumstances. Similarly, Young concluded that the informal nature of the programme may have made it easier for local people to come forward and feel at ease as volunteers (Young, 1986: 11). The weakness in the arrangement clearly lies in being over-reliant on one person, who had to take the responsibility for the programme's performance and future.

Wilson's first task apart from setting up points of liaison with other local agencies was to recruit and train local volunteers as mediators. Initially, volunteers were recruited from approaches to local organizations and community groups in the area. Eleven were inducted in two stages of intake. Of the eleven, nine were women, five Afro-Caribbean, four white; two men, one Asian and one Afro-Caribbean. The weakest aspect of the volunteer group was the lack of Asian representation which clearly limited the effectiveness of the scheme in handling Asian referrals, both in terms of cultural understanding and, in some cases, language. Part of the barrier to Asian involvement may be that the role of mediator as currently practised is not acceptable to a cultural tradition which places greater emphasis on dispute settlement within the family or by referral to community elders in the local temple or mosque.

The training programme was largely constructed around the ideas, experiences, and views of the volunteers. The worker's first task was to instil confidence from the volunteer's point of view. Few had previous experience of volunteering or mediation techniques and some found the prospect quite daunting at first. At a later stage, the leader introduced role play methods which familiarized part-icipants with some of the real life situations they would encounter.

In practice, the neighbourhood disputes were, as we have seen, referred by voluntary and statutory agencies and individuals themselves. Once a referral is accepted by the worker, normally two people from the project (two volunteers or the worker and a volunteer) visit the referring party and explore the issue in some depth. The mediators then visit the other party to the dispute and undertake a similar analysis of the problem. Wilson reported that a joint mediation session involving all parties was rare. Most disputants preferred to negotiate individually through the mediators. This process differs sharply from the American models of mediation which rely little on individual negotiation and almost entirely on organizing joint sessions. Wilson suggests an explanation for this tendency:

> Many possible explanations exist for this, including cultural differences, which may affect how people react to such conflicts (i.e. in America people generally are found to want to face up to, and take responsibility for such a problem, whereas in Britain the tendency is to call in an outside expert and wash one's hands of it). We would feel that we are in fact reversing this tendency by involving people directly with the processing of their problem, even if it is via the scheme rather than directly with the other party. (Wilson, 1986: 9)

Young's evaluation of the scheme, based on consumer evaluation, throws up some different perspectives. Of the 59 neighbours interviewed, 40 said the scheme's intervention had been to no effect and that difficulties continued as before. Twelve respondents thought that the scheme had been instrumental in reducing the tension between them and their neighbours. The cases in which the scheme had the most success tended to be those in which several visits were made to each party and those in which joint meetings were held. Where the scheme visited only one of the parties to a dispute or visited each side once only, the results tended to be negligible. In relation to these findings, Young concludes that the modest success rate should not be taken as a sign of the project's failure. The successes were achieved in the most unpromising of situations, where other agencies had already tried and failed to resolve the problems: 'There does seem to be a place for an agency which specializes in dealing with neighbour problems using a mediative approach, even if spectacular results are unlikely to be achieved' (Young, 1986: 48).

By contrast, the scheme had some success in achieving its aims with victim/offender mediation. Young suggests that victims often agree to such a meeting out of a sense of social responsibility. They consider they ought to meet the offender if by doing so the young offender can be deterred or dissuaded from crime in future. Secondly, offenders may think they have little option but to agree to attend a meeting with their victims. These considerations do not necessarily apply to neighbours, who have not spent several months enmeshed in the decision-making process of the criminal justice system. Third, the scheme does not always suggest meetings to neighbours in dispute, despite the possibility that in some cases such a suggestion would have been welcomed. A greater promotion of the value of face-to-face meetings with neighbours may help dispel generalized notions of unwillingness (Young, 1986: 48–9).

What of the future?

This chapter has attempted to explore some of the influences which led to experimentation in neighbourhood dispute resolution and victim/offender mediation over the last decade in Britain, and to outline the experiments undertaken. The projects, all the subjects of research, have encountered implementation difficulties not unfamiliar to pioneer undertakings. The Sandwell mediation scheme was rushed in terms of development and did not live up to some of the original hopes. Yet even if such projects do not lead to a measurable diversion from the criminal justice process there is evidence that the presence of the workers and volunteers helped to ease tensions and stress within the community. It is probably right that Probation should withdraw from a project at this stage so that an agency like the Citizens Advice Bureau with a more neutral image could assist the local community in Sandwell to own the project more decisively in the future, always provided that local funding bodies are willing to express support for a long-term approach.

What is the future of victim/offender mediation programmes in terms of their assimilation into the mainstream work of statutory and voluntary agencies dealing with offenders? As with the development of community service orders, the lessons of mediation, of a more reconciliative approach to justice issues, have to be absorbed by mainstream staff if programmes are not to be written off as marginal, irrelevant, and elitist. In a general sense the recent focus on the impact of crime and the consequences for victim and offender alike have not been lost on practitioners, even if the lessons have not been wholly absorbed. Supervision programmes with juveniles frequently concentrate on the significance of offending behaviour and the impact of victimization; staff will make tailored arrangements for offenders to meet their victims if both sides agree. Likewise, such meetings are often used as an adjunct to the police caution, in work with juveniles. But the practice does raise doubts about as to whether the juvenile would have been prosecuted in any event: another form of net widening? The independence of the newly created Crown Prosecution Service and the prosecutors' possible willingness to cooperate with a risk-taking alternative to prosecution may help project staff clarify this dilemma.

Few projects have used victim/offender mediation in a pre-trial setting where agreements between the parties are lodged with the court on the offender's initial court appearance. Three principal difficulties arise that are also linked to intervention at the post-conviction stage: first, the court may take little account of what has gone before, thus nullifying the agreement between victim and offender; second, the whole process of getting victim and offender together, whether through the efforts of paid project staff or volunteer mediators as in Wolverhampton and Hampshire, is time-consuming, needing considerable planning and coordination with the courts by both statutory agencies, such as probation officers responsible for court liaison, and by independent ones such as mediation projects. If mediation programmes are to be absorbed in mainstream budgets after the experimental funding period, then project staff will have to define selective target groups for intervention, particularly where victim/offender encounters not only aid the process of justice but give meaning and purpose to the principal actors involved in the aftermath of a criminal incident.

Finally, an issue not resolved by the current round of experiments: can mediation and reparation be successfully grafted on to an essentially retributive criminal justice process? Is it appropriate to link mediation with the court appearance either pre-trial or post-conviction? Does it become another exercise in diversion open to elements of confusion, misunderstanding, and manipulation for the court, for the offender, for the victim? Would mediation be more successfully integrated into practice as part of the requirement of probation or supervision order, always provided that an investigating officer had checked out questions of suitability, willingness of parties to proceed, etc.? Mediation would be thereby freed from the court appearance and could become a selected feature of many probation and supervision orders, involving probation officers, volunteer mediators, and community organizations without necessarily enlarging budgetary demands.

Much has been learnt about the experience of crime both for victim and offender from these experiments. The danger, as funding ends, is that the lessons of reconciliative acts, which are neither contrived nor coerced, can be easily lost. Project staff and management will need to seek ways of centralizing this dimension of justice into the everyday supervisory practices of agency staff and volunteers, without additional demands on budgets.

References

Christie, Nils (1977) 'Conflicts as property', *British Journal of Criminology*, 17 (1): 1–15.
Coventry Reparation Scheme (1986) *Victim Offender Mediation, Six Monthly Report: 23.9.85–21.3.86.* Coventry: CRS.
Eccles, Graham (1975) 'Knife man meets his victims', *Melbourne Herald*, 25.2.75: 4.
Freeman, John, John Harding, Helen Reeves and Martin Wright (1982) *Establishing a Local Mediation Centre.* London: National Association of Victims Support Schemes.
Galaway, Burt (1983) 'The use of restitution as a penal measure in the United States', *Howard Journal*, 22 (1): 8–18.
Harding, John (1976) 'Restitution: paying back the victim', *Social Service News*, 20 (5): 8.
Harding, John (1980) 'A realistic payment for crime', *Social Work Today*, 12 (2): 20.
Harding, John (1982) *Victims and Offenders: Needs and Responsibilities.* London: Bedford Square Press.
Image, Terry (1986) 'Mediation and reparation in Wolverhampton', *West Midlands Probation Service Bulletin*, July 1986, 22–8.

Klein, Andrew R. (1981) *'Earn it'* – *the Story so far*. Quincy Court, 50 Chestnut Street, Massachusetts MA 02169.

Marshall, Tony and Martin Walpole (1985) *Bringing People Together: Mediation and Reparation Projects in Great Britain*, Home Office Research and Planning Unit Paper 33. London: HMSO.

Priestley, Philip (1970) 'What about the victim?' Regional Information Paper No. 8. Bristol: NACRO.

Priestley, Philip (1974) 'The victim connection and penal reform', speech to Margery Fry centenary proceedings, Bromsgrove, England. Unpublished.

Priestley, Philip (1977) 'Victims the key to penal reform', *Christian Action Journal*, Summer: 30–1.

Quaker Social Responsibility and Education (1979) *Six Quakers Look at Crime and Punishment*. London: Quaker Home Service.

Ruddick, Rose (1986) *Victim Offender Agreements, Coventry Reparation Scheme, 23.9.85–1.7.86*. Coventry: CRS.

Wilson, Deryck (1986) *Sandwell Mediation and Reparation Scheme 1985 Report*. Leagowes School Hut, Oldbury Road, West Smethwick, Birmingham.

Wright, Martin (1977) 'Nobody came: criminal justice and the needs of victims', *Howard Journal*, 16 (1): 22–31.

Wright, Martin (1983) *Victim/Offender Reparation Agreements: A Feasibility Study in Coventry*. Birmingham: West Midlands Probation Service.

Young, Richard (1986) *Sandwell Mediation and Reparation Scheme: An Evaluation*. Birmingham: Institute of Judicial Administration, University of Birmingham.

Zehr, Howard (1982) *Victim/Offender Reconciliation Program: Organizer's Manual*. Mennonite Central Committee, 220 West High Street, Elkhart, Indiana.

3

The Victim Support Perspective

Helen Reeves

If mediation arrived in Britain too late for the enthusiasts, it came just a little too early for Victim Support. Victims of crime were not yet properly provided for and their needs were only beginning to be recognized and understood. From the perspective of the National Association of Victims Support Schemes, the idea of mediated agreements between victims and offenders was born prematurely from an unusual union between policy-makers and penal reformers concerned primarily with an ailing criminal justice system which was in urgent need of a new direction. The concern for victims which was emerging in the early 1980s was seized upon as a potential means of diverting cases from the over-stretched courts and offenders from the crowded, unmanageable prisons.

The concept of applying mediation to the criminal justice process was introduced into Britain in the late 1970s by people who had been impressed by the restitution projects in North America. The programmes they described (Harding, 1982; Wright, 1977, 1981) contained a fundamental element of financial compensation or service in recompense for harm which had been caused. As a result, the idea appealed to supporters of punishment who were attracted by the ideas of offenders having to 'pay' for what they had done, as well as to exponents of the rehabilitation principle, who recognized in mediation the possibility of helping offenders to grow through a deeper understanding of the effects of their actions. By 1984, when the idea was adopted by the Conservative Home Secretary, Leon Brittan, he announced:

> The idea of reparation appeals to me for three reasons. First, through reparation, the criminal justice system can concentrate its attention on the individual victim whose interests must never be ignored. Secondly, the principle of reparation can be used to ensure that the wider interests of society are better served, and thirdly, nothing is more likely to induce remorse and reduce recidivism among a certain, all too numerous, kind of offender than being brought face to face with the human consequences of crime. (Brittan, 1984)

The problem at this stage was the absence of information as to the views or attitudes of victims of crime towards the proposed new practices. It came as a shock to enthusiasts when letters began to appear in the press questioning the acceptability of mediation. 'If I have just been burgled, the last thing I want is to have the grinning crook brought round to my door by some do-gooding social worker', ran one memorable contribution to the debate, printed in the *Daily Mirror*. The National Association of Victims Support Schemes,[1] launched in 1979, was still, by 1984, struggling against the odds to establish an identity and to secure even basic funding. Its officers were cautious about the new interest in reparation. Not only was the potential value to victims unclear, but the amount of excitement generated by this new treatment of offenders was already being confused with Victim Support by public and professionals alike. Volunteers visiting victims to offer assistance began to report anxious questions as to whether or not the offender would have to be involved, and the National Office of Victim Support soon became deluged with enquiries from probation officers, police, and press about how reparation and mediation projects should be run.

It must be said that many members of Victim Support had been interested in both reparation and mediation from the outset. As early as January 1980, the association had been approached by officials at the Department of Health and Social Security to ask if NAVSS would establish a juvenile reparation project to run alongside some of the victims support schemes in membership. Funding was mentioned which would have far exceeded the £15,000 government grant which had been made that year for the whole of Victim Support nationally. The new national council, which was still trying to raise enough money to open its first office, was naturally tempted by the proposal. However, after lengthy deliberations, it had been decided that the two issues should be clearly separated in order to safeguard the identity of Victim Support and to establish a service designed solely for victims of crime as a priority in its own right.

The criminal justice 'industry', focused almost entirely on the treatment of offenders, was substantial and influential. Any innovation related to the treatment of offenders was certain to attract much interest from the media. It was feared that, if Victim Support had become associated with experiments in reparation and mediation too early in its career, its primary objective could easily have become overshadowed. Even worse, if reparation had failed, like so many earlier attempts to deal with offenders, Victim Support might also have become regarded as a short-term fashion, rather than the fundamentally new response to the problems of crime which the association intended. The reparation proposal, together with the possibility of new funding, was therefore rejected.

The confusion between the two ideas persisted, however, in spite of NAVSS's decision. By 1981, almost every agency that was interested in running a mediation or reparation project had contacted NAVSS to ask about other developments in the field. To save time in passing on the valuable information which had accumulated, NAVSS decided to produce *A First Survey of British Developments in Reparation and Mediation* – a modest document, typed and photocopied in the new office, several hundred of which were issued to interested parties (NAVSS, 1981). From 1981, meetings were arranged at six-monthly intervals, to which everyone on the now substantial reparation mailing list was invited. This way, interested parties could meet and talk to each other without NAVSS staff having to pass on addresses or convey messages. Finally, in 1984, the new Forum for Initiatives in Reparation and Mediation (FIRM) was born of these informal meetings, hosted by Victim Support. Offender reparation had continued to attract rather more public and official interest than Victim Support, and the association was even more determined that the two issues should be clearly distinguished from each other (Reeves, 1984).

By now the association was, quite correctly, being accused of having an ambivalent attitude towards the new developments. Opinions among the membership varied considerably, particularly as there was still no evidence that mediation or even reparation, financial or otherwise, would prove to be in the victim's best interests. It would do little for the credibility of a victim-centred organization to jump onto a bandwagon which might later prove to make matters worse. Even more importantly, there was a genuine anxiety that, whereas the potential advantages for both offenders and for the criminal justice system itself were fairly straightforward, the reasons which had been postulated as to why victims might benefit from mediation and reparation may not be as sound as they at first appeared.

To begin with, much was made of the possibility that victims would benefit from financial compensation or service from the people who had offended against them. Such a source of compensation can hardly be regarded as adequate, and there were fears that acceptance of this notion could mask the need for a fully comprehensive system of compensation designed to benefit all victims. Less than 30 per cent of property offenders are detected and few offenders have the means to pay for the damage or loss they have caused. The chances of victims who need compensation being matched with offenders who can pay it are fairly remote. When compensation orders are made, offenders are given time to pay, usually small amounts on a weekly basis. A study in 1978 had revealed that, after 18 months, 25 per cent of orders had not been completed, including 10 per cent which had not been paid at all (Softley, 1978: 24). Compensation orders may therefore raise victims' expectations and the initial anger and distress may be prolonged unnecessarily if these expectations are not met.

For those who have insurance, the money should, in any case, be repaid to the insurance company, while for those who do not, the money arrives in small, irregular instalments over a long period, making replacement of goods almost impossible. Personal attitudes to financial compensation also vary. Some people will feel insulted by the idea that money can put things right, while others will feel bitter at the small amount which can be ordered when offenders' means are taken into account. It may be that a sincere apology may prove to be both more practical and more acceptable.

The 'ownership of conflict' was another idea which had gained considerable prominence, introduced by the Norwegian criminologist Nils Christie (1977). The relationship between victim and offender was said to involve a personal conflict which had been stolen by the state, leaving the victim with feelings of loss and frustration. There was certainly a good deal of evidence that victims do feel neglected and angry about the lack of information they are given regarding the progress of their case, but no evidence that victims would like the responsibility of deciding what should happen to the offender (Shapland et al., 1985). While it might sound attractive to give people more personal involvement, the criminal justice system was introduced to protect victims from the fear of threat or retaliation which might result from personal intervention, and to protect offenders from unreasonable or vindictive victims. There would need to be very good evidence of advantage before removing these safeguards.

Finally, with increasing knowledge of the effects of crime, it was now recognized that most victims do pass through a phase of searching for an explanation as to why the crime has occurred. Some might experience less persistent effects if they knew the identity of the offender(s), particularly if they could achieve some insight into the motivation and factors which had precipitated the crime. Some people will already know the offender and have to see him or her again anyway, so that a first meeting in a controlled setting could reduce the possibility of fear or retaliation. Another possible advantage, identified by Victim Support but rarely appearing in the literature at that time, was that many victims might appreciate an opportunity to put their negative experience to positive use by helping the offender to recognize the harm he or she has done in the hope of preventing further crimes.

These potential advantages are based upon the victim's attitude and state of mind at the time of being invited to meet the offender. If the intention of a project is to help meet some of a victim's emotional needs, it follows that cases should be selected according to the victims involved. The length of time between the offence and the offer of a meeting will also be of critical importance. Unfortunately, most of the earlier discussion had focused instead upon the selection of cases according to the suitability and wishes of offenders and their position in the sentencing tariff. Referrals were most likely to be generated according to the progress of the case through the criminal justice system, typically when either prosecution or sentence are being decided, regardless of the time which had elapsed since the offence.

The already extensive interest in reparation and mediation gained momentum in 1984, when the Home Secretary announced that money would be made available during the following year to fund a small number of reparation projects based on mediated agreements to test their effectiveness in the context of criminal justice. There was an explosion of interest throughout the country and far more projects were proposed than could be funded. Most proposals came from probation services and other agencies already dealing with offenders, so that the lack of contact with victims soon became recognized as a major obstacle. People who had previously shown little interest in Victim Support were now proposing to set up new schemes as part of their reparation programmes. NAVSS moved quickly to discourage such ideas. There was serious concern that victims and their own needs might be regarded as secondary to other objectives, such as diverting offenders from prosecution or imprisonment. References in some of the proposals to 'cooperative' or 'uncooperative' victims, and the fact that victims would usually only be asked about their willingness to meet after the offender and the court had already expressed interest did nothing to allay these fears. NAVSS encouraged its members to become involved with any local projects which might develop in order to safeguard the interests of victims and to monitor the results. No overall opinion was expressed as to the value of mediation, and judgement was reserved until more facts were known from the victim's point of view.

Four reparation projects were finally selected for funding in 1985, and their two-year experimental period came to an end in 1987. Only their interim findings are so far to hand, but other projects have in the meantime yielded some results. The second British Crime Survey sought reactions to the question of mediation from all respondents who had been victims of crime during the previous 12 months (Hough and Mayhew, 1985). Victims were told that the purpose of such a meeting would be 'to agree a way in which the offender could make a repayment for what he had done', but there was not, of course, any possibility of the meeting actually taking place in the context of this research. Overall, 49 per cent said they would have agreed to a meeting; the proportion was 52 per cent among those who had reported the crime to the police. Positive responses were considerably lower for victims of violent offences and threats, including less than one-third of the victims of assault and robbery, compared with approximately 60 per cent of those who had experienced property crimes, including burglary. When asked if they would like an agreement to be reached without having to meet the offender, the proportion who said they would rose from 49 to 69 per cent. Of these, only one-third would have regarded a mediated agreement as an alternative to criminal justice proceedings (Maguire and Corbett, 1987: 227–31).

In their survey of victims support schemes, Maguire and Corbett also considered the level of interest in mediation amongst victims. Fifty-two people, of whom half had been visited by Victim Support volunteers and half had not, were asked how they would react to the idea of meeting the offender to enable him or her 'to make personal amends'. Of those who had been visited, 43 per cent said they would have agreed to a meeting, compared with 32 per cent of those who had not (1987: 230), and the former group also expressed considerably less punitive feelings towards the offender (p. 170). Overall, the level of interest among victims was rather lower than that recorded by the British Crime Survey, possibly because of the slight difference in the question, or possibly, as the authors suggest, because the crimes referred to Victim Support were rather more serious than many of those uncovered by the British Crime Survey. The reasons most commonly given spontaneously by people who would have agreed to a meeting were: 'to know why he did it' or 'to see what he was like'. After prompting, 'the arrangement of financial compensation', 'letting the offender see the effect of his crime', and 'telling him what the victim thought of him', rose to equal prominence. Most common reasons for not finding the idea attractive were: 'fear', 'lack of interest', and 'anger' (pp. 230–1). Once again, victims knew that there was no possibility of a meeting actually taking place as a result of these interviews.

In a shorter study of one victims support scheme in Merseyside (Walklate, 1986), 28 victims who had been visited by Victim Support were asked if the offender could make amends for his offence. Only 30 per cent expressed positive interest, and apparently most of these interpreted making amends in financial terms or as the return of stolen property. Walklate describes a high level of anger and bitterness among her sample of victims, resulting in 11 of the 28 saying that 'making amends would be impossible.' It is difficult to explain the differences in the results of these two studies, as insufficient information is available, but differences in the geographical area, the schemes giving support, the wording and position of the questions or the attitude of the researchers are all possibilities.

One further survey which is worthy of note was carried out by Elaine O'Brien (1986) for the Gloucestershire probation service. The survey considered the effects of crime on individual victims and the closely associated factor of the relationship between victim and offender, as well as the level of interest in mediation. The sample consisted of 86 victims of all types of personal offence referred to the survey team by the police, specifically for the purposes of this research. Almost a quarter of victims interviewed were found to have known the offender well, and a further quarter to have known him or her slightly. O'Brien concluded that the closer the relationship between the victim and the offender, the more seriously the victim regarded the offence, the more serious were the effects, and the longer they lasted. She also found that victims of the more serious offences or those who knew the offender well were least likely to want mediation. Those who had been most frightened or angry were also least likely to welcome an opportunity to meet; but at the other end of the scale, those who thought the offence was a minor affair could see little point in pursuing the matter.

Although only 34 per cent of the sample would have been interested in a personal meeting with their offender, almost a half of all those questioned would have welcomed an apology, and more than half expressed some interest in group meetings with other victims and offenders. Two-thirds would have liked the offender to carry out voluntary work for others. It should also be noted that responses between the two towns selected for this study varied considerably, 48 per cent expressing interest in mediation in one and only 28 per cent in the other.

Genuine opportunities for victims of crime to meet their offenders have so far been fairly limited, and the results of the Home Office funded projects are not yet available. Some early information has been provided from a probation project in South Yorkshire which started work independently in 1983, and also from the first year of the Home Office funded project in Coventry. Cases for each of these emanate directly from the courts. In the case of Coventry victims are referred specifically for consideration of mediation, while in South Yorkshire all cases which were remanded on bail for social inquiry reports within the project catchment areas were considered. The catchment areas were small, definable communities within the towns of Barnsley and Rotherham. Victim responses to an offer of mediation in the first year of each project are shown in Table 3.1. Considerable variation in victim responses is suggested: a third agreeing to meet the offender in Coventry, nearly a half in Barnsley, and a quarter in Rotherham. An additional item is included in the South Yorkshire report, where 12 out of the 104 victims had already had a satisfactory meeting with their offender since the offence and therefore did not need mediation. This inevitably raises the question of whether similar cases occurred in other surveys, and if so, in which category they were recorded.

Table 3.1 *Victim responses to an offer of mediation in the first year of two mediation projects*

	Coventry		South Yorkshire Barnsley		Rotherham	
	No.	%	No.	%	No.	%
Victims referred/contacted in 1st year	115		66		38	
Victims agreeing to meet their offender	38	33	30	45	10	26
Already met	—		7	11	5	13
Agreeing to apology via mediator	26	23	12	18	3	8

Sources: South Yorkshire Probation Service, 1985: 3, 5; Coventry Reparation Scheme, 1986: 31.

More questions are raised by the differences in the level of interest expressed than can be answered. Writing about the South Yorkshire project in 1984, Smith et al. (1985) suggested that the higher level of interest in Barnsley resulted in this being an area where there was a higher proportion of private victims (whereas most of Coventry's victims were corporate and institutional), where more offences were committed by local people (although O'Brien suggests that increased knowledge of the offender reduces take-up), or resulted from the styles of the various workers involved. They do not say whether the Barnsley team were more helpful to the victim or if they exercised more persuasion!

Some findings, however, are remarkably consistent throughout the limited work available so far. Victims' main reasons for being interested in mediation relate to what the researchers describe variously as 'curiosity', 'wanting to know more about the offender', and 'why he did it'. The second most prominently reported reasons are to let offenders learn how their actions affect others, in the hope that it may prevent them from committing such crimes again, and to 'let him know what they think of him', 'let off steam', or 'give him a piece of their minds'.

What victims in general do not appear to want is tangible reparation in a form which might be measured and recognized by a court, although financial compensation, in part if not in full, is sometimes acceptable to confirm an apology. Even more importantly, victims do not wish to usurp the authority of the courts, for, to quote Peter Dixon, director of the South Yorkshire project: 'For victims, the public response to a crime is seen as something quite distinct and separate from any private settlement' (South Yorkshire Probation Service, 1985). The reasons given by victims who do not wish to mediate are also very consistent and fall into the broad categories of people being too angry or fearful, or not believing that there would be any useful purpose served.

To summarize, the main determinants of a victim's interest or otherwise in mediation appear to lie in the level of fear or anger they were experiencing, the questions which they want to have answered, and the degree to which they feel it would be useful to educate offenders about the effects of their crimes. Much of this is very familiar from a victim perspective. At an early stage following a crime, all victims are more likely to experience considerable fear and anger. For more distressing cases or more vulnerable victims, these feelings may persist over a long period, or even become permanent, particularly if people are not offered support. An offer of a meeting in these circumstances could cause more distress, although some may appreciate an opportunity to give vent to their feelings.

At a later stage, people attempting to come to terms with a crime are likely to be preoccupied in searching for a reason or explanation of what has occurred. It is perhaps not surprising that the most common reason for accepting a meeting is to find out more about the offender and why he or she did it. Finally, for those more fortunate people who have been able to come to terms with what has occurred, or at least to have put it behind them, an offer of mediation may well be regarded as pointless or a waste of time, unless of course they recognize in this a possibility of preventing further crime. What must be avoided at this stage is the possibility of reopening old wounds which could postpone the eventual recovery.

The central questions which should be asked, therefore, relate more to the victim than to the offender. The length of time which has elapsed since the crime occurred is likely to have a major bearing on the victim's state of mind, as will the degree of severity which victims attribute to the particular crime and the way in which they are managing to cope with the experience, including the amount of support which is available. As mentioned, the cases referred to mediation projects so far have tended to be selected by the stage the case has reached in the criminal justice process and by the attitudes of the offender at critical points in that process.

Far more information is needed about any detrimental effects which offers of mediation might have produced, particularly if the approach from the mediator constituted the only direct intervention from the system to the victim. While we know from the early findings that those who did agree to mediate were largely appreciative of the result, we know little about the effect upon the majority who did not. Is it possible that they were left feeling more guilty or more fearful of revenge from the offender, or simply more angry with a society which appeared to be concerned only with diverting offenders from the courts and not with helping the healing process for the person most concerned? It must surely be said that victims approached in this way must have services provided for them in their own right, and separately from the mediation programme. Support should be available before the offer of mediation is made and continue where necessary, even when the offer has been rejected.

In 1986, the government issued a discussion document on reparation, seeking views as to the possible relevance of mediated agreements in the context of criminal justice (Home Office, 1986). Almost all agencies and professions responding (the Justices' Clerks Society was an exception) by now took the view that mediation was of value in certain cases, but that it should not become a formal part of the criminal justice system. The concept of a reparation order was therefore abandoned and mediation did not appear in the Criminal Justice Act which followed. Some of the original anxieties regarding victims being put under pressure to accept the responsibility of helping determine the offender's future were therefore removed.

Also in October 1986, the Home Secretary announced substantial new funding for victims support schemes, which by then had achieved not only an identity but also proper recognition for the services they could provide for previously neglected victims of crime. It is now a matter for speculation whether Victim Support would have been more able to play an active role in mediation had it been introduced five years later, and if so, whether this would have resulted in the projects being more focused on victims and less contentious than they have so far proved to be.

Note

1 The National Association of Victims Support Schemes was established in August 1979 and began operation in January 1980. For those not familiar with its work, it is an Association of local schemes through which trained volunteers receive referrals, mainly from the police, shortly after the crime has been reported, and visit victims of crime at home to offer whatever support and assistance is needed. The most usual form of help is to provide people with an opportunity to talk about the experience and to get things into perspective. When necessary, practical assistance is provided – for example, in claiming criminal injuries or other compensation – and advice is given about crime prevention or other agencies who can offer help. It is offered to all victims, young or old, male or female, and for all types of crime where the victim is a private citizen. The only exceptions are for domestic violence and child abuse, in which other agencies already have the expertise to offer specialist help.

The primary aim of Victim Support is to help people to cope with the effects of crime. The NAVSS does not hold a view on the treatment of offenders, except where such issues as compensation are involved, and it has avoided the type of promotional activities which could increase the effects of crime, particularly fear. Each of the independent local schemes has a management committee which must include a representative of the local police, as well as statutory and voluntary social work agencies. The National Association maintains a code of practice to which all local schemes in membership agree to comply. It provides an information service on all issues relating to victims, develops policies related to practice, and, more recently, administers the new government funding which has been made available to local affiliated schemes.

References

Brittan, Leon (1984) 'Home Secretary's speech to the Holborn Law Society', 14 March 1984, unpublished.

Christie, Nils (1977) 'Conflicts as property', *British Journal of Criminology*, 17 (1): 1–15.

Coventry Reparation Scheme (1986) *First Twelve monthly report, 23.9.85–22.9.86*. Coventry: CRS.

Harding, John (1982) *Victims and Offenders: Needs and Responsibilities*. London: Bedford Square Press.

Home Office (1986) *Reparation: A Discussion Document*. London: Home Office.

Hough, Mike and Pat Mayhew (1985) *Taking Account of Crime: Key Findings from the 1984 British Crime Survey*, Home Office Research Study 85. London: HMSO.

NAVSS (1981) *A First Survey of British Developments in Reparation and Mediation*. London: NAVSS.

Maguire, Mike and Claire Corbett (1987) *The Effects of Crime and the Work of Victims Support Schemes*. Aldershot: Gower.

O'Brien, Elaine (1986) *'Asking the Victim': A Study of the Attitudes of Some Victims of Crime to Reparation and the Criminal Justice System*. Gloucester: Gloucestershire Probation Service.

Reeves, Helen (1984) *The Victim and Reparation*. London: NAVSS.

Shapland, Joanna, Jon Willmore and Peter Duff (1985) *Victims in the Criminal Justice System*. Aldershot: Gower.

Smith, D., H. Blagg and N. Derricourt (1985) 'Does mediation work in practice?', *Probation Journal*, 32 (4): 135–8.

Softley, P. (1978) *Compensation Orders in Magistrates' Courts*, Home Office Research Study 43. London: HMSO.

South Yorkshire Probation Service (1985) *Victim/Offender Mediation Project: Interim Report on First Twelve Months, November 1983–October 1984*. Sheffield: SYPS.

Walklate, Sandra (1986) 'Reparation: a Merseyside view', *British Journal of Criminology*, 27 (7): 287–98.

Wright, Martin (1977) 'Making the criminal help his victims', *The Times*, 3 August.

Wright, Martin (1981) 'Crime and reparation: breaking the penal logjam', *New Society*, 10 December, 444–6.

PART II

MEDIATION IN PRACTICE

4

Reconciliation Procedures and Rationale

Mark Chupp

> When I faced my victim, it scared the living daylights out of me and it hurt . . . but when I had to sit there and tell somebody 'Hey, I ripped you off,' . . . it created a relationship with me and them. (ABC, 1982)

Rarely have offenders had to face their victims and the human impact of their crimes. Offenders perceive their victims to be deserving of the crime and able quickly to recover losses. Victims have not only been overlooked by their offenders but many times by the entire criminal justice system. Furthermore, crime breeds suspicion, fear and anger, destroying the fabric of trusting relationships in a community.

In 1974, in an effort to address these concerns, the Kitchener, Ontario, project (see Peachey, this volume) was founded. Within fifteen years nearly seventy-five communities across Canada, the United States, and the United Kingdom have established programmes along the lines of this initial experiment. The essence of the Victim/Offender Reconciliation Program (VORP) is a face-to-face meeting between those caught up in crime – the victim and offender, facilitated by a community mediator. It offers opportunities for reconciliation to people who, although often previously unrelated, are now related in conflict by the criminal act. In cases where there is more than one victim or offender, each victim/offender pairing is treated as a distinct case. (For a history of VORP see Bender, 1986.)

This chapter describes the victim/offender reconciliation process, and provides a brief rationale for each programme procedure, drawing on actual case examples for illustration. The victim/offender reconciliation process is based on training materials developed by the Kitchener and Elkhart programmes and on the common practices that have evolved from the numerous VORPs in North America. For training purposes, the original programme developers divided the VORP process into four steps (Zehr and Sears, 1980: 8). I will proceed through each step, outlining the programme activities and giving the rationale for them. The four

Figure 4.1   *Four steps in the victim/offender reconciliation*
process (Zehr, 1983: IV.5)

steps are given in Figure 4.1. Although numerous VORP programmes have applied the process to various points in the criminal
justice system and with various types of case referrals, this four-step
process remains consistent among the programmes. The chapter
aims to describe this process from the perspective of programme
practitioners and therefore does not include a thorough critique of
the procedures and rationale.

Step 1: Intake, screening, and assignment to volunteer mediator

The majority of victim/offender reconciliation programmes receive
case referrals for primarily non-violent offences at a post-conviction
stage, often as one of several sanctions in a community sentence.
Some programmes, however, operate at a pre-trial level as a
diversion programme for juveniles or adults. Many VORP practitioners prefer to work with cases referred at the time of sentencing
to avoid any questions of guilt or innocence, and to prevent
offenders from performing in VORP to satisfy the sentencing judge.
The most common offences in VORP are burglary and theft, crimes
where the victim and offender are often strangers to one another.
But increasingly, a number of programmes are beginning to work
successfully with serious violent offences (see Umbreit, this volume).
The more common property offences for which VORP is used as a
post-trial diversion will serve as many of the examples in this
chapter.

   Once a referral is made to VORP, the programme staff conduct
the necessary intake procedures – checking for complete information on the referral, logging the case in, and completing any other
paperwork. The second activity is to screen the case to ensure that it
is an appropriate referral. Many programmes utilize written case
criteria to assist in identifying and screening cases. The staff review
the referral to see if there is any evidence of overt hostility between
the parties, and to make sure there is clearly a reason to meet – the
need for reconciliation and/or restitution. Assuming the case is
accepted, the VORP staff then assign it to a community volunteer
who has been trained in mediation. Volunteers will be referred to in

this chapter as volunteers or mediators, some of their functions adhering to a strict definition of mediation while others would be more accurately defined as community support work. Although it has been more common for one person to work on a case, many programmes prefer, and are beginning to use, co-mediators. In especially difficult cases a staff person might assist the volunteer or handle the case alone.

Criminal justice professionals have at times questioned the use of volunteers for such important, sensitive programme work. Through every step of the VORP process, however, there are clear benefits to using volunteers. A volunteer underscores the power of the participants themselves, pre-empting reliance on a paid professional to solve their problems. The volunteer role gives the community a renewed participation in the criminal justice system. VORP is intended as an attempt not only to empower the offender and the victim, but the entire community as well. Additionally, volunteers can avoid being partial to one party over the other and, with adequate training, can function in a professional manner. Many programmes have a minimum of fifteen hours of training for all volunteers, which is often followed by observing another mediator on a case before actually being assigned a case. A burglary victim who managed a magazine distribution company referred to the VORP volunteer in his case as 'very business-like and fair-minded. She looked out for the interests of those kids, making sure that they weren't shafted [unfairly taken advantage of] by us and that we benefited, too. Everything was done on a most professional level' (*Langley Advance*, 1985).

Step 2: Preliminary meetings with offender and victim

With very few exceptions a volunteer holds separate meetings with the offender and victim before considering a joint meeting. This is the first task of the volunteer and the first personal contact from VORP, although the victim might have received a form letter from the VORP office. There are six objectives for the individual meetings with the victim and offender. Even though the agenda is different for victims and offenders and, therefore, the separate meetings have different characteristics, the overall objectives remain the same. The volunteer attempts to:

1   introduce her- or himself and the VORP programme;
2   listen to the person's story – to gain understanding about the crime, but more importantly, to give the participant a chance to express themselves and feel heard. This is also a time for the volunteer to do the final screening of the case to confirm the appropriateness of proceeding;

3 explain the VORP process, including the role of the mediator, role of each participant, and the benefits for everyone involved;
4 secure agreement to meet with the other party;
5 make arrangements for the meeting, the time and place;
6 explore restitution possibilities, providing information about realistic options given who the participants are in this particular case.

The initial meeting with the offender is often conducted first, so that specific information on the offender and his or her ability to make restitution can be taken to the meeting with the victim. This also precludes the possibility of gaining the victim's agreement to meet with the offender, only to discover that the offender is unwilling to meet, which could further victimize the victim. This meeting allows the volunteer an opportunity to encourage voluntary participation by the offender. Many offenders feel a real pressure to participate in VORP since non-participation would be a negative reflection before the court. More than one offender has said to the volunteer: 'Tell me what I am supposed to do and I will do it.' On the contrary, the volunteer makes every effort to have the offender own the process. The format of the initial meeting (specifically, the story-telling) demonstrates to the offender that the VORP process places the responsibility squarely on his or her shoulders, to speak and act according to his or her own preference. While coercion still exists, the mediator tries to minimize it by allowing offenders to decline to participate and by turning the nature of their participation over to them.

The initial meeting also provides a safe environment for the offender to tell his or her story. In traditional proceedings offenders are rarely asked to tell, from their perspective, how the crime occurred and what took place during the arrest and court process. VORP allows the offender a chance to express what happened in her or his own words and is an outlet for any frustrations which may have developed either during the court processes or from lack of opportunity to discuss the offence. This is also a time for offenders to prepare their thoughts before meeting the victim, an encounter offenders usually face with fear and trembling. One offender said before meeting his theft victim: 'You know I'm really scared to death. I hope this guy doesn't kill me' (Zehr and Sears, 1980).

Thirdly, the initial meeting should help the volunteer gain credibility and trust with the offender. Unlike representatives of the adversary system, the volunteer stresses the mediators' impartial and non-coercive role. Since most offenders are frightened at the prospect of meeting their victims, establishing some rapport provides the bridge for the offender to enter that VORP meeting. The offender just referred to could face his victim because of his trust in the VORP volunteer. Fourthly, the volunteer attempts to explore with the offender a possible resolution of the crime. If there are physical losses, the volunteer can assist the offender in thinking through how she or he might be able to make restitution. The volunteer stresses the negotiating aspect to determining restitution, even asking the offender to come to the meeting with a specific proposal. Lastly, the volunteer tries to alleviate any unfounded fears on the part of the offender by answering questions and stating what will *not* happen at the joint meeting with the victim.

In the same way the initial meeting with the victim provides the volunteer with a time to establish credibility and trust, alleviate unfounded fears, and prepare the victim for the joint meeting. One major difference, however, pertains to the willingness to participate. There are no external coercive powers pressuring victims to participate, and the majority are initially reluctant to meet the offender. The volunteer does not present a 'hard sell' to the victims but, on the contrary, offers to listen. The story-telling process provides, probably for the first time, an opportunity for the victim to feel heard and validated by someone connected to the criminal justice system. The volunteer shows support and care for the victim by listening, empathizing with their pain, loss, and frustration.

After listening to the victim's story, the volunteer suggests the possible benefits of participating in the VORP meeting. Many victims have heard little about their case and have had little-to-no say in the outcome. They usually have many outstanding questions about their crime which can be answered by meeting the offender, not to mention the financial restitution they might receive. The volunteer might also provide a brief verbal sketch of the offender(s) in order to eliminate any fear of the unknown. At this point many victims express their interest in meeting the offender without further encouragement. One could argue that while there are not external pressures on the victim, there are internal ones urging them to participate: the fact that the offender has agreed to meet and the encouragement by the volunteer might be real coercive factors affecting the victim. For this reason, volunteers are discouraged from using coercive language during the initial meeting with the victim. After securing agreement to meet the offender, the volunteer explains in detail the procedure, to alleviate his or her fears, assuring the victim that the volunteer will prevent further victimization.

As in the meeting with the offender, the volunteer pursues potential resolutions to the crime by going over the victim's losses and outlining various restitution possibilities. Many victims assume restitution must be a cash payment, a hard-to-come-by commodity for most offenders. The volunteer might give examples of agreements on work and future behaviour from previous cases. The volunteer might also give a general assessment of what restitution the offender can realistically provide. The volunteer can also 'plant seeds' for future agreement by suggesting options they might want to consider. The volunteer tries to avoid getting caught in 'shuttle diplomacy', not striving for resolution before coming together but saying only enough to promote a positive joint victim/offender meeting.

In these initial meetings with the victim and offender, the volunteer goes beyond the role of a mediator or neutral third party. Without jeopardizing the capacity to stand in the middle or mediate, the volunteer offers support and encouragement to each party. The reconciliation process recognizes that crime causes a breach not only between victims and offenders, but in the entire community. Victims and offenders feel alienated from the community, neighbours become suspicious and fearful after hearing of the crime, and the entire community experiences a loss of trust and security. The volunteer, as a representative of the community, breaks the cycle of mistrust and validates the trauma each party has experienced, extending support that may lead to a renewed sense of trust in the community. As victims and offenders feel support from and reconciliation with the community, they gain confidence to be reconciled with one another. Through listening and reflecting, the volunteer also models the type of communication desirable in the joint meeting.

Step 3: The victim/offender reconciliation meeting

There are three basic aspects to the victim/offender meeting, commonly referred to as 'facts, feelings, and restitution'. The volunteer, who will function as the mediator during this portion of the process, sets the atmosphere and the stage for the meeting by planning a balanced seating arrangement, providing smooth introductions, and opening the meeting in a relaxed yet professional manner. The formal part of the meeting begins with the mediator reviewing the process, the roles of the mediator, victim, and offender, and ground rules, and emphasizing the confidentiality of the meeting.

The volunteer encourages each person to state factual information and express their past and present emotions. The victim usually begins the story-telling, going back to the time of the crime itself. The volunteer shifts the focus to the offender's story once the victim has spoken. The offender then engages in story-telling, stating why and how the crime took place. Once both sides have had an opportunity to complete their stories, the mediator opens a discussion period where outstanding questions can be addressed.

By the end of this part of the meeting, the victim should understand the offender's motivation for committing the crime, the impact of the arrest and court proceedings, and the offender's response to the victim's story. The offender should understand the various levels of impact the crime has had on the victim, including physical losses, fear, anxiety, mistrust, suspicion, anger, secondary victimization by the system, and the victim's response to the offender's story.

Reconciliation is not forced upon participants. The mediator will, however, ask the participants to express themselves freely. If communication is awkward or slow, the mediator might ask one party to paraphrase what the other person has said and felt, or ask how each party feels now that they have heard the stories. An apology often emerges at this stage, even though the offender might have gone into the meeting vowing not to apologize to the victim. The power of the personal face-to-face encounter breaks down many stereotypes and previous hostilities. Many victims will in turn offer some type of acceptance of the apology or extend forgiveness to the offender, despite their earlier intentions.

After the factual and emotional content of the meeting is covered, and any reconciliation has occurred, the mediator shifts attention to the written resolution. Now that some understanding has been reached about the crime, the mediator asks what the offender has to offer to 'make it right' to the victim. The offender is encouraged to offer some tangible form of restitution based on the losses which were stated in the earlier part of the meeting. This is a negotiation process where victims might state what they would like to receive and offenders respond according to their willingness and ability. The mediator encourages the participants to work out the agreement themselves and does not make suggestions unless there is a stalemate. Once the parties reach an agreement, the mediator offers to write up the details on a contract form provided by the VORP office. The contract could include any combination of financial payments, work for the victim or the community, or even agreements as to future behaviour. At times, the victim might agree to do something as well, such as employing the offender until enough funds have been earned to make restitution. The contract includes commitments made by both victim and offender. A projected completion date is written on the contract.

The many functions in the victim/offender meeting and accompanying rationale have evolved over time, in the context of case experiences. Some are still not utilized by all programmes or mediators. The ground rules, for example, were developed in order to prevent inappropriate behaviour and to have guidelines to fall back on in the event of a sudden outburst. Some mediators do not find this necessary, while others spend time securing agreement to such things as 'no name-calling', 'no interrupting', and 'no shouting'. This is all part of establishing an atmosphere and stage that will be conducive to open communication and reconciliation.

The story-telling, as mentioned earlier, validates each perspective without passing judgement. The mediator often asks the victim to begin in an attempt to offset the neglect he or she might have already experienced from the criminal justice system. There are stereotypes and misconceptions held by both victim and offender that need to be overcome in the session, and if the mediator determines that this will occur more effectively by the offender telling his or her story first, then the mediator will do so. When offenders are faced with the responsibility of admitting involvement in the crime, the story-telling allows them to stress their perspective.

Reconciliation comes about as the offender realizes for the first time the human consequences of her or his actions, the personal fear, trauma, loss, and anger that has resulted, and when the victim begins to see the offender as a person rather than some violent monster he or she has conjured up. A burglary victim whose home was broken into while he was away on his honeymoon exemplified this when he said:

> At first I kind of wish I would have been home so I could have shot him . . . But the more I talked with him, the more I found out the kind of problems he was faced with, and how the both of us kind of felt the same, thought the same. (ABC, 1982)

The expression of emotions encourages people to direct their feelings toward the cause rather than lashing out at society or others working in criminal justice. Once the victim has aired feelings, he or she can better listen to the offender and understand what motivated the act.

Reconciliation is based largely on breaking down stereotypes and the victim and offender arriving at a new understanding of each other. Although many cases end without a verbal apology and for-giveness, a degree of reconciliation may have occurred simply by the new understanding and respect for one another. This same burglary victim acknowledged that some reconciliation had occurred:

> As a matter of fact, when he left . . . he offered his hand in friendship and I took it, we shook hands, which I knew I would not have done before he came through the door. But when the evening was over with, I actually felt for him. (ABC, 1982)

The mediator encourages the participants to wait to discuss any restitution until after the reconciliation process. This promotes an easier negotiation of a restitution contract and promotes more creative, less rigid agreements. The offender is encouraged to propose some way of 'making it right' to the victim, which gives the offender an active rather than a passive role, contrary to the position taken by many offenders in the criminal justice system. In addition to helping the offender move away from seeing himself or herself as a victim, this demonstrates a level of sincerity to the victim. When the restitution is negotiated, rather than dictated, the result is a more realistic agreement that meets the needs of both parties, and is more likely to be fulfilled because the offender has more ownership in the agreement.

Restitution is not the goal of the process, but one major component of the desired reconciliation. Making it right to the victim, through tangible reparations, often embodies the less tangible verbal reconciliation attempted in the victim/offender meetings. For some it is 'icing on the cake', an extra which in many ways symbolizes or demonstrates the reconciliation that has already happened. As one victim said: 'I believe you are sorry but I want you to prove it to me.' At other times, the agreement furthers the reconciliation process. When restitution involves work for the victim, the relationship between the offender and victim is strengthened as the offender completes the task. In fact, in one case where two high school students vandalized their principal's car, the offenders agreed to take the principal and his wife out for dinner after they had completed restitution. At times the agreement can be an educational process, as in a case where the offender agreed to read the book on a particular ethnic group represented by the victim and write a report about the book (Friesen, 1985).

Not all cases end in reconciliation; for these cases restitution takes on a different meaning. The offender's attempt to make it right can soften a victim's tough attitude. Or, the contract might be behavioural: 'Bill will not have any contact with Larry', thereby stopping the conflict from escalating. The primary goal of the VORP process, though, is a more complete reconciliation; agreeing to some type of resolution might be the first step in a reconciliation process that takes months or even years.

Step 4: Reporting, monitoring and follow-up

After the VORP meeting the volunteer writes a narrative report with four short sections: (1) Preliminaries, (2) Reconciliation meeting, (3) Restitution agreement, and (4) Evaluation and summary. The report, along with the case packet and contract are returned to the VORP office. The staff, after reviewing the case with the volunteer, edit the report and send it and the contract to the referral source. The contract is monitored by the VORP staff until completion. Occasionally, the contract is not fulfilled by the projected date, so the VORP staff will schedule an additional VORP meeting, mediated by the same volunteer, to discuss what action will be taken. A new contract can be negotiated based on the current status of the offender's income and time. Some programmes have initiated a 'closure meeting', after the contract has been fulfilled, where the victim and offender have an opportunity to reflect on the process and the completed restitution. In this final meeting there are clearer signs of reconciliation and actual resolution of the crime.

This final step in the VORP process links the work of the volunteers with the office and referral sources. The report and oral review of the case give the staff an opportunity to monitor volunteers' work and provide advice and training. The staff edit and send the reports to the referral source in order to maintain a consistent format and a clear communication channel. Likewise, the staff monitor the agreements until completion. This also relieves volunteers of tedious work that is often difficult to accomplish outside the office. Volunteers are encouraged to check on the status of their cases from time to time.

Additional victim/offender meetings are necessary if the offender has lost his or her job or for some other reason is unable to abide by the agreement. Naturally, the same mediator is used as much as possible. This is also true of closure meetings, held once the restitution contract has been fulfilled. While many of the programmes do not yet hold these final meetings, most programme staff and volunteers see this as an important process. Reconciliation is often tentative at the first meeting, but the participants are usually more relaxed when they meet a second time, knowing the offender has actually completed what might have sounded like empty words earlier. This process also allows the offender once again to look the victim in the eye and say 'I offended you', but now they can also say with relief 'I made it right.' To reinforce this positive self-image some programmes have given the offender a certificate upon completion of the agreement.

Conclusion

Victim/offender reconciliation is a method designed to empower the victim, offender and community to solve their own problems, based on a win–win model of conflict resolution. Together, the victim and offender are to seek a mutually satisfactory agreement. And in the process, the larger community is to participate in the form of volunteer mediators and benefit from decreased suspicion and hostility and increased harmony and trust. Offenders are no longer to be seen as outcasts, but are to be integrated back into the community.

While this process has undoubtedly proven to be a healthy and effective one for many participants, a number of limitations have been realized. When VORP is a post-trial intervention (where VORP is utilized most), the victim and offender have already received many messages from the criminal justice system that hinder the reconciliation process. The nature of the adversarial system pulls the parties in conflict further apart, exaggerating and distorting the nature of the conflict. VORP participants, then, must go through a re-education process. For example, many victims have been told not to have any contact with the other party and not to give in to any compromise.

Another limitation to the reconciliation process relates to the voluntary nature of participation. There is certainly coercion from the criminal justice system on the offender to participate. As mentioned earlier, the victim also might experience subtle pressure to participate, since the offender and the volunteer are willing and ready to proceed with the meeting. Such coercion can inhibit personal responsibility and impede a free-flowing dialogue.

Once the parties come together there are several limitations affecting the outcome, the degree of reconciliation achieved. Victim/offender reconciliation is a process heavily dependent on communication skills. If a participant has difficulty expressing him- or herself, the other party might misinterpret this as an uncooperative attitude. The mediator, someone skilled in communication techniques, can intervene with some degree of success, but, ultimately, the parties themselves are to play the lead roles and reconciliation can be limited by their communication skills.

The final, and perhaps most significant, limitation to the reconciliation process hinges on the individual power of the victim and offender in a criminal conflict. The offender often comes to VORP feeling somewhat inferior, since he or she is the criminal. This sense of powerlessness can be quickly compounded by the potential power the victim might have that comes with wealth, age, social standing, and education. As a result, the mediation session can be very imbalanced from the outset – a situation possibly too difficult for even an experienced mediator. Furthermore, the results of overcoming this imbalance of power might go against a larger sense of justice. What might be considered a successful resolution could actually reinforce a notion that the wealthy get their dues and the poor continue to be oppressed. Some programmes have addressed this issue by developing job training and placement for unemployed offenders.

Yet even with these limitations, victim/offender reconciliation represents a model of justice rarely attempted, or even imagined, by many criminal justice professionals. VORP is an alternative sanction, but more basically it is an alternative to the adversarial process. The primary communication is shifted away from the powerful state to those directly caught up in crime – the victim and the offender. Rather than being adversarial, communication is collaborative. Figure 4.2 illustrates this fundamental shift.

The volunteer mediator attempts to balance the personal power of each participant. The mediator, as a third party but unlike a judge, directs communication away from her- or himself and facilitates communication between the victim and offender. This process does not focus on issues as defined by others (e.g. the judge,

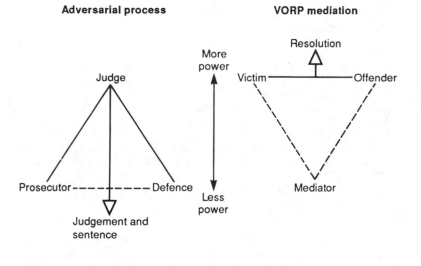

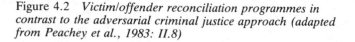

Figure 4.2 *Victim/offender reconciliation programmes in contrast to the adversarial criminal justice approach (adapted from Peachey et al., 1983: II.8)*

prosecutor, and defence lawyer), but on the concerns raised by the parties themselves. The four steps in the VORP process ensure that this collaborative communication will be likely to occur.

The reconciliation process, regardless of whether the victim and offender were previously acquainted, recognizes past injuries and the rights of individuals to work at their own solutions. The victim/offender conflict is valued and given priority. But instead of focusing solely on what happened, the reconciliation process offers an opportunity to decide what will happen in the future so that community members can live together peacefully (Zehr, 1985). Justice, according to this model, occurs when the offender has taken responsibility for his or her past behaviour, the victim has moved beyond the victimization event, and the anxiety in the community has subsided.

References

ABC Documentary Special (1982) *Going Straight*. Hollywood: Dave Bell Associates.

Bender, John (1986) 'Part I: Reconciliation begins in Canada' and 'Part II: Reconciliation Spreads to the US', *Mennonite Central Committee Peace Section Newsletter*, 16 (1): 1–5. Akron, Penn.: Mennonite Central Committee.

Friesen, Ray (1985) *Mediation: An Alternative Within the Criminal Justice System*. Manitoba: Mennonite Central Committee.

Langley Advance (1985) 'Magazine employees VORPed into new jobs', 15 May. Langley, British Columbia.

Peachey, Dean E., Brian Snyder and Alan Teichroeb (1983) *Mediation Primer: A Training Guide for Mediators in the Criminal Justice System*. Kitchener, Ont.: Community Justice Initiatives.

Zehr, Howard (ed.) (1983) *The VORP Book: An Organizational and Operations Manual*. Valparaiso, Ind.: PACT Institute of Justice and Mennonite Central Committee, Office on Criminal Justice.

Zehr, Howard (1985) 'Retributive justice, restorative justice', *New Perspectives on Crime and Justice*, 4. Elkhart, Ind.: Mennonite Central Committee, Office on Criminal Justice.

Zehr, Howard and Earl Sears (1980) *Mediating the Victim Offender Conflict*. Akron, Penn.: Mennonite Central Committee, Office on Criminal Justice.

5

Pre-Court Diversion for Juvenile Offenders

June Veevers

After the 1969 Children and Young Persons Act, cautioning by the police was the main method of diverting juveniles from the criminal justice system. The city of Exeter, Devon, has developed a structured system of cautioning, as will be seen below, and has had a high cautioning rate in the past; a careful assessment of the type of referrals, however, suggested that such a disposal was often unnecessary, and perhaps additional lower-tariff sanctions were appropriate, together with reinforcements or diversion. Much juvenile offending is of a minor nature. Policies which reflect this reduce the risk of drawing juveniles into 'the system'; at the same time they create an opportunity to work informally with the juveniles whose situation causes concern, and to develop preventive strategies.

The Exeter Joint Services Youth Support Team was formed in October 1979 after obtaining a five-year Urban Aid grant. The creation of the Youth Support Team meant that for the first time in this country police officers, social workers, and probation officers worked together on a full-time basis. The team has four main objectives:

- to develop effective policies for the prevention of juvenile crime;
- to divert juvenile offenders from the criminal justice system and courts;
- to coordinate local efforts in combating delinquency in Exeter;
- to establish community involvement projects, including self-help schemes, in conjunction with the statutory services.

Philosophical and theoretical basis and objectives

The team's reparation scheme evolved as one of the diversionary schemes from the second objective, beginning in 1980; it was aimed mainly at work-based reparation and voluntary monetary compensation. From this, victim/offender mediation developed about two years later. We were looking for appropriate responses to juvenile offending: ways in which the offender might 'pay back' the victim of the offence. This was seen as having a punitive element, but also as seeming 'fair' to all parties. In 1983 I put forward the following concept of reparation on behalf of the team, in the cementing of the reparation scheme as a formal integral part of the team's diversionary schemes; it will be seen that the idea of mediation was also introduced.

Reparation
'The act of repairing, restoration, satisfaction for injury or making amends'.

Reparation is seen by the Youth Support Team as an attempt to impress upon the young person the effect of anti-social behaviour on their 'victims' and to involve the community in an active response to the problems of juvenile delinquency. This is hopefully brought about by creating a sense of awareness through the discussion of the offence, culminating in an agreement that voluntary work will be carried out by the offender for the victim. The Scheme is NOT CONDITIONAL and, if a child or parent refuses to participate the caution is administered and that is the end of the matter.

Once a decision to caution has been reached and reparation is considered appropriate, the victim is approached to obtain his/her views. The programme of reparation is agreed by the team co-ordinator (who will also consult the young person's social worker or supervisor, if appropriate) and the victim. Victims generally prefer to meet the offender at the onset of reparation as opposed to a prior meeting.

Care is taken to arrange a meaningful programme as a result of which the victims will feel adequately compensated and the offenders will consider that they have contributed constructively and have been fairly treated. It is appropriate on occasions that compensation in cash form may be arranged together with a personal apology by the offender. This meeting to be supervised by either the scheme co-ordinator and/or the offender's social worker/supervisor by mutual agreement. In no circumstances should money be handled by a third person. In certain circumstances and situations, a personal apology or a letter of apology may be adequate.

In cases where reparation [Categories 1 and 2 below] is found to be impossible to arrange, and it is felt that the offender would benefit from performing some community based task, the reparation co-ordinator should consider the possibilities of the use of community reparation.

The reparation scheme is planned with a view to assisting the young person to integrate within his community in a positive way, e.g. by taking practical steps to 'put right' wrongs by methods which will hopefully benefit the offender and the victim and consequently the community as a whole.

Categories of reparation and mediation
Our experience of incidents where reparation may be appropriate

has resulted in the division of reparation and mediation into four categories:

1 *The single victim*: reparation when, for example, the victim is a householder or owner of damaged or stolen property.
2 *The corporate body*: (a) large businesses, factories and the like; (b) the local council parks department, highways department, etc.
3 *Community reparation*: community-based tasks where reparation is impossible to arrange under categories 1 and 2 and it is felt that the offender would benefit from performing a community-based task.
4 *Mediation after disputes*: in cases of assaults where the victim and the offender each have a percentage of the responsibility (e.g. 60/40) for the occurrence. The parents of the victim and the offender meet at the Youth Support Team, together with a police officer and social worker from the team, when all aspects leading up to the assault are discussed and alternative methods of resolving the issue are explored.

Levels at which introduction of reparation may be considered appropriate

The team, with the approval of the respective agencies, developed an 'extended' range of cautions which can be given at different levels. At the lowest level, no further action is taken. An 'informal warning' may be given by a police sergeant, and a 'formal warning' by an inspector. The formal warning is recorded in the team's records, but cannot be cited at any future court proceedings. The 'official caution' is administered by a police inspector, provided that it is accepted by the juvenile and signed by the parents. If the juvenile offends again and reappears before the court, the official caution can be cited in the same manner as previous convictions, that is, the court may be made aware, before passing sentence, that the juvenile has been cautioned for a previous offence. The next step on the tariff is prosecution.

Reparation can be considered in conjunction with an official caution, or higher on the tariff as an alternative to court; but it should not generally be considered when a person is being cautioned for the first time, unless the offence is appropriate and this course of action is thought beneficial to the accused. What is 'appropriate' may be illustrated by examples. One case might be an assault with such surrounding circumstances that mediation may be of more benefit to the offender and victim than a caution being administered to the offender; another would be an occasion when reparation would be seen to have positive results in terms of prevention and/or community involvement. These factors should be considered primarily in respect of the offender in terms of his or her 'best interests'.

In these situations a low tariff caution, for example, a warning by a police sergeant, is to be used in preference to the 'official caution', thereby preventing the offender climbing the 'tariff system' with undue rapidity, if he or she were to re-offend. This will leave the option open in decision-making for reparation to be considered with regard to re-offenders, where appropriate, accompanied by the official caution either as a reinforcement of the caution or as an alternative to court.

The use of mediation

As mentioned, the concept of mediation was preceded in the Youth Support Team by the development of the reparation scheme, and the experience of mediation within the reparation scheme encouraged the team to develop mediation as an integral part of the main scheme. The decision to use mediation was originally based on the following assumptions.

1   *Leading to reparation*: that it might provide the initial vehicle for intervention out of which reparation might be suggested or agreed by both parties.
2   *Effective communication*: that it might provide better communication between the offender and victim and hence a better understanding of each other's responsibilities for the incident and subsequent actions.
3   *Community responsibility*: that it could put the responsibility for the incident and future behaviour on to families, who often come from the same community.
4   *Diversion for offenders*: that it might well provide an effective diversion for offenders 'against the person'. It was noted that many 'assaults' and cases of 'actual bodily harm' were incidents in which some contributory behaviour could be identified in both parties. (We were also looking for evidence that neither was likely to re-offend.)
5   *Effective addition or alternative to the police cautioning system*: that it should provide a useful and acceptable addition or alternative to the formality of the police caution.
6   *Youth Support Team cooperation*: that it might provide a useful model within which the constituent agencies of the Youth Support Team could actively cooperate and to which they could contribute their respective knowledge and skills.

Practical arrangements

We agreed to have a police officer and a social worker involved in each mediation and, ideally, the same people involved throughout a number of cases. This allowed for a development of specialization and a more confident reinforcement of roles. The variety of experiences in each mediation could also be compared and monitored. It seemed most important that the two people involved in the mediation be responsible for setting it up, and it seemed to be appropriate to use the police officer as the contact with the victim and family because of the assumed authority and 'protection' often seen as invested in the police.

It was felt that ideally the mediation should take place on 'neutral' ground, and the Youth Support Team is fortunate in being able to provide a fairly anonymous city-centre office for this purpose, being apart from either the police station or the social services office.

In particular, we felt that the use of mediation in offences against the person could prevent on-going conflicts within the community and encourage youngsters, through understanding of incidents which lead to physical assaults, to find other methods of resolving their difficulties. Perhaps by seeing the effects of their respective behaviour on others, they could learn methods of modifying behavioural patterns, and thereby avoid physical confrontation.

Mediation prerequisites

We have established five basic criteria to decide whether a case is appropriate for mediation.

1 That there is evidence in the police file sufficient to establish a *prima facie* case.
2 That the offence is admitted by the alleged offender.
3 That both parties (and the parents of juvenile offenders, and victims) agree to mediation.
4 That the liaison meeting agrees that mediation with or without a caution is an appropriate disposal of the case and that the caution is acceptable to the offender and parents.
5 That the youngsters will probably benefit from mediation and that it will be a positive experience for them in terms of prevention of a recurrence.

In addition to using mediation in cases of assault, the team uses it in cases of theft, criminal damage, and minor burglaries, by way of personal apologies to individuals, shop and factory managers, and so on. In these situations victims are encouraged to explain to the youngster the effects of their actions on themselves and others and their feelings. The youngsters are encouraged to discuss and explain their own actions and their feelings 'after the event' – how they feel in retrospect and the effect on themselves and their families and thoughts regarding their future behaviour.

The ground is carefully prepared by the mediator beforehand both with the victim and the youngster, to enable them both to contribute meaningfully to the session.

The mediation process

In order to present the mediation process, it is necessary to describe the unique process of decision-making within the Youth Support Team where the final disposal of each case is determined by a liaison meeting consisting of the senior social worker, the probation officer and the police inspector from the team. If a pre-liaison visit has been made, the team member making that visit will also be invited; if the youngster already has a social worker, that social worker will be invited to the meeting. The total membership of the Youth Support Team is as follows: one senior social worker; two social workers; one probation officer; one police inspector; two police sergeants; one police constable.

The police members have an additional responsibility for the investigation and monitoring of child abuse within the police division. The police inspector is able to make the final decision vested in the police by virtue of delegation of responsibility by the divisional commander. Thus referral decisions do not have to be ratified by the divisional senior officers unless the offences are very serious ones, which are dealt with at a higher level after consultation. In cases where agreement cannot be reached by the liaison meeting, the police divisional commander and the divisional director of social services will meet and make the decision. Failure to reach agreement has been rare during my seven years with the team – not more than half a dozen cases, and in these agreement was reached at the higher level after consultation.

The path of the referral

Every juvenile who comes to the notice of the police, whether the incident is offence-based, or for any other reason (e.g. missing from home, behavioural problems at home or within the community) is referred to the team on a 'juvenile referral form' giving full details of the young person and the problem. The official police file follows when completed.

If the youngster is giving cause for concern, the liaison meeting may decide that before any decision is made, a pre-liaison visit should be made by a member of the team in order that the meeting is aware of all the facts surrounding the youngster, the family, and the background to the incident. If the youngster already has a social worker then he or she will be invited to make this visit and make recommendations to the meeting in person.

At this stage, should reparation or mediation be considered a possible part of the disposal of the case, this would be discussed with the parents and the youngster at the pre-liaison visit, to ascertain whether it would be of benefit to the youngster and whether the parents were likely to consent. Such consent is purely voluntary and no approach will yet have been made to the victim. (The offender is also visited first at Coventry: see Ruddick, this volume.)

Once the reports are available to the liaison meeting, a decision is made on the outcome. If reparation or mediation is part of the decision then the file is passed to the reparation coordinator to arrange the reparation/mediation.

The coordinator will visit the victim to ascertain his or her willingness to participate and, if the victim agrees, to explain the reasons for the mediation so that the meeting can be constructive and the youngster can gain knowledge which may help him or her to moderate future behaviour. It is of the utmost importance that victims are so briefed and that they do not see the meeting as a chance of an extra berating or 'telling off' of the youngster. Mediation needs to be seen to have advantages for both the victim and the offender. When both parties have agreed to take part, arrangements are made for a meeting.

Simple mediation
At the lower end of mediation is the simple 'personal apology' plus, occasionally, some form of voluntary compensation, covering thefts and criminal damage. In these cases a member of the team (either the coordinator or the social worker involved, decided by mutual agreement between the two) will accompany the youngster to visit the victim at the place of the offence, e.g. shop, office, or home, to make the apology. At these meetings the youngster is encouraged to express his or her feelings and give reasons for his or her behaviour. The victim is encouraged to describe to the youngster the effects of such behaviour on herself or himself and others in close proximity.

Both are then encouraged to come to their own conclusions and express them to the other, and, after the meeting, to discuss with the mediator their opinions of the outcome of the meeting. Did they consider it worthwhile; what have they individually gained from it or otherwise; will it affect the youngster in modifying his or her future behaviour? This form of mediation is fully discussed with parents, who are invited to attend if they wish. To date, none have.

It is made clear to the parents that the mediator in these instances will be acting in the youngster's and parents' interests during the meeting.

With careful preparation of the ground before the meeting with both offender and victim, we have found that this type of mediation is beneficial to both parties.

Mediation in more serious offences

In more serious offences such as assaults, similar preparations are made for mediation, but the meeting is arranged at the Youth Support Team offices. We then have two mediators, usually a police officer and a social worker from the team. People contributing to the mediation session consisted of offender(s) and parent(s), victims (and parents, if juveniles). As a general rule, leading up to the meeting, the social worker makes contact and arrangements with the offenders and parents and the police officer makes the contacts and arrangements with the victim(s) and parents.

The mediators have not always stuck to their official, agency role. The police officer usually introduces the session and gives the official summary, including the decision made by the liaison meeting. The social worker is instrumental in putting all those attending at ease, encouraging both parties to discuss their feelings about the offence and the effect on them as individuals, and reflecting on 'statements' made by each party.

To set up the meeting it has been found that a simple circle of chairs was all that was necessary. Both sets of participants are invited to attend at the same time and admitted to the room together. This allows a free choice of 'territory'. On most occasions this left chairs for the mediators to sit opposite each other, thus allowing effective non-verbal communication between them.

A mediation may be accompanied by a caution or a warning or no further police action. If a caution or warning is part of the decision then that is completed prior to mediation to ensure that the attendance at mediation is voluntary. Again, the voluntary attendance is emphasized. If at, or after, the caution the offender refuses mediation, then that is the end of the matter.

After the mediation session, contact is made with the offender and victim by the mediators to discuss any comments and reflections that they may wish to make on the session and to evaluate its usefulness. The mediators will then discuss the session and its outcomes, and record them.

As referrals to the scheme increased, other members of the team were trained to make the initial contact with victims and build up that particular expertise.

Mediation issues and problems

The time factor
It was noted that the most effective mediations with youngsters were those arranged as soon as possible after the offence, when the details were clearly remembered by both parties to mediation. This depends on prompt arrangement of the pre-liaison visit, arrival of the police file and the administration of the caution, where appropriate. Where possible, the mediation is arranged within a week of the caution or warning being administered. Where mediation alone is decided upon, the meeting is arranged as soon as possible after the decision is made by the liaison meeting.

Non-attendance by the victim
Non-attendance by victims has not been a major problem, but has occurred on a few occasions. In these situations it was felt that the offender had made the effort and this would be fully discussed with the mediators, and then the matter was dropped, the outcome being recorded. The victim was then contacted to ascertain the reason for non-attendance, and informed of the decision arrived at.

The reasons for non-attendance by adult victims were either that they had forgotten or that they had pressing business elsewhere and had not bothered to contact the mediators. These were very few, but impossible to foresee. Where juvenile victims and their parents did not attend, the reasons were that they had forgotten or there were transport problems. The latter could be resolved in further similar cases by the mediator in contact arranging to collect the juvenile and parent(s). There has been no experience of victims consenting to mediation and then refusing to attend.

In the years from the start of the project in 1983 (1984, 1985, and the first seven months of 1986 [to 31 July]), the total numbers of

Table 5.1 *Mediation outcomes in Exeter, 1983 to July 1986*

Cases referred to reparation scheme	1983	1984	1985	1986[a]
Total	31	92	93	48
Specifically for mediation	11	36	50	28
Achievements				
Personal apologies	11	35	45	24
Mediation	0	1	5	4
Refusals				
Victims	0	1	4	3
Offenders	0	0	7	0

The types of offence included theft (1983 only), assault (1984 onwards), damage, and burglary.
[a] To 31 July.

offenders referred to the Youth Support Team for all types of crime were, respectively, 659; 799; 702; and 380. The numbers referred for mediation are shown in Table 5.1.

Case histories

'Wendy' (14 years old) and 'Helen' (12 years old)
Wendy was reported to the Youth Support Team by the police after Helen had been taken to the hospital with a broken jaw, caused by a fight on local playing fields. Wendy had freely admitted the offence and the liaison meeting of the Youth Support Team (Juvenile Bureau) were having to consider a court hearing in the light of the seriousness of the offence.

The reporting police officer had highlighted in his report that there had been a series of arguments between these two girls leading up to the fight. Wendy is a first-time offender and neither girl was officially known to the police. It was agreed to caution and to try mediation. The visits to parents were carried out quickly. The social worker involved in the mediation had already visited Wendy for a pre-liaison assessment and a woman police sergeant was dispatched to the victim and parents. Both sets of parents agreed, but the following week only the mothers and their daughters turned up at the office.

Helen proved to be a quiet girl, very responsive to adult disapproval, and much of the mediation meeting centred on her. The two workers and both mothers encouraged her to talk and she was able to admit that she could be very destructive in the way that she sought friends by using cruel gossip. Wendy proved much more powerful, but again the mothers, with the help of the workers, were able to impress on her that she had used inappropriate means to stop Helen's gossiping. Wendy eventually contributed to a pictorial, social skills presentation of how she could avoid fights in the future. She was then able to offer a clear apology which was accepted by Helen and her mother.

Wendy's mother was also powerful, and she brought many aspects of the school and community to the discussions. It seemed that the dynamics of this community had contributed to this fight, with the girls being goaded and 'set up' by others. Helen's mother could identify with all this, and made subsequent contributions. The atmosphere developed out of the formal into a very comfortable interchange of ideas which could be diverted into positive expressions of what could be achieved next. The two girls worked out ways in which they could coexist with minimum contact. They were determined not to be friends. The mothers went further and promised to communicate more because, as mothers on this particular estate, they had a lot in common.

It was interesting that while Wendy had always been the stronger of the two girls both mothers noted how this had altered since the fight. Helen had become the wounded party and had gained a lot of sympathy and status in the community for this, which created problems as Wendy had started to reassert herself; but meanwhile Wendy had developed regular enuresis. This meeting seemed to have allowed for a natural but less traumatic reassertion of the previous pattern and both Wendy and Helen seemed happy that they now knew where they stood with each other. The meeting broke up with a very positive air, both sides saying that they thought the experience had been worthwhile and cleared the air. Both mothers said they were glad that Wendy had not been taken to court, but said that by sitting in this meeting and listening to the criticism she had received, she had been punished. The free delivery of the apology had seemed to be most significant.

In the follow-up, it was noted that Wendy soon grew out of the enuretic stage. Over the following year she developed into a much more confident but less abrasive character. Helen has regained her position in her peer group and shows few problems at school or in the community. The immediate neighbours of these two families on the estate, who seemed to do such a good job of gossiping about the offender, have now concentrated their efforts on different subjects.

'David' (14 years old) and 'Thomas' (14 years old)
David was reported to the Youth Support Team by the police after assaulting Thomas at school, causing him actual bodily harm (heavy bruising around the face and head). David admitted the offence and the reporting police officer included in his report the fact that there had been a lot of verbal provocation by Thomas prior to the assault. Thomas's mother had made the initial complaint to the police, although the incident had been reported at school. Both boys were known to the Youth Support Team for minor offences, but none of this nature. It was decided to caution and try mediation.

The social worker, involved in the pre-liaison visit, made the visit to David and the woman police sergeant visited Thomas. Both mothers and the boys agreed to the meeting and came to the office the following week. It transpired that the mothers knew each other slightly: the boys had, until fairly recently, been friends but had drifted apart. Neither parent had realized the identity of the other boy, although both parents had been in contact with the school and the police officer and had questioned their respective sons.

As a result of this discovery both mothers encouraged the boys to talk their way through the incident and the events leading up to it. It became apparent that up to this point Thomas had been totally unaware of the effect of his verbal provocation on David, and David had been unable to react other than by hitting out. With the help of parents and the two workers, Thomas and David were able to discuss alternatives and methods of recognizing the effect of their respective behaviour on others. David was then able to apologize to Thomas, who was able to acknowledge the provocation in his own behaviour.

Both sides said that they felt the experience had been worthwhile and Thomas's mother was glad that David had not been prosecuted. The parties left the meeting to travel home to their estate together in an easy relationship. The follow-up revealed that David and Thomas remained within the same group of friends and neither presented further problems.

Conclusions and recommendations

Experience of the reparation/mediation scheme, over the three years of its main operation, has shown the need to recognize cases suitable for reparation or mediation, where the experience would be positive and meaningful for the offender and meet the needs of the victim. Having obtained the consent of both parties, there must be careful preparation of the ground beforehand, including the exploration of the expectations of each participating party. Close consultation and planning is needed between the mediators in order to guide the direction of the meeting of the parties to a satisfactory conclusion.

In using the same people as mediators for a number of meetings, expertise is acquired in dealing with various situations which can be passed on to other members of the team. Regular meetings of the team have been found necessary to monitor the scheme and query its direction and, if necessary, to lay down new or amended guidelines. These queries have been picked up quickly by the coordinator, who has an overview of what is happening within the scheme. Doubts or queries can be discussed and ironed out (see *Reparation Scheme Review*, March 1985, Exeter Joint Services Youth Support Team).

Keeping within aforementioned guidelines, it is generally accepted within the Youth Support Team that mediation has beneficial and lasting effects when used with youngsters of 14 and over within the juvenile system. Provision is made for the use of reparation/mediation within the scheme on more than one occasion with the same offender if, under the particular circumstances, it is thought to be beneficial. The joint reparation/mediation scheme has a wide range of options to facilitate what may be considered to be a 'higher tariff' option, if thought necessary.

In my view, the multi-agency approach has a distinct advantage over a single agency, in that the scheme will have a wider and sounder basis and support. Also, it will more easily retain continuing support for future development.

6

A Court-Referred Scheme

Rose Ruddick

In February 1985 the government announced funding of four experimental reparation schemes over a two-year period, based in Cumbria, Leeds, Wolverhampton and Coventry. These pilot schemes represent a few of the mediation/reparation initiatives currently taking place in Britain at different points in the criminal justice process and with a mix of objectives. Support for the development of these early initiatives was drawn from concerns about

1 the search for a new sanction which would be community-based and yet punitive enough to be seen to 'fit' the crime;
2 increasing awareness of crime victims and a wish to see victims offered better acknowledgement by the criminal justice system, and reparation for the harm caused;
3 the developing movement towards seeking alternatives to the formal justice system for resolving both civil disputes and criminal offences. Christie (1977) argues, in relation to victims and offenders, that both parties have lost the right to partici-pate in the resolution of their own offences, clarify norms, put right anxieties and misconceptions and, for offenders, have direct responsibility for the consequences caused by the offend-ing act.

Strands from all the above areas and the growing experiences in North America presented in Britain by advocates of reparation such as Harding and Wright from the early 1980s onwards have variously influenced the aims and objectives of initiatives in Britain during the last few years; projects are also diverse in terms of funding arrangements, administration and structure.

This chapter considers one of the three court-based Home Office funded schemes, at Coventry, drawing on the scheme's experience and results and available research material over the first two years of operation – all outlined in the CRS report (1988).

Background to the Coventry scheme

The Coventry Reparation Scheme (CRS) began its operation in September 1985 as an experimental court-based project aiming to test the value and practicability of victim/offender reparation and mediation. In addition to Home Office funding, charitable grants were also provided during this period which were extended in 1987, along with new funding from the West Midlands Probation Committee, to enable the scheme to continue for a further two years.

Locally, interest in the development of a mediation and direct reparation scheme began in 1983, after discussions between magistrates and the West Midlands Probation Service about a dissatisfaction with available methods of dealing with low- to mid-tariff offenders, particularly those who commit offences against property and whose financial position is not strong enough to enable them to make adequate compensation or pay the level of fines that the court felt would be commensurate with the seriousness of the offences. John Harding, then Deputy Chief Probation Officer in the West Midlands, had traced the development of restitution schemes in the USA in which victims and offenders, with the assistance of a mediator, agreed a plan for the recovery of losses. Harding's interest in this alternative way of dealing with offenders also influenced local thinking in considering this new approach.

A local committee, consisting of representatives from different court-user groups (including magistrates, justices' clerks, Crown Prosecution Service, probation, the local Law Society) and the Coventry 'Care of Victims' Scheme, was then convened by the probation service to look further into the possibility of a reparation scheme. With the assistance of a grant from the Barrow and Geraldine S. Cadbury Trust, Martin Wright (a former Director of the Howard League of Penal Reform and author of *Making Good* (1982) in which he argued for a criminal justice philosophy which would emphasize offenders making amends to victims) was commissioned to prepare a feasibility study in Coventry. In his report (1983), Wright considered the possible types of cases, referral system and staffing requirements suitable for a court-based reparation scheme and the various methods which victims and offenders could agree, with the assistance of a volunteer mediator, whereby direct reparation could occur – either by way of direct service or by payment of compensation.

Increasing interest also began to be shown nationally in the notion of direct reparation. An All-party Penal Affairs Group of MPs recommended developments in this area (Parliamentary All-party Penal Affairs Group, 1984) and in his speech to the Holborn

Law Society in 1984, the then Home Secretary, Leon Brittan, asserted that 'offenders . . . should be required to make positive reparation for their crimes'. The time was ripe, therefore, for the Coventry scheme and others to make successful applications for Home Office funding.

Between the announcement of government funding in February 1985 and the offer of charitable assistance and the project leader's appointment in June 1985, two main issues began to be considered which had an influence on future decision-making. The first was the emphasis in Martin Wright's study on compensation and the part this could play in reparation agreements. The study's proposals in relation to the development of 'Earn-it' schemes (i.e. providing temporary work to unemployed defendants to enable them to pay compensation to the victim) caused some concern locally; given the increasing levels of unemployment, for some this concern related to queue-jumping, and for others the dangers of offenders being exploited as cheap labour. The second issue related to the experiences of a senior probation officer (Lionel Smith) during a visit to mediation/reparation schemes in the USA and the view he formed from this that a reparation scheme should operate in as neutral a setting as possible, its independence from a major statutory agency needing to be apparent in order to ensure the recognition of the victim as well as the offender-focus of such a scheme. In recognition of this varied focus the scheme sought to operate outside mainstream probation activities and management for the initial period and independent premises were obtained.

Structure

The recipient of the project's grants is the West Midlands probation service which employs all members of staff and services the scheme. There is, however, an independent management committee of representatives from all court user-groups and the victim support scheme. This committee is responsible for the policies and everyday operations of the scheme and the staff are directly accountable to it. The three staff members appointed in 1985 (plus a secretary) were from varied work backgrounds – probation, industry, law; a replacement staff member after one year, with a background in social work, took over as the scheme's project leader in February 1988.

Aims

The CRS aimed to test a number of hypotheses during this initial period, relating to victims' and offenders' wishes for mediation and reparation, offender education and reducing re-offending, the uses which the local courts might make of the provision of a reparation scheme, and the value of operating as an independent service.

The aims of the reparation scheme include:

1 Offering *victims* reparation, an opportunity to express feelings and views, and obtain information which may assist in coming to terms with the offence and its consequences, and providing victims with better acknowledgement by the criminal justice system and an active participation in a process which may divert the offender from similar criminal behaviour in the future.
2 Encouraging *offenders* to accept personal responsibility for their actions, to consider the victim and to make constructive use of opportunities for making reparation, apologizing and expressing feelings, and for reviewing future criminal behaviour intentions.
3 In cases where victims and offenders have a prior relationship the mediation/reparation process also offers the opportunity for conciliation or reconciliation between the parties.
4 Providing the *court* before sentence is passed with a report containing further insight into the offence and its consequences gained from the mediation/reparation process, the victim's views, the offender's attitude towards the offence and details of attempts to put matters right.

Method of operation

The scheme provides a service to victims, offenders and the local court by accepting court referrals of criminal cases, and facilitating through the *mediation* process communication between victims and offenders about the offence and its aftermath, and encouraging *reparation* (that is, the making of emotional and/or practical amends) to occur through an apology being offered and, when agreed, by the completion of a practical reparation agreement. Feedback about the mediation/reparation process is then presented to the court by way of a written report.

Table 6.1 outlines the types of cases considered for referral from the magistrates', juvenile and (experimentally) the crown court, referral procedures, the process of mediation/reparation under-taken, and method of feedback to the court.

Cases and outcomes

The main focus of the scheme's work during its initial two years was in the magistrates' court and 158 referrals were made during this

Table 6.1 *Method of operation (court-based)*

	Magistrates' court	Juvenile court	Crown court
Date of commencement of referrals	September 1985	April 1986	June 1987
Types of cases considered for referral	Cases where there is: 1 a guilty plea 2 an identifiable victim 3 a willingness by the offender to cooperate with the scheme's aims	Cases where there is: 1 a guilty plea 2 an identifiable victim 3 an offender and victim aged 14 years or over (save in exceptional circumstances) 4 a willingness by the offender and his/her parents to cooperate with the scheme's aims	Same as magistrates'/juvenile court cases
Referral procedure	1 Following plea and before sentence a court referral to the scheme may be prompted by one of the scheme's officers available daily at court or by any court user 2 If the magistrates agree to refer, the case is adjourned for 28 days 'for assessment by the reparation scheme' (decisions regarding the need for social inquiry or other reports are made separately)		Practice direction 18 March 1987 1 Potential cases are identified by the scheme or defence solicitor prior to committal to crown court 2 If requested by the defence solicitor following discussion and instructions from the defendant, the scheme offers the defendant an appointment to explain the scheme and its aims; prosecution details are also read 3 The scheme then writes to the defence (copy to crown court office) indicating scheme's views regarding the appropriateness of seeking a referral 4 On committal for trial, defence confirm an anticipated guilty plea and the scheme informs the magistrates' court office requesting adherence to the 4-day rule for transmission of papers to the crown court which then immediately drafts the indictment 5 Within 7 days of committal the case is listed for plea; on that date the prosecution and defence sign an abridgement of time consent

when the defendant is arraigned (the defence solicitor will be present although with no right of audience and the CPS representation will be available for other court business; pre-existing bail terms will not be subject to variation at this arraignment hearing)

6 Following the guilty plea the judge, if he/she agrees that the case is suitable for referral, warns the defendant that willingness to participate will not determine the sentence, although it may affect it, and directs that the reparation procedure be undertaken

7 In cases where a referral is made, the crown court notifies the CPS and the case reverts to the ordinary listing procedure

Mediation/ reparation process	In relation to *both* parties emphasis is placed on: ● voluntary participation in the mediation/reparation process ● the mediator's equal and active concern ● facilitating constructive communication (about issues agreed and in conflict) ● protecting and ensuring the parties' security 1 The mediator begins with reading the prosecution file and becoming familiar with available details about the offence and its consequences 2 During an initial go-between stage, the mediator has discussions with the offender and then the victim. The aims here are to explain the scheme and how it works, to understand more about what happened and its consequences and each party's feelings now 3 Both victim and offender are assisted, if they wish, to consider whether communicating with each other through a third party or by way of a joint meeting could be helpful. The aims of such communication are drawn out and the victim and offender helped to prepare for meeting each other when this is to occur. Discussion about reparation possibilities also takes place 4 The mediator conducts joint meetings by introducing the parties, facilitating communication between them and checking out details regarding agreement/understanding reached 5 Individual discussions with victim and offender take place following joint meetings to discuss what took place and on-going contact occurs when the mediator is involved in direct/indirect supervision of reparation agreements NB The mediator may also have contact during this process with other parties, e.g. victim's or offender's family
End of adjournment period	1 Written reports are presented to the court before sentence is passed. No recommendation regarding sentence is made. Reports include details of the mediation/reparation process and information about the offence, its consequences for the victim, the victim's views and offender's attitude towards the offence and details of any attempts to make amends 2 If a reparation agreement has been agreed but not completed the court may be requested to further adjourn the case, defer sentence, or the reparation agreement may be completed (voluntarily) post-sentence

period. The juvenile court extension, which occurred after the first six months, yielded 26 referrals and 12 referrals were received during the first few months of a pilot extension into the crown court setting during 1987.

There were 69 joint meetings from the above cases (involving 67 offenders and 64 victims) and mediation on a go-between basis took place in a further 57 cases. Seventeen offenders carried out a privately agreed practical reparation (10) or compensation agreement (7), 16 of these offenders appearing in the magistrates' court and 1 in the crown court.

The CRS was the subject of three research evaluations during the 1985–7 period, the most detailed and broad report, by Unell and Leeming, independent researchers appointed by the Home Office Research and Policy Unit (HORPU), being the major evaluation available to the Coventry scheme to date. Permission was given to include information from this report in CRS (1988) and the report's findings will be included in Marshall and Merry (forthcoming) which collates all the research into reparation schemes in Britain undertaken by or on behalf of HORPU. The following comment on aspects of the scheme's practice draws on Unell and Leeming (1988) in addition to the staff's evaluation of experience to date.

Court-based referrals

Any court user may prompt magistrates to refer to the scheme. It is hoped that the court's participation in the system of referral will encourage more consideration of information which is then fed back by way of a written report. Referrals are not confined to particular categories of offence nor related to the criminal background of the offender; rather the court is encouraged to consider the circumstances of the case as a whole, the offender being the vehicle by which a referral is then made. Cases involving a wide variety of offences (especially dishonesty, assault and criminal damage) and offender background have been referred, ranging from minor to relatively serious matters and involving personal and corporate victims. This has been helpful in letting us learn more about the possible value of mediation and reparation in different circumstances, although it has also meant that obtaining suitable referrals has been rather 'hit and miss'. A focus on victims as well as on offenders when considering possible referrals in a court-based scheme is difficult to achieve, as very little information about the victim is normally available to the court. For example, from magistrates' court referrals, 32 per cent of victims did not consider that mediation or reparation on a go-between or joint meeting basis would be of any assistance. Despite the difficulties of adopting a victim focus in a court-based system of referral, which tends to concentrate on the offender, at least there is less danger that victims will be let down further, when they express a wish to meet the offender, but he or she, on being approached, does not agree to take part.

The researchers (who concentrated on magistrates' court cases) found that the scheme's dependence on the cooperation of magistrates and court users and the restrictions imposed on its operation by court procedures contributed to the low rate of referrals in relation to the total number of cases passing through the court, and the time limits placed on the mediation/reparation process could also place at risk the quality of service offered by the scheme. Initial thinking surrounding the system of referrals had related to encouraging all those involved in the operation of the criminal justice system locally to be introduced to the notions of mediation and reparation; and also influencing sentencing. Unell and Leeming (1988), however, suggest that the notion of the 'court' making the actual referral may not be justified. Their evidence suggests that many court personnel have been introduced to the ideas of mediation and reparation and have given considerable thought to their operation in relationship with the criminal justice system but not more so than in Wolverhampton (also a Home Office funded court-based reparation scheme) where referrals did not have to be obtained from the court itself. Again, although the Coventry scheme's operation may well have mitigated the eventual sentence received by an offender, a comparison with the Wolverhampton scheme does not suggest that this scheme's influence was greater through the court's 'ownership' of the referral system. This may be because in Coventry the magistrates referring a case were rarely the same magistrates who would be sentencing, so the sentencer's interest in the offender's involvement in the reparation scheme was not always strong. It is also recognized that there was perhaps less incentive for magistrates to refer cases to the scheme when it was unlikely that they would be sitting on the case when sentencing took place. During the second two-year funding period (1987–9), therefore, the scheme aims to explore alternative means of obtaining referrals in addition to current procedures.

Victim and offender involvement in joint meetings

Unell and Leeming (1988) interviewed victims and offenders who had taken part in joint meetings. Their interviews with offenders suggested that the actual meeting with the victim was perceived as the most important aspect of their involvement in the mediation/reparation process and that the opportunity to make practical reparation was of marginal significance. Most offenders acknowledged that the initial reason for becoming involved in the scheme related to obtaining a lesser sentence but subsequently they emphasized more interpersonal and psychological gains – seeing the victim as a real person and understanding more about the human consequences of their behaviour. Unell and Leeming indicate that offenders were more receptive to the points of view of sympathetic victims. They also felt that more follow-up by project staff with offenders following joint meetings could assist in making better use of opportunities provided by the mediation process for offender learning. Generally project staff were perceived by offenders as impartial and sympathetic.

The report found some victims to have benefited variously from involvement in the scheme and in joint meetings, being helped to come to terms with the offence, receiving information about the court process and sentencing, and assisting offenders. Most victims did not see the scheme as involving them in the criminal justice process and did not express a wish to be given an increased role in this process. Corporate victims had particularly valued the opportunity for obtaining more information and the deterrent possibilities of joint meetings were seen by *most* victims to be the *most* worthwhile potential outcome of their participation. Victims' views about the scheme operating before the offender was sentenced were mixed. In general victims were not keen on practical reparation; Unell and Leeming considered that the scheme had not 'sold' reparation as enthusiastically as it could have done although in a number of cases victims had declined the reparation offered for various sensible reasons. The study also suggested that mediation on a go-between basis would not, in the views of victims and offenders who had participated in joint meetings, have resulted in comparable benefits to them.

Practical experience as mediators has sometimes led the project staff to see considerable value in go-between mediation and the view that the only useful communication between the two parties is a direct face-to-face meeting is, therefore, questioned. For any number of reasons, particularly in the scheme's experience following the commission of more serious crimes, a face-to-face meeting may not be desired by the victim and/or the offender despite a wish to share information and views with the other party through an intermediary and to receive feedback as to how this was received. The scheme has also sought to pursue possibilities of offender learning through the more detailed and personalized account of the consequences of their offence obtained from the victim. Through direct contact with victims and offenders, the scheme's mediators became aware from the early stages of practice onwards that reparation alone (in the traditional criminal justice sense) cannot necessarily address many of the issues raised for the parties by an offence. Over the first two years, therefore, the value of shared communication between victims and offenders and possibilities for offender education were given greater priority.

Impact on re-offending patterns

Unell and Leeming (1988) recognized that the pattern of re-offending needed to be approached 'with caution', particularly given the relatively small number of cases being examined. Their evaluation contains a detailed analysis of 75 offenders from Coventry, their criminal history (77 per cent had previous convictions) and level of involvement in the scheme (8 had had no involvement, 13 some involvement, 16 involvement on a go-between basis and 21 had participated in joint meetings, with 3 of these completing reparation agreements). Their results suggest that offenders who had some contact with the scheme or who participated in a joint meeting benefited from the experience and that this benefit was reflected in their future criminal behaviour pattern, that is, they committed fewer offences or offences of less severity. The result also suggested that offenders whose involvement with the scheme did not include direct contact with the victim also responded positively and that this may have been because the project staff still became involved in discussions with offenders even where the victim was unwilling to participate. Their tentative conclusion, therefore, is that this early analysis is 'encouraging'.

Survey of views of court-user groups

Unell and Leeming undertook a postal survey of the views of court users and concluded that the scheme did promote itself effectively. Many professionals remained uncertain of the scheme's benefits, particularly in relation to the value for victims and the deterrent value with regard to offenders. Many court users felt that reparation should be the scheme's primary objective. A substantial majority of court users felt that a mediation and reparation service should continue, and should start at the same point in the criminal justice process, although few supported the notion of a separate reparation order. The majority of those wishing mediation/reparation to continue supported the notion of integrating it into the probation service although the professional groups were divided on this point.

Impact on sentencing

Unell and Leeming's evaluation suggests that most offenders taking part in the mediation/reparation process received a reduced sentence from the magistrates. In a third of cases considered there were indications of a movement towards a conditional discharge in place of a fine and in a further third it was estimated that offenders received an alternative to what otherwise would have been a custodial sentence. A movement in a small number of cases towards lower compensation orders was discerned and the researchers, therefore, felt that any potential financial cost to a victim resulting from participation in the scheme should be made clear to them by project staff.

In relation to compensation, in 48 per cent of the referred cases sentenced the court did make a compensation order. Although acknowledging, therefore, that such compensation orders were often for amounts which in the victim's view did not realistically reflect their loss, the scheme's staff began to form the view (backed up by discussions with defence solicitors) that without the reparation report some of these compensation orders would not have been awarded at all. Reports served to remind magistrates about the victim and also provided a much more detailed account of the victim's material and non-material loss. In this way the role of reparation may have been enhanced by the operation of the scheme albeit by a different process than had originally been envisaged. If so, the scheme has returned to many of the issues which led to the initial interest of the early architects of the project – particularly, that of dealing with offenders by reparative means who are not in a financial position to pay adequate compensation or fines.

The scheme's own survey of defence solicitors' views about sentencing at the end of each case in the magistrates' court generally correlates with Unell and Leeming's (1988) evaluation regarding the impact of the scheme on sentencing. Out of 141 offenders sentenced, defence solicitors considered that a reduction in sentence had occurred in 21 per cent of cases where no mediation/reparation had taken place and in 54 per cent of cases where there had been mediation/reparation on a go-between or joint meeting basis. (The sentence had not been affected in the other cases.) In his comment concerning the pilot Crown Court extension, 'Reparation in the Crown Court' in CRS (1988), the Honorary Recorder of Coventry states that 'as far as the Crown Court judges are concerned, the depth of the Reports by the Reparation Officers has provided an insight into the particular offence which neither the Social Enquiry Report nor the Prosecution papers can provide either severally or jointly. In all the cases, the Reparation Reports had a direct relevance to sentence'.

Victim/offender mediation and the mediator's role

One of the most valuable outcomes of this first two years has been the learning of skills to facilitate the communication between victims and offenders. Coventry was fortunate in having sufficient funding for the employment of a small full-time staff group. One project officer works on each case, although joint work is occasionally undertaken when parents are involved in joint meetings for training purposes and so forth. This hopefully allows victims and offenders to receive a consistent experience of the scheme and encourages the building of trust between the parties and the mediator. The project officers have a working knowledge of the criminal justice system, prepare reports for the court which outline the results of the mediation/reparation process and are able to offer counselling when appropriate. We have increasingly seen the distinction between offering a mediation service and offering counselling as often in practice becoming blurred and unhelpful. Project staff also undertake an explicitly educative role, particularly with offenders, sharing and discussing the views of victims even when no joint meeting is to take place and assisting and encouraging offenders to consider points and issues raised so that this may inform their future behaviour. The tasks undertaken by the scheme's staff and their method of operation, therefore, influenced the decision to continue without developing a role for volunteer mediators within the project during this period.

The basic method of approach to the mediation/reparation process as undertaken at Coventry is outlined in Table 6.1. It begins with a set of practice statements which for *both* parties relate to ensuring their voluntariness and security, facilitating constructive communication about agreed and other issues, and offering active and equal assistance to both parties.

A small team of Home Office funded researchers from Bristol university, directed by Gwynn Davis, observed the mediation process and mediator's role at Coventry for a short period at the end of 1986. Unell and Leeming (1988) also considered this aspect of the scheme's work drawing on their own direct contact with victims and offenders. In a thoughtful and challenging report Davis et al. (1987) criticize mediators at Coventry for undertaking too much preparation work, particularly with offenders, and suggest that this practice could intrude on the notion of voluntary participation and undervalue the actual victim/offender encounter as the most effective means of achieving offender education – one of the scheme's major objectives. Unell and Leeming (1988), however, argue for greater preparation of both parties before joint meetings, given the need to ensure their security, assist them both to obtain as much benefit as possible, and to fulfil the potential of the mediation/reparation process for offender learning. Their evaluation also suggested that the scheme needed to provide offenders and victims with greater opportunities to discuss their experiences following the mediation/reparation process and obtain a more detailed feedback via the mediator from the other party in the court. (Often only one such contact takes place with each party.)

Unell and Leeming acknowledge the importance attached to the objective of offender education by the majority of victims who became involved in the mediation/reparation process. Indeed they recommended that 'many victims need to be treated as partners rather than clients in the mediation process, given that their motivation to take part in the Scheme is often fuelled by notions of helping offenders and deterrent objectives' (Unell and Leeming, 1988). This recommendation is acknowledged by the scheme's staff up to a point, although the more serious the consequences of the crime the less appropriate and reasonable it would be for victims to participate in mediation/reparation out of a sense of social responsibility alone. In our experience victims who often present themselves as motivated primarily by an interest in offender education also have an interest in obtaining information, ventilating feelings and obtaining reassurance. Adequate acknowledgement of these needs is an essential part of a process which includes the aim of making offenders recognize that victims are real people who have suffered unpleasant personal consequences because of their actions.

These research reports and the scheme's direct experience all suggest that victims and offenders who do meet generally attach considerable importance to the encounter. In Coventry, therefore, the mediator does aim to help both parties to prepare for the joint meeting – working out what their basic aims will be, where potential conflict may lie, and how this might best be addressed. Through this preparation the mediator also becomes familiar with the aims and issues of each party and so can better facilitate a useful exchange when this takes place. Preparation is aimed at supporting each party and assisting them to do their best according to their own criteria. With regard to the dangers of 'pressure' on offenders, it goes without saying that any number of external pressures may be placed on offenders to cooperate with the scheme – from the court, solicitor, probation officer, family members, community feeling. Most offenders referred to the scheme are aged between 17 and 24, many of them have been through the courts before, but none are likely to be familiar with the values and aims of this type of scheme. Without full discussion many offenders would either not become involved with the scheme because they have not been given the opportunity and assistance to think it through, or they might take part in the process but misunderstand or miss altogether some aspects and opportunities arising from it. This would be neither to the offender's nor to the victim's benefit. Together, the research reports give a general impression that victims and offenders perceived the scheme's staff as caring and from our experience, offenders did not see the preparation as moral (lecturing) pressure but responded fairly positively to this approach.

Davis et al. (1987) interestingly compare the approach of the mediators in Coventry to many conciliators in the area of divorce disputes, where often there is little or no preparation of parties before joint meetings, although the conciliator may then take on a more active role than at Coventry to facilitate communication, draw out common ground and areas of potential conflict. Victim/offender mediation is a new area, however, and there are marked differences between the two contexts. In the divorce setting the parties know each other, are likely to have some measure of expectation of one another at a joint meeting, have a 'clear' fundamental dispute to address and resolve, and the issue (usually a child) means that some ownership of the dispute is likely to be accepted by both individuals. In the victim/offender setting the parties may know nothing of each other or the expectations likely to be held; the aim in entering mediation may relate less to specifics than to a general curiosity and wish to clear the air or exchange relevant information and views. One party has already been labelled at fault and an apology is often perceived as relevant. There is a good deal, therefore, of walking into the unknown for both parties and, in the scheme's view, one of the mediator's main responsibilities in this setting is to reassure them in advance that he or she understands certain points and aims. Joint meetings between victims and offenders are unlikely to occur more than once if no practical reparation agreement is forthcoming. It is important, therefore, to work towards achieving the most benefit for both parties; the emphasis in preparation on offender learning and a heightened awareness on the offender's part of the victim's position is both necessary and relevant to victims as well if they are to feel that their personal needs and the deterrent possibilities of the mediation/reparation process are all being addressed.

Although not always trying to avoid areas of conflict between the two parties, the scheme has aimed to facilitate constructive communication between victims and offenders. Given this protective aim of conferring positive benefit from a decision to become involved in the scheme, in addition to the aims of education and ensuring each party's basic security, the scheme's staff as mediators are at times assertive, give advice or counselling and attempt to be as flexible as possible so as to respond to the needs of individual cases. It is recognized, however, that there could be a danger of the scheme taking on responsibility for avoiding areas of real conflict and seeking only an unrealistic consensus on all issues. This would certainly reduce the potential for spontaneity and meaningful exchange between victims and offenders. Unell and Leeming (1988) point to the need for issues relating to mediator authority to be openly addressed; as practice develops further the scheme will need to work towards achieving an acceptable balance between these competing concerns.

During the first two years CRS has tested and continues to test these and other issues relating to the aims of mediation and the role of the mediator in this type of victim/offender scheme. It is hoped that practical experience obtained in Coventry alongside the work undertaken by other schemes, in conjunction with the Forum for Initiatives in Reparation and Mediation, UK, will encourage the development of good practice guidelines that can ensure safeguards and assist the work of mediation initiatives in the future.

Conclusions

When the CRS began in 1985 external expectations were varied – the government was looking for a new method of dealing with some offenders that could possibly achieve a punitive objective while also recompensing the victim in a practical way; the probation service's interest lay in reducing sentences, possibly providing an alternative to custody, and in offender learning; the mediation movement from this period onwards was increasingly interested in mediation and reparation as complete alternatives to the formal justice system which had failed to resolve the personal nature of crime and its consequences for both parties.

From the way in which the scheme has been received by the local courts it does appear that sentencers are increasingly interested in seeking ways of showing victims that they have not been forgotten (partly in an effort to maintain the court's credibility with the public) and providing opportunities for offenders to own personal responsibility, hear about and learn from a more intimate know-ledge of the effects on somebody else of their crime. There is evidence from some cases that the court welcomes more in-depth information about the offence and its consequences for both parties and is prepared to take into account the offender's own attitude – tested through the mediation process – about his/her offending behaviour, and attempts to repair the harm caused, before passing sentence.

The experience of the Coventry scheme with regard to the few practical reparation compensation agreements has encouraged greater consideration of the therapeutic benefits of face-to-face meetings or indirect communication between victims and offenders. Concentration on therapeutic benefits makes a clear assessment of the success or otherwise of the scheme in achieving its objectives even more difficult than just using the more measurable and enforceable qualities of direct reparation. Although the lack of practical reparation agreements emerging from the scheme's intervention has not assisted towards developing a new sentence for the court, reparation reports do appear to have helped the court in making alternative uses of current sentencing options, including reducing the sentence. There have also been encouraging signs, albeit tentative, that the learning process provided to offenders may have a constructive effect in reducing re-offending rates.

Victims may find both a public role, offender education, and also private benefit, reassurance and the breaking down of stereotypes which, fuelled by the media, are responsible for much of the widespread fear of crime. Public duty is often emphasized by victims who have taken part in this and other schemes. Any impact on reducing re-offending is, therefore, of added relevance.

The idea of victim/offender mediation and reparation has now been introduced locally at Coventry and the scheme's staff have also begun to explore the notion of mediation as an approach to community-based dispute resolution through links with police and the local housing department. Many cases appearing in the criminal courts are not appropriate for mediation/reparation and it is a form of intervention which can be time-consuming and hence costly. The real benefit emerging from practice so far, however, appears to be the quality of this response to a criminal act and its personal consequences, and the insight that can be provided to assist in criminal justice decision-making.

During the second period of funding (1987–9) the CRS aims to continue with its court-based activities and extend further into the community setting. Two years was considered by all concerned to be too short a time to evaluate fully the major focus of the scheme's work in the magistrates' and juvenile courts and in the recent pilot extension into the crown court.

A court-based mediation scheme cannot operate without satisfactory links with all court-user groups and in this respect the Coventry scheme has been fortunate in the support provided by its inter-agency management committee; this committee's role initially in ensuring a degree of independence for the scheme from the probation service also assisted the scheme's operation in many other respects. The West Midlands probation service nevertheless has an important role in the running of the CRS; since 1987 this has included part-financing of the scheme for a period. From being an interesting but peripheral development in the field of criminal justice, however, the experience gained by the Coventry and other mediation schemes so far, particularly with regard to offender education, working with victims and exploring reparation possibilities, will hopefully have much to offer the probation service as it considers its future priorities and also current government thinking with regard to harsher community-based sanctions which include a stronger emphasis on making reparation.

References

Brittan, Leon (1984) 'Home Secretary's speech to the Holborn Law Society', 14 March 1984. Unpublished.

Christie, Nils (1977) 'Conflicts as property', *British Journal of Criminology*, 17 (1): 1–15.

Coventry Reparation Scheme (CRS) (1986) *First Twelve Monthly Report, 23.9.85– 22.9.86*. Coventry: CRS.

Coventry Reparation Scheme (CRS) (1988) *Mediation and Reparation: Report 1985– 1987*. Coventry: CRS.

Davis, G., J. Boucherat and D. Watson (1987) 'Report of an observation study of the Coventry Reparation Scheme.' University of Bristol: unpublished paper.

Harding, J. (1982) *Victims and Offenders: Needs and Responsibilities*. London: Bedford Square Press.

Hough, M. and P. Mayhew (1983) *The British Crime Survey: First Report*. Home Office Research Study 76. London: HMSO.

Marshall, T.F. and S. Merry (forthcoming) *Crime and Accountability: Victim/ Offender Mediation in Practice*. London: HMSO.

Parliamentary All-party Penal Affairs Group (1984) *A New Deal for Victims*. London: PAPPAG.

Unell, J. and A. Leeming (1988) 'An evaluation of the mediation and reparation schemes in Coventry and Wolverhampton.' Unpublished report to the Home Office, London.

Wright, M. (1982) *Making Good: Prisons, Punishment and Beyond*. London: Burnett Books/Hutchinson.

Wright, M. (1983) *Victim/offender Reparation Agreements: A Feasibility Study in Coventry*. Birmingham: West Midlands Probation Service.

7

Violent Offenders and their Victims

Mark S. Umbreit

The growing North American and European network of programmes attempting to mediate victim/offender conflict focus
nearly exclusively on the non-violent offences of theft and burglary
(Umbreit, 1986b). The development of the Victim/Offender Reconciliation Program model (VORP) is perhaps best representative
of this growing network. (See Peachey, this volume; Harding, this
volume for the background.) There appear to be a number of
benefits resulting from the VORP process, for victims, offenders,
and the larger community.

The idea of applying victim/offender mediation techniques in
cases of certain violent crimes against persons requires a thorough
assessment of the initial victim/offender reconciliation model and
the identification of elements of that model which may require
significant modification. Many professionals and volunteers working
within the criminal justice system see cases involving violence as
clearly beyond the acceptable limits of this relatively new justice
reform effort. Yet, as the case-studies reported in this chapter
indicate, some of the most fundamental goals of the VORP model
appear to be even more relevant when applied in some cases
involving violent victim/offender conflict. After reviewing the
current VORP model, with its focus on non-violent offences and
restitution, five cases in which the victim/offender mediation
process was used with very violent offences will be presented.[1]
Finally, specific and preliminary implications for modification of the
initial victim/offender mediation and reconciliation process will be
identified.

Victim/offender mediation and reconciliation

The victim/offender reconciliation process as initially developed
involves bringing convicted offenders who are referred by the court
(most often for burglary or theft) face to face with their victims in
the presence of a trained mediator. (See Chupp, this volume, for

details of the process.) The primary goal of these victim/offender reconciliation programmes is to facilitate conflict resolution between the parties involved, by first allowing time to address informational and emotional needs, followed by a more practical discussion of determining a mutually agreeable restitution obligation (e.g. money, work for the victim, work for the victim's choice of a charity, etc.) as a symbol of reconciliation. Part of the theory of this intervention is that through face-to-face communication, in the presence of a trained mediator, the conflict can be humanized, tension reduced, and stereotypes of each other modified. The mediation process is believed to result in a more satisfactory experience of justice for both victim and offender (Umbreit, 1985).

In most cases the victims and offenders involved in the programme had no prior relationship. VORP is not meant to be an offender rehabilitation programme. Nor is it only a victim assistance programme. Rather, it is designed to address the needs of both victims and offenders in a manner which personalizes the process of justice by providing both parties with an opportunity to resolve the conflict at a community level (Umbreit, 1986a).

Zehr and Sears (1980) provide a theoretical basis for the VORP concept. They begin by pointing out the strong religious value base, premised upon a biblical perspective that views crime as a rupture, a wound in the health of the community which needs to be healed. They state that from this perspective, the emphasis is upon re-establishing right relationships through reparation rather than retribution. This must involve addressing the underlying feelings of frustration and anger caused by crime. VORP is to offer the courts an alternative conflict resolution process involving a restorative rather than a punitive sanction. It is meant to humanize the justice process, to strengthen offender accountability, to provide assistance to victims, and to divert some convicted offenders from costly incarceration, providing some relief, however small, to the extensive overcrowding in penal institutions.

Despite many important sub-goals (e.g. offender rehabilitation, victim restitution, alternatives to incarceration), the primary goal of reconciliation remains. Attitudes, feelings, and needs of both victim and offender must be taken seriously. Restitution is important but should not be the only purpose of the victim/offender meeting (Zehr, 1983).

The major theoretical elements of the victim/offender reconciliation model can be summarized as follows:

- Crime should be viewed as relational; emphasis is on the conflict among people rather than primarily on an offence against the state.

- Response to crime is to be restorative rather than retributive.
- Response to crime should address the needs of both victims and offenders, allowing for expression of feelings and opportunities for healing of emotional 'wounds'.
- Victims and offenders should be empowered to work out the conflict between them and to participate directly in the justice process.
- Reconciliation of victim/offender conflict should lead to greater understanding of each other, the events that occurred, and a more humanitarian understanding of crime and its impact.
- Reconciliation of victim/offender conflict leads both victims and offenders to hold less stereotyped views of each other.
- The negotiation and completion of restitution (either monetary or non-monetary) by the offender to the victim is an important symbol of reconciliation.
- The process of mediation involving a neutral third party with no coercive power is integral to the victim/offender reconciliation process.

Extending the VORP model to crimes of violence

As the VORP model has developed over the past decade, both practical experience and preliminary research have found a number of important benefits for both victims and offenders. Coates and Gehm (1985; and this volume) found a high level of satisfaction with the process; a perception of fairness related to VORP as a criminal justice penalty; a high degree of actual restitution payment; and a perception that meeting each other was beneficial for both victim and offender. This research also found that some victims were critical of the lack of follow-up involved in specific cases. On the other hand, an earlier and less rigorous evaluation of VORP in Canada conducted by Dittenhoffer and Ericson (1983) was more critical of the model. Focusing primarily on the systemic impact of VORP, they concluded that the programme did not serve as an actual alternative to incarceration, as its initial developers intended. While still recognizing the potential for VORP to address important victim needs, including the possibility of conflict resolution with the offender, Dittenhoffer and Ericson concluded that the VORP projects they assessed tended to be preoccupied with the issue of restitution, rather than 'reconciliation', despite rhetoric to the contrary.

After reviewing the theoretical base of the current VORP model, several important questions emerge.

- If crime is viewed as conflict between people and the importance of addressing the emotional needs of both victims and offenders is so central to the model, why does VORP focus so much on non-violent property offences in which the emotional trauma experienced by victims is probably often not as great as in crimes of violence?

- If the model operates from a restorative rather than a retributive paradigm of justice (Zehr, 1985), why is VORP so closely linked to the concept of restitution, which many regard as merely another form of retribution and punishment? (The Reagan administration, for example, supports restitution as part of its commitment to get tough with criminals.)

- Even with the nearly exclusive focus on non-violent property crimes, if the VORP model is committed to viewing crime as conflict between people and reconciliation as the primary goal of the process, why is only one meeting lasting an average of one hour, with rare exceptions, conducted between the victim and offender, rather than scheduling follow-up meetings? Is it realistic to think that 'reconciliation' will occur in such a brief encounter?

- To what extent is the very goal of the model, that of reconciliation, more an ideological and symbolic value statement of its originators, rather than a grounded and realistic goal that has a clear meaning to victims and offenders participating in VORP?

While the early development of the victim/offender reconciliation concept and its replication in a growing number of communities has continued to focus upon non-violent property crimes, there is certainly nothing inherent in the model to suggest it must be limited to property offences. As a number of victims of violent crime have pointed out themselves, mediation can often have a significant impact in facilitating the healing process and moving beyond one's sense of vulnerability. The case studies presented below illustrate the manner in which the process of victim/offender mediation has been found to be meaningful in the context of violent victim/offender conflict.

Case studies

Armed robbery

'Carl' was taking the final readings on the gas pumps as he was closing up the station at 10 p.m. Two young men approached him and asked him if they could have change for a ten dollar bill. Having sensed that these men might be preparing to rob him, Carl gave them the change, went outside and called the police. When he returned to the station he was ordered to turn over all of the money and to go to the back room where one of the men was waiting for him with a butcher's knife. He ran out, but the police had not yet arrived and before long one of the robbers caught up with Carl. As they fought on the ground, the police finally arrived and arrested the two men. Although Carl had not been stabbed, he was punched in the face and had hurt his knee badly when he fell to the ground during the scuffle.

Soon after the offence, Carl began receiving help from the Genesee County Sheriff's Department Victim Assistance Program. He was later asked how he would feel about meeting 'Jim' and 'Al', the two offenders. Carl was eager to do so. Even during the actual robbery, he had tried to talk to both Jim and Al and to encourage them to stop what they were doing and just leave. Immediately after their arrest, Carl wanted to approach them both and ask why they had decided to rob his gas station. He was curious about what type of young men would do such a thing. The actual mediation session gave Jim and Al an opportunity to explain their motivation, describe some of their background, and to apologize to Carl. Many answers to Carl's questions were provided. He learned that Jim and Al were themselves very frightened during the robbery and had no intention of killing him. He was also able to express his need to forgive Jim and Al for what they had done. Because he had a religious background, this opportunity for forgiveness was very important to Carl. He stated:

> after meeting them, I found that they weren't really hard individuals and I found out they were younger people too . . . if these guys go to prison . . . they would definitely be messed up . . . they would be useless to society and then they would really be hard and the next 'time they probably would kill the guy if they robbed a gas station.

In this case of armed robbery, Carl expressed many of the same questions and concerns experienced by crime victims in non-violent VORP cases. His need to know why *his* gas station was selected for the robbery, and to learn what type of individuals would commit such a violent crime were particularly important issues. The degree to which the concept of a victim/offender mediation and reconciliation is based on a relational perspective on crime is certainly validated by the conflict exemplified by Jim and Al's armed robbery of Carl. Through the mediation process, several needs of both Carl (the victim) and Jim and Al (the offenders) were met, all at a post-conviction level of intervention.

Sexual assault

'Karen' was only 5 years old when her 13-year-old uncle raped her. She was under pressure from her uncle not to tell her mother, and frightened at the prospect of seeing her uncle at a planned family gathering. Karen's mother could not understand why she was so anxious about going to Grandma's house. On learning that it was because Uncle 'Jack' would be there, her mother began to ask probing questions. Within minutes she learned that Karen had been raped by Uncle Jack. According to Karen's mother, after first learning this, 'I was ready to go over to my mother's house and shoot my brother, kill him.'

After receiving assistance from the Genesee County Sheriff's Department Victim Assistance Program over several months, Karen's mother was asked if she thought a victim/offender mediation session might be helpful, in order to confront her brother and work out the anger and hostility she felt toward him, as well as helping her brother understand the full human impact of his behaviour. While hesitant at first, her mother later agreed to participate in a victim/offender reconciliation meeting. The key question expressed during this encounter was 'Why did you do this to Karen?' Feeling embarrassed and ashamed, her brother explained that a neighbour friend of his had teased him and dared him to do it. At this point he felt terrible about what he had done to Karen. Many weeks after the mediation session, Karen's mother stated that had it not been for the mediation session she would probably not have been able to go to any family gatherings where her brother might have been present. She was still angry at her brother, but the intensity of that anger had been lessened and she felt more in control of her feelings.

As is true with so many victims of crime, Karen's mother could not understand why her daughter was sexually assaulted. Her anger and confusion were heightened because her brother was the offender. While it is very unlikely that many victims of sexual assault would even consider the mediation process prior to court adjudication of the case, Karen's mother found it helpful in dealing with the very real 'relational' element of the violent crime committed against her daughter.

Assaulting a police officer

'Carol' was the only woman state trooper in the Rock Valley area of southern Wisconsin. She noticed a car going through a stop sign, made it pull to the side of the road and asked its driver, a young man aged 19, for his licence. The offender, 'Bob', lied to Carol since he had lost his licence as a result of drunk driving. He panicked and sped off. She pursued him for nearly 10 miles in a high-speed chase which ended when Bob's car spun out of control. Bob was again ordered out of the car and told to put his hands on the squad car. As Carol prepared to put her handcuffs on him, he again panicked, tackled her, fell to the ground and struggled for control of her gun, which was now under Carol's chest. Her whole life flashed before her as she anticipated her death. Yet before a shot was fired, a truck driver who saw the scuffle ran over to the fight and pulled Bob, who now had control of the gun, away from Carol. Soon other state troopers arrived and took control of the situation.

Bob was later convicted of the felony of endangering a police officer. He had no previous criminal convictions, and received a sentence of six months in jail, probation, and community service. Nearly eight months after the incident, Carol and Bob were approached by Missy Henderson of the newly established Victim/ Offender Reconciliation Program of the Rock Valley Correctional Programs agency in Beloit about their possible interest in participating in a mediation session. Probation staff had indicated to the VORP project that Carol was having a very difficult time recovering from the trauma she had experienced, particularly since her fellow officers (all male) provided little understanding and support. As a single parent, Carol was worried that her daughter was being followed by Bob and might be the object of retaliation. Probation staff also indicated to the VORP project that Bob had no prior court record and was extremely shaken up about what he had done while he had been drunk that evening.

While Bob was the first to agree to a meeting with Carol, far more time was necessary for Carol to sort out how she felt about confronting Bob. As she struggled to regain a sense of control within her life and to move beyond her feelings of helplessness and vulnerability, Carol came to realize that meeting Bob in the presence of a trained mediator and co-mediator might help her. Numerous contacts were required by the VORP project with Carol before she finally agreed to participate. It became clear that the very process of building trust with the VORP staff person and expressing her feelings had triggered the beginning of her healing.

By the time both Carol and Bob came together in a mediation session, with co-mediators, both had given a great deal of thought to their feelings. Bob was particularly ashamed of his actions, found it difficult to even look at Carol, and apologized for his behaviour. Carol was able to find out why Bob had reached for her gun. He thought that she might have shot him. Carol told him that it was against police policy to draw a gun in a traffic offence, but that once he took her gun Bob was then open to being shot by any police officer. His act of defence had actually made Bob more vulnerable to being shot by other officers coming to the scene. Bob had not thought of this. As they shared information about their backgrounds, Carol and Bob found out that both had suffered from alcoholic parents and its related abuse. Carol kept stressing to Bob: 'If you had only talked to me about your licence. If I had known you only had two more weeks to go before getting it back, I wouldn't have arrested you.'

In full recognition of how both had come within seconds of being killed, Carol and Bob were later able to joke about the foolishness of the event, as well as sharing the hardship of living with alcoholic parents. In response to Bob's apology, Carol openly expressed her forgiveness of Bob and her hope that he would get help for his drinking problem.

Once again, the type of issues addressed in more typical property-related crimes that are referred to victim/offender mediation were present. Carol was able to find out why Bob had reached for her gun. Bob was able to apologize directly to Carol for having assaulted her. Both were able to gain a more human understanding of each other and a greater sense of closure on the criminal event that brought them together.

Negligent homicide

'Cathy' was driving home one evening when she heard over the radio that a terrible head-on collision of a car and a large truck had just occurred, resulting in the death of the driver of the car. She felt a terrible pain within her, though she was uncertain why. Before the evening ended, she learnt that her husband of thirteen years, 'Andy', had been killed in that accident. The other driver was later convicted of negligent homicide. The impact of Andy's death on Cathy and her eight children was excruciating.

Shortly after Andy's death, Cathy and her children were contacted by Dennis Wittman, the director of a Victim Assistance Program operated by the Genesee County Sheriff's Department. Dennis, a friend and neighbour of Cathy's family, offered her support and assistance; after several months he mentioned the possibility of Cathy meeting the man who had killed her husband in a victim/offender reconciliation conference. While the Genesee County Sheriff's Department works with many victims, it is only in a relatively small number of cases that they encourage a direct face-to-face meeting with the offender if the victim feels this might be helpful. Nearly all their approximately twenty mediation sessions have been with violent felony offenders.

At first, Cathy was very uncertain as to what she might gain from such a meeting. Yet, as she realized that she had many unanswered questions about the incident and a growing sense of bitterness, she agreed to meet the offender. When Cathy and 'Tom', the offender, were brought together in the presence of a mediator, Cathy soon realized that Tom had an enormous amount of guilt over what he had done. As a family man with no prior criminal background, Tom and his wife, as well as their children, were having a very difficult time coming to grips with what had happened. While Cathy spoke of the pain felt by herself and her children over the loss of Andy, Tom gained a far greater understanding of the full impact of the criminal behaviour that had resulted from his drinking. Many months later, Cathy said that it was only after meeting the person who killed her husband, face-to-face, that she was able to move beyond the bitterness in her heart and to gain a greater sense of peace.

In a case involving the death of a loved one, it is difficult to imagine any process which could effectively help the surviving victim to come to terms with such a loss and the offender to comprehend fully the effect of such a crime, while also assisting them in dealing with their own sense of guilt. Through participation in mediation prior to court adjudication of the case, a process was offered to both Cathy and Tom which appeared to be helpful in addressing many of the issues emerging from a negligent homicide offence. Like many victims of property crimes involved in mediation, Cathy was able to get answers to many important questions and to gain a more human understanding of 'the criminal'. She was able to move beyond her anger and bitterness, toward closure and healing.

Sniper shooting
Dennis Wittman also mediated, with the assistance of a co-mediator, the first known sniper-shooting case to be referred into a programme providing victim/offender mediation and reconciliation services. This occurred before the trial. The two victims, who were shot and nearly killed, were brought face to face with the young offender, who had pulled a rifle out and began shooting across the main street in a small rural community. After a break for lunch, a second meeting was held with all of these individuals plus six community representatives (a minister from a church near where the shooting occurred; a former judge; a housewife involved in promoting drug-abuse programmes; the investigating police officer at the time of the shooting; an estate agent; and a local attorney).

This very violent offence had received banner headlines in all the local newspapers and frightened the entire community. Therefore the direct involvement of a number of community representatives was seen as important in order to work toward reconciliation between the community at large and the offender.

Despite a significant amount of tension and stiffness initially, the two mediation sessions appeared to go very well. The two victims were able to get answers to a number of questions, particularly whether they had been shot because of a dispute with a girlfriend that both the victims and the offender knew. The offender eventually admitted that 'the girl' was part of what led to the shooting, but not entirely. He was depressed, had attempted suicide several times before, was high on both alcohol and drugs, and claimed he had no recollection of the shooting, or of the fact that after shooting at and hitting the two victims he had shot himself in the head with the rifle. Both victims indicated that they were glad to finally get this issue cleared up.

While one victim did not believe the story about not remembering the shooting, the other victim mentioned his own problems with drugs and thought it was very possible that the offender had had a blackout. This same victim told the offender toward the end of the first meeting that while he could never forget what had been done to him (having been shot a quarter of an inch from his heart), he could forgive the offender. The other victim still harboured a great deal of resentment and anger. At best, the mediation process appeared to take the edge off his anger, according to his statements. Community members present expressed a high level of satisfaction with their involvement in such a controversial and violent case in which they felt their entire community had been victimized. The offender and both victims expressed their satisfaction with being able to confront each other and sort out some of the issues all were facing.

Even in this extremely violent and unusual case, the issues found in more typical mediation cases were present. Many lingering questions that the victims had were answered by the offender. The offender gained far more understanding of the full human impact of his behaviour. Both the direct victims of the shooting, and the secondary victims represented by the community representatives, were able to understand more clearly why this terrible crime had occurred, and what type of individual had committed it.

Summary

During the last several years there has been a small but growing amount of evidence to suggest that face-to-face contact between certain victims and offenders may be appropriate in some cases involving violent criminal behaviour; that is, for those victims who voluntarily chose to enter the mediation process because of potential benefits that they perceive. This recognition is grounded in the statements of victims of violent crimes who have been able to confront their offender, and the direct experience of Dennis Wittman, this author, and others in trying to apply mediation in a relatively small number of cases involving violent victim/offender conflict. While the VORP model was explicitly designed for application in non-violent property crimes involving a restitution obligation, the findings reported in this chapter would suggest that the VORP model is no less appropriate in selected crimes of violence. Drawing on the most fundamental element of the model, that of promoting reconciliation and healing within a context of viewing crime as relational (e.g. conflict between people, not just between the offender and the 'state'), serious consideration should be given to modifying the initial VORP model significantly, so as to include a major new initiative in making the service available to victims and offenders involved in violent crime. This new initiative should include the development of appropriate training materials for practitioners in the field.

Conclusions: modifying VORP

Mediation of violent victim/offender conflict is certainly at an early and experimental stage of development. In the relatively few cases in which the victim/offender mediation process has been used, it appears that it can be a very helpful intervention for those victims and offenders who choose to participate. The potential for further application of the mediation process in certain violent cases seems clear. Yet a great deal of caution must be exercised in doing so. Three basic principles need to be emphasized.

1 Sensitivity should be exercised as to when victims involved in crimes of violence should even be approached about the opportunity to confront the offender in a mediation process. Experience in Genesee County would suggest that several months must often elapse, after normal support systems begin to fade, before suggesting the possibility of VORP.

2 Extreme sensitivity is also essential in working with victims of violent crime. The different rhythm in which people deal with their feelings must be recognized. At no point should a victim of a violent crime (or even a non-violent one) be forced, coerced, or manipulated into the mediation process with the offender. To do so would place the programme in the victimizer role and would violate its basic integrity. Nor must a victim be placed in the position of feeling he or she 'should' be reconciled with the offender. Any reconciliation that may occur must be genuine.

3   Victims and offenders involved in crimes of violence are likely to
be in need of more extended counselling and support services
than the more typical VORP case. Cases will often require far
more frequent contacts with both the offender and the victim,
over an extended period of time. Therefore, it will be important
for mediators either to offer additional counselling and supportive services directly or to assist the victim or offender in securing
them. (For supportive services for victims see Reeves, this
volume.)

As one moves from the presentation of the above basic principles
to actual preliminary guidelines for the practice of mediation with
victims and offenders involved in violent crimes, the task becomes
more difficult.

While the goal of reconciliation and healing is present with both
property or violent cases, the symbol of any reconciliation that may
occur is likely to be different. While restitution is the obvious
symbol of conflict resolution in property offences, the concept of
reparation (e.g. rather than restoring an actual financial loss, a more
general expression of compensation for the harm done) is likely to
be appropriate. It could be argued, however, that rather clear items
of financial loss exist in nearly all violent crimes (e.g. medical costs,
low wages), even though no 'property' was taken. Therefore
perhaps both the concept of direct restitution and reparation may be
appropriate in crimes of violence.

The experience in Genesee County indicates that far more time is
required for each case. Rather than the usual single meeting with
the victim and the offender, prior to the joint session, at least three
or more individual sessions with both parties are likely to be
necessary. Dennis Wittman was involved in as many as 15 to 20
individual meetings in some cases. The average time per case is
probably going to be closer to 15–20 hours, rather than the 4–6
hours per case currently experienced by many VORP projects.

Because of the much longer time involved in working with violent
cases and the far more traumatic effects upon the victim, the role of
mediators is likely to be different from what is required in non-
violent cases involved in mediation. Rather than trained community
volunteers doing the mediation, which is the practice of many
VORP projects, more extensively trained and experienced professional mediators will need to be available. This is not to suggest,
however, that all volunteer mediators would be inappropriate. For
example, it is quite possible to recruit a highly trained and
competent mental health professional to serve as a 'volunteer'
mediator.

Mediators' training will need to be significantly increased from its present 12–15 hours in many programmes to 40–60 hours, in order to cover post-traumatic stress, grief counselling, and provide familiarity with local mental health resources. Because of the complexity of issues involved in violent crime, training will need to include the role of co-mediation and appropriate follow-up strategies, including follow-up victim/offender meetings in some cases. Whereas most current victim/offender mediation programmes do not regularly schedule follow-up meetings, even though there is some evidence to suggest the effectiveness of doing so, such a strategy may be more frequently required in crimes of violence.

Finally, it would seem as though referrals to a mediation programme working with certain crimes of violence are likely to come not only from probation officers, as in most VORP projects,

Table 7.1 *Extending the VORP model to crimes of violence*

	Current VORP model	Modified VORP model
Goal	Reconciliation of victim/ offender conflict	Reconciliation of victim/offender conflict
Cases	Non-violent property offences (e.g. theft, burglary, vandalism)	Violent offences (e.g. robbery, assault, manslaughter)
Symbol of reconciliation	Negotiation of restitution	Negotiation of restitution or reparation, if appropriate
Mediator	Usually volunteer	Usually professional
Co-mediator	Rarely involved	Frequently involved
Training	12–15 hours	40–60 hours
Training components	VORP process, CJS[a] information, mediation skills, victim/offender experience	VORP process, CJS information, mediation skills, victim/offender experience, grief counselling skills, severe trauma intervention skills, familiarity with local mental health resources
Preliminary victim meeting	1	3 or more; up to 15–20 in some cases
Preliminary offender meeting	1	3 or more
Joint victim/ offender mediation sessions	1	1 or more when appropriate
Follow-up victim/offender meetings	Usually 0	1 or more when appropriate
Average time per case	4–6 hours	15–20 hours; up to 100 hours in some cases
Referral source	Usually probation	Probation, prosecutor, or victim support scheme

[a] CJS = criminal justice system

but also from the prosecuting attorney's office or even local victim assistance agencies. A longer process of building trust with the victim and providing support is certainly going to be required and, therefore, the earlier the case can be referred, the better.

Table 7.1 should be understood as an initial and rather modest attempt to begin identifying important implications in extending the VORP model to crimes of violence.

It is hoped that the above provides a framework for further development of the victim/offender mediation process as it attempts to adapt to the needs of victims and offenders involved in violent offences. Without question, far more research and experimentation is necessary before it should be widely practised. If developed properly, mediation of violent victim/offender conflict may become one of the more creative and humane responses to crime and victimization in the coming years.

Note

1   The cases presented in this chapter are based on the pioneering work of Dennis Wittman, of the Genesee County Sheriff's Department in upstate New York, and Missy Henderson, of the Rock Valley Correctional Programs in Beloit, Wisconsin. The author served as a co-mediator in two of the five cases and interviewed victims in the other three cases. The names used in each case-study are fictitious.

References

Coates, Robert B. and John Gehm (1985) *Victim Meets Offender: An Evaluation of Victim Offender Reconciliation Programs*. Michigan City, Ind.: PACT Institute of Justice.

Dittenhoffer, Tony and Richard Erikson (1983) 'The victim offender reconciliation program: a message to correctional reformers', *University of Toronto Law Journal*, 33: 315–47.

Umbreit, Mark S. (1985) *Crime and Reconciliation: Creative Options for Victims and Offenders*. Nashville, Tenn.: Abingdon Press.

Umbreit, Mark S. (1986a) *Victim Offender Mediation: Conflict Resolution and Restitution*. Washington, DC: US Department of Justice.

Umbreit, Mark S. (1986b) 'Victim offender mediation: a national survey', *Federal Probation*, December.

Zehr, Howard (ed.) (1983) *The VORP Book: An Organizational and Operations Manual*. Valparaiso, Ind.: PACT Institute of Justice and Mennonite Central Committee.

Zehr, Howard (1985) 'Retributive justice, restorative justice', 4. Elkhart, Ind.: Mennonite Central Committee, Office on Criminal Justice.

Zehr, Howard and Earl Sears (1980) *Mediating the Victim Offender Conflict*. Akron, Penn.: Mennonite Central Committee, Office on Criminal Justice.

8

Victim/Offender Groups

Gilles Launay and Peter Murray

For the past three years, victims of burglary in the Medway towns, Kent, have been offered the opportunity to meet, not their own burglars, but young offenders convicted of burglary and incarcerated in the nearby Rochester Youth Custody Centre.[1] The objective is twofold: first to help victims to come to terms with their burglary; second to confront offenders with the results of crime. The scheme has been called Victims and Offenders In Conciliation (VOIC) to reflect that the victims and offenders find common ground in that neither has a 'voice' in court and that the meetings give to victims and offenders the opportunity to voice their feelings.

Victims are referred to the scheme by victims support scheme volunteers (Reeves, this volume) and the Crime Prevention Officer from the local police. They are nearly always victims of unsolved crimes and therefore would not have the chance to meet their own burglars. The offenders serving a sentence at Rochester Youth Custody Centre are aged between 15 and 21. They are usually recidivists with a long history of offending and previous experience of imprisonment. Victims and offenders, four to six of each, meet as a group for three 1½-hour discussion and role-play sessions spaced at weekly intervals. Fourteen sets of meetings (i.e. 42 sessions) have been organized since the inception of the scheme in 1983. So far 52 victims and 48 offenders have taken part.

In this chapter we present the rationale for bringing victims and offenders together, drawing on recent evidence from the fields of victimology and offender rehabilitation. We describe the main aspects of VOIC (the referral system, the activities participants take part in, their reactions to each other) after giving an overview of related schemes. Finally we discuss the results of the evaluation of VOIC and some of the problems encountered.

Theoretical basis

The setting up of VOIC was influenced by two major developments in the field of criminology in the early 1980s. The first was the sudden upsurge of interest in and concern for the needs of victims of crime. Several victim surveys were conducted in Britain in the early 1980s (Maguire, 1982; Shapland et al., 1985; Hough and Mayhew, 1985) which showed that as a rule victims are not vindictive but in need of information, explanations, and a forum to ventilate their feelings of anger, helplessness, and resentment. The rapid growth of the Victims Support Scheme movement (see Reeves, this volume; Maguire and Corbett, 1987) shows that these needs are now recognized. The experience of the first author in his work as a VSS volunteer is that the questions victims of burglary ask themselves (and the VSS volunteer) often concern their unknown burglar and sometimes reveal some extreme and unnecessary anxieties: 'why did they pick on me?'; 'who would do such a thing?'; 'how do burglars feel when they break into a house?'; and 'do they ever think of the people they are burgling?' Thus, the first objective of VOIC is to address and reduce the fear and anger of the victims by giving them the opportunity to question, confront, and get to know offenders.

The second development of the 1980s is the (apparent) shift of attitudes among practitioners and academics towards offender rehabilitation. In the 1970s the general stance was epitomized by the 'nothing works' doctrine (Martinson, 1974; Brody, 1976). Following data reanalysis (e.g. Garrett, 1985; Thornton, 1987) which suggests that treatment initiatives with offenders can be effective, a more positive attitude is breaking through in the 1980s. Recent publications urge practitioners to tackle offending behaviour directly (Thorpe et al., 1980; McGuire and Priestley, 1985). They argue that it is insufficient to help offenders merely by improving their social skills or their educational standards, and that the offenders' delinquent values and the way they rationalize their criminal behaviour should also be confronted.

McGuire and Priestley (1985) argue that most offenders are not committed to delinquent values. They are better described as being in a state of confusion, bewilderment, and having 'mixed up emotions and feelings'. What Rogers (1977) calls 'value blurring' enables them to rationalize their criminal behaviour and neutralize any guilt they may feel (Sykes and Matza, 1957) by using psychological techniques which have been well researched (Priest and McGrath, 1970; Velarde, 1978; Scully and Marolla, 1984). Scully and Marolla in their study of rapists make the useful distinction between the *excuses* given for a crime which admit criminal acts to be bad or inappropriate but deny full responsibility, and *justifications* which accept responsibility for those acts but deny any wrongdoing. They found that some rapists justify themselves by claiming that victims deserved to be or enjoyed being raped. For example, one rapist was quoted as saying 'she semi-struggled but deep down I think she felt it was a fantasy coming true' (1984: 535). Another rapist claimed that since his victims were prostitutes and therefore '. . . dirty sluts . . . everything I did was justified' (p. 537).

The excuses usually involved drug or alcohol intoxication or a fatalistic feeling of being plagued by 'a problem'. One rapist in the study said 'the fact that I'm a rapist makes me different. Rapists aren't all there. They have problems. It was wrong so there must be a reason why I did it. I must have a problem' (p. 539).

The parallel rationalizations used by burglars tend to cite victims as benefiting from being burgled (e.g. financially from insurance claims or from the attention received, briefly, as a 'celebrity'), or deserving it (because they are excessively rich or dishonest themselves). How is one to challenge these rationalizations? This is notoriously difficult for professionals responsible for offenders (such as probation officers, psychologists, or prison officers); the offenders' 'immune response' (McGuire and Priestley, 1985: 51) to moralistic lectures has been well documented. Akerstrom for instance describes how offenders 'switch off' when faced with a 'professional do-gooder who tries to educate them about right attitudes', which the offenders merely interpret 'as a way of getting them to be more like their teachers' (1985: 90).

The second objective therefore in bringing victims and offenders together through VOIC is to challenge the offenders' justifications for their criminal behaviour by confronting them with the human consequence of crime.

VOIC and other victim/offender groups

The fact that VOIC operates within a particular Youth Custody Centre is a result of historical circumstances. Rochester Youth Custody Centre just happened to be the place where the theories met the practical need for such a scheme. There is nothing within the theoretical precepts of VOIC which would inhibit such a scheme operating in other settings, including non-custodial ones (Wall and Hopkinson, 1987).

There have been other custodial schemes where sentenced offenders have met unrelated victims in both the UK and the USA; most have been poorly documented, but two examples are fairly well known. In the USA the Western State Hospital experiment brought together victims of rape and rapists for one highly confrontational meeting. (This scheme has received much publicity, e.g. the television programme QED, broadcast on BBC2, 12 March

1986.) A similar scheme operated at Maidstone Prison, in the UK, between 1979 and 1981; although this scheme also brought together victims of rape and rapists, the approach taken was more sensitive (Hawkins, 1986). (See also Victim-related therapy for sexual offenders in Hameln prison, Dünkel and Rössner, this volume.)

Avon probation service runs a scheme in which attendance at a victim/offender group is a condition in a probation order (Wall and Hopkinson, 1987). The scheme is restricted to offenders convicted of domestic burglary and takes place over six sessions. The scheme is primarily aimed at 'adult' as opposed to 'young' offenders.

It is interesting to compare victim/offender groups such as VOIC and the others cited above, which all operate after sentence, with schemes such as Matchmate, run by Stoke City Football Club, which involve meetings between opposing groups when no offence has, as yet, been committed. The Matchmate scheme brings together opposing sets of football supporters to participate in social activities, the aim being to diffuse possible tensions before a football match (Graham, 1986). McWhirter (1985) has also reported some evidence to show that it is possible to promote positive attitude change in Irish Catholic and Protestant children by taking them on common holidays. Similar, but less successful ventures have also been reported in the field of race relations (Goldwyn, 1986). The latter schemes share many aims and objectives with VOIC and the other victim/offender groups. The intention is to bring about attitude change, and ultimately behaviour modification, through increasing the mutual understanding of the groups involved.

VOIC and other conciliation schemes
It is difficult to discuss victim/offender groups without reference to other schemes currently operating which involve victims and offenders. The framework illustrated in Table 8.1 enables VOIC, and other groups referred to above, to be placed in context with schemes bringing together individual victims and offenders, and those which aim to reconcile individual offenders and the community.

In Type A schemes, protagonists meet face to face with a mediator or mediators in order to resolve their conflicts and possibly to reach some form of reconciliation. At stage 0 they may aim to resolve a dispute when no offence has (yet) been committed (Marshall and Walpole, 1985: 7–12; or see Shaw, this volume). At stage 1 an offender may volunteer to meet and make amends to his or her victim after a police caution (Blagg, 1985; or see Veevers, this volume). At stage 2 victim and offender meet after the offender has been convicted, to agree on a contract of reparation which may be taken into account by the sentencing court (Smith et al., 1985; or

Table 8.1 *Conciliation and the criminal justice process (CJP)*

Who is involved	Stages in the CJP				
	Pre-CJ involvement (0)	Pre-conviction (1)	Pre-sentencing (2)	Post-sentencing	
				Non-custody (3a)	Custody (3b)
One-to-one (A)	Dispute resolution schemes (Victim Services Agency, New York)	Mediation/reparation schemes (personal victim) (Exeter Youth Support Team)	(Coventry reparation scheme)	Rochdale and Bury scheme	
Group (B)	Matchmate-type schemes	(no scheme presently in operation)		Avon Scheme	VOIC
Community (C)	Informal control from community	Mediation/reparation schemes (corporate victim) (Exeter YST)	(Coventry reparation)	Community service	Prisoners' community work

The *columns* show the stages in the criminal justice process at which the schemes operate. *Stage 0:* no offence has been committed or at least none reported. Participants may, however, be in dispute and/or at risk of breaking the law. *Stage 1:* an offender has been caught by the police; he/she may have been cautioned or may be awaiting a decision whether to prosecute. *Stage 2:* the offender has been convicted but not sentenced. *Stage 3:* the offender has been sentenced.

The table *rows* show the approach taken in bringing together disputants or victims and offenders.

see Ruddick, this volume). At stage 3 victim and offender meet in order to resolve their conflict either in a non-custodial or in a custodial setting (see the account of the Rochdale and Bury scheme in Marshall and Walpole, 1985: 26; also, in another context, Gadsby and Thompson, 1985).

In Type B schemes, which have been described in the previous section, groups of protagonists meet in which the victims and offenders are unrelated. The purpose is to increase mutual understanding rather than reach agreement. Schemes at stage 0 are those such as Matchmate and schemes at stage 3 include the Avon scheme and of course VOIC. To the authors' knowledge there are no schemes operating at stages 1 and 2 which make use of group techniques. However, such schemes could exist in practice, attendance at a group being linked with a caution at stage 1 or deferment of sentence (or even during remand in custody) at stage 2.

In Type C schemes an attempt is made to reconcile offenders not with their own victims but with the community as a whole. Stage 0 refers to the informal control exercised over offenders in small communities. An example would be the local teacher or vicar 'asking' a minor delinquent to make good some act of vandalism. Stages 1 and 2 refer to reparation made to an institution, e.g. a factory or school, rather than to an individual (Blagg, 1985; Smith et al, 1985). At stage 3, a non-custodial example would be attending for community service (Pease, 1985). A custodial example would be the type of scheme under which the inmates in a penal institution produce goods for sale, the proceeds of which go to the victims of crime in the community (Marshall, 1984: 33).

VOIC: the referral system

Victims

Victims are referred to the scheme either by the local victims support scheme (VSS) or the local Crime Prevention Officer. The VSS usually contacts victims of residential burglary, while the police find victims of commercial burglary. There is some degree of selection in the sense that the referring agencies tend to refer people they think are likely to be interested. Indeed, most victims contacted show some interest in the scheme, although only a proportion of these are willing or able to participate. The percentage of victims who volunteer was found to be higher for VSS referrals (around 30 per cent) than for police referrals (around 15 per cent). Maguire and Corbett (1987: 230) similarly found that victims who had been visited by a VSS worker were more likely to volunteer to meet their own offender than victims who had not benefited from a VSS visit. The reasons victims give for volunteering are various, the prime one being curiosity about burglars. Victims also want to give offenders 'a piece of their mind', and they hope to have a positive influence on them and make it less likely for other members of the public to suffer what they have been through.

Offenders

Offenders are selected purely on grounds of their offences. Only offenders who demonstrate serious discipline problems in the institutions are excluded. Almost all offenders who are approached want to take part. They look forward to a break in the institution routine and to meeting people from 'outside'. They also say that they want to justify themselves and show victims that they are not 'animals' (which is how some offenders think they are perceived by the general public). They want victims to see, for instance, that they have an elaborate ethical code which involves not stealing from friends, the poor, the old, and so on.

Matching victims and offenders

A lesson learnt from the VOIC meetings is that offenders are highly skilled at arguing that they are not concerned with the particular offence under discussion if it is not precisely one they have committed themselves, or would commit. It is therefore important that the victims invited to the meetings should have experienced very similar types of offences to those committed by the offenders they meet. This is the reason why separate meetings are organized for commercial and residential burglaries. When victim and offender participants are paired in the role-play exercises further effort is made to match the type of burglary suffered by the victim and the type of burglary the offender specialized in.

VOIC: the process

Victims and offenders meet for three sessions. Although the content of the discussions clearly varies from group to group, common themes emerge which are illustrated below (see also Launay, 1985: 205–7). The first session brings together all the participants: the victims, the offenders, the scheme organizers and the VSS or police representatives, who come to act as a support to their referrals. Discussion begins with the victims being asked to describe their reactions when they discovered that they had been burgled. Occasionally victims (usually young men) report that their burglaries had caused them little or no distress, arguing that burglary is a common occurrence for which they were prepared and that their stolen property was easily replaceable. Most victims however report some or considerable distress, extreme cases being women who felt they had to clean their house from attic to cellar to erase any trace or memory of the burglars' intrusion, or people who have had to move house as the result of their burglaries. Some offenders, in response, demonstrate an understanding of the distress of the victims. They often report feeling guilty and ashamed as they listened to the victims describing their experiences. Other offenders however found it difficult to accept that victims should suffer from a mere loss of property, which, through the offenders' eyes, seems generously compensated by insurance pay-outs. It is only in the ensuing discussion that offenders begin to understand the psychological aspects of burglary which had been previously unknown or alien to them (the loss of the victim's peace of mind, the intrusion of privacy, the loss of property of sentimental value, etc.).

120 *Gilles Launay and Peter Murray*

Once they have admitted that their criminal behaviour hurts people, offenders usually (as in the Scully and Marolla study already quoted) use one of two further lines of self-defence, either excusing their behaviour or justifying it. Excuses include lack of money, unemployment, dearth of organized leisure activities, poor education, and poor family background. To a large extent victims are sympathetic to the offenders' description of the miseries of 'life on the dole' and are surprised and shocked by the offenders' lack of 'proper' family life. They do, however, using examples of deprivation from their own lives, forcefully argue that such difficulties could and should be surmounted without resorting to crime.

The other line of defence used by offenders which has even less success with the victims is to argue that their acts, even though harmful, are justified. They argue, for instance, that most victims deserve to be robbed because of their excessive wealth or because they are dishonest themselves. Indeed they often claim that burglars are no more dishonest than most people who cheat on their income tax returns, Value Added Tax or insurance claims.

Although offenders do not always accept the validity of the victims' criticisms (e.g. when victims compare burglars to rapists since both invade their victims' privacy), it is significant that they are at least prepared to discuss these views. This contrasts with the reaction of offenders in a control group who were confronted by VSS representatives with descriptions of the consequences of their crimes (see below). Here, such criticisms evoked aggression and denial on the part of the offenders, culminating in a refusal to contribute to the discussion. It would seem therefore that offenders regard recent victims as having, as some offenders expressed it, 'the right to an explanation', unlike criminal justice officials whose motives offenders are suspicious of.

The exercises and role-plays in the subsequent two sessions all serve to cement personal relationships between victims and offenders. In the role-play, victim and offender participants are asked to enact a mediation/reparation meeting where a victim and his own offender try to agree on a reparation contract which may be taken into account when sentencing the offender. Both victims and offenders find the role-playing difficult, especially when they are asked to reverse roles so that the offender plays the role of a victim, and the victim plays an offender. By working as a team to surmount these difficulties (or failing to surmount them) individual victims and offenders are brought together and invariably this leads them to a degree of amicability and mutual personal respect, to the extent that they find it difficult to part at the end of the last session. Indeed, ending the last session is usually only achieved because of the threatening consequences of breaking the institutional curfew.

Issues

Actual v. unrelated victim and offender

The decision to involve unrelated victims and offenders, rather than victims and their own offenders, in the VOIC scheme was based on the following considerations. Firstly, a scheme limited to actual victims and offenders would exclude victims of *unsolved* crimes (the majority of burglary victims) who may well feel more in need of expressing their frustration and helplessness than victims of solved crime. Secondly and more pragmatically, in view of the large catchment area of a Youth Custody Centre, the matching and bringing together of victims and their own offenders would have been a costly and time-consuming enterprise. Finally, involving unrelated victims and offenders offers the possibility of bringing them together as a group.

Groups v. one-to-one meetings

The main reason for favouring groups rather than one-to-one meetings is that groups have been found to be effective agents of attitude change (Reich and Addock, 1976). In a victim/offender group, participants are presented with a wide range of views and attitudes. Offenders do not all justify their acts in the same way or to the same extent; victims differ widely in their reaction to crime and criminals. An example of group dynamics is the way peers influence each other. Offenders often 'change sides' to challenge some of the more outrageous rationalizations made by their peers. Similarly victims often find arguments to explain the behaviour of offenders which convince other victims better than the offenders' own explanations.

Sentenced v. unsentenced offenders

The main drawback of involving offenders awaiting a court decision is that their contribution to the meeting is likely to be influenced by the possibility (real or imagined) that the judicial decision is going to be affected by the outcome of the meeting. This is vividly illustrated below by an offender's cynical but honest view of mediation meetings. Meetings which involve sentenced offenders (or offenders whom it has been decided to caution: see Veevers, this volume) have the advantage that participants have nothing to gain or lose from the meeting and so the proceedings are not encumbered by selfish aims and bargaining.

Custodial v. non-custodial schemes

Arguably, a scheme which aims to promote a better understanding between offenders and victims should take place in the community.

If the offenders feel better accepted by the community as a result of the encounter they should be allowed to test this new-found confidence in the community, not locked up in their cells! The relative merits of custodial victim/offender groups like VOIC and non-custodial groups such as that run by Avon probation service will no doubt be the subject of future empirical investigations. In the meantime there is no reason of course why both types should not be developed in parallel.

Type of offence

Burglary was an obvious choice of crime for VOIC because of the wide discrepancy between the severity of its impact on some victims and the offenders' perception of the crime (e.g. Landau, 1974). Other crimes, such as car theft, although arousing less anxiety for the victim (Hough, 1985) are also promising candidates. Although there have been some apparently successful encounters between victims of rape and rapists (Hawkins, 1986), clearly particular care should be taken over the needs of victims of such traumatic crimes. One danger, for instance, is to overburden the rape victim with the added problems of offenders when she is trying to cope with the aftermath of her own trauma. Annis et al. (1984) suggest that a better strategy is to confront offenders with therapists who help rape victims rather than the victims themselves (see also Dünkel and Rössner, this volume).

Are some types of victim or offender unlikely to benefit from VOIC?

When a victim/offender group was tried out in 1984 at Maidstone Prison (a training prison for long-term adult offenders in south-east England), which also brought together burglars and victims of burglary, it soon became clear that meetings involving hardened professional criminals (such as those likely to receive a long sentence for burglary) were unlikely to benefit victims or offenders. The victims understandably were not reassured in any way by meeting professional burglars, who were untypical since most burglars are young people. The professional burglars in turn seemed little affected by accounts of the victims' suffering. Although it is too early to make rules about who is not likely to benefit from the encounter, professional, hardened criminals appear to be poor candidates.

The experience of the VOIC sessions would suggest that victims who had no previous contact with offenders (the great majority) benefited most from the experience and contributed most to the progress of the group. The victim volunteers who had had extensive dealings with offenders (two magistrates, one social worker, two headmasters/teachers) tended to talk in general terms rather than about their specific experiences as victims. They also tended to 'take the side' of the offenders in a way which the offenders found patronizing, for instance by providing sociological explanations for the offenders' behaviour.

Finally, a tentative research finding from the evaluation of VOIC (Launay, 1987) is that another group of participants, elderly female victims, did not seem to benefit in terms of measurable attitude change. This group showed no anxiety reduction after the meetings, and was the only group not to rate the offenders more positively. This result is not unexpected since the elderly women did seem to find it more difficult than the other victims to achieve rapport with the offenders. It is, however, an unfortunate finding since it appears that many elderly women are among those who suffer most when they are victims of burglary (Maguire, 1982). If the finding is replicated it suggests that individual needs should be better assessed and catered for on the VOIC programme.

Risks of exploitation

A common concern on the part of practitioners contemplating the setting up of a victim/offender conciliation scheme is that they might exploit the victim in order to help the offender, or vice versa.

Practitioners may be somewhat reassured by the evidence of VOIC (Launay, 1987), which demonstrates that as a rule both victims and offenders benefit. An analysis of VOIC sessions suggests that, through the encounter, victims and offenders will either form personal relationships from which both parties benefit; or, exceptionally, they will not get on, but remain suspicious of each other, in which case the experience is not likely to benefit either of them.

Conciliation v. confrontation: the role of the facilitator

Maintaining the right balance between confrontation and conciliation is a main concern for the VOIC facilitator running the meetings. The creation of a good rapport between victims and offenders is a crucial element. It is instrumental in reducing the victims' fear and anxiety and makes it more likely that the offenders will accept the criticisms and challenges of the victims.

A successful session, however, is more often than not one where the social climate alternates from a good-humoured friendly mode to one of confrontation which requires victims as well as offender participants to justify themselves. It is up to the facilitator to ensure that the timing of the confrontation is right. If the participants are challenged too early and too successfully they may be left with no escape route and refuse to take part any further. On the other hand confrontation might prove difficult to establish once the participants have formed friendly personal relationships.

Visitors to the scheme, who significantly are only invited to the third and last session, have commented that victims and offenders seem to be getting on almost *too* well by the end of the encounter and have questioned whether this easy relationship might not lead the offenders to feel complacent about their criminality. Again the facilitator should be alert to this problem and make offenders aware that being accepted as human beings by the victims does not make their delinquency more acceptable.

Outcomes

The objective of VOIC is to promote a better understanding between victims and offenders. The evaluation (see below) provides some evidence to suggest that this has been achieved. This section attempts to complement that evidence by describing some of the reactions of the participants after the meetings.

The most common response for both victims and offenders has been that the encounter was a totally new experience. Offenders (who usually come to Rochester YCC with a wide experience of rehabilitation programmes) claimed that it was the first time they had been given the chance to put across 'their side of the story' and made to think hard about their motives and excuses. They did not expect that recent victims would be prepared to listen to them and sympathize with their problems.

Victims were surprised that the offenders were, in their words 'just ordinary young men', and found meeting them an enlightenment rather than an ordeal. A victim participant commented after the last session: 'It has been fascinating. Girls at work were saying "I don't know how you can do it!" but I thoroughly enjoyed it. I suppose I have really learned a lot. It has been a new experience in my life, something else I have experienced.' The answers to a feedback questionnaire (Table 8.2) administered to 26 victim participants at the end of the meetings held in 1984 support this anecdotal evidence. As a rule victims discovered that offenders were friendly and ordinary and that the meetings were useful and enjoyable.

In the light of recent experiments in victim/offender reparation (Davis et al., 1987), it is interesting to consider the comments of victims and offenders towards the type of reparation meetings which may affect the sentence of the offender, after they had role-played

Table 8.2 *Victims' answers to the feedback questionnaire* (N = 26)

	Strongly agree		Agree		Undecided		Disagree		Strongly disagree	
	No.	%	No.	%	No.	%	No.	%	No.	%
1 Coming to meet offenders at Rochester YCC has been a waste of time.	0		2	7.7	1	3.9	5	19.2	18	69.2
2 The meetings have helped me to understand why young burglars offend.	4	15.9	11	42.3	4	15.4	5	19.2	2	7.7
3 Such meetings might be useful for some victims but not for me.	1	3.9	2	7.7	1	3.9	10	38.5	12	46.2
4 I have found that during the meetings the offenders were honest.	4	15.9	8	30.7	12	46.2	2	7.7	0	
5 I have found it rewarding to talk about the experience of being burgled with other victims.	12	46.2	13	50.0	1	3.9	0		0	
6 I am glad to have had the opportunity to confront burglars with the results of their actions.	12	46.2	13	50.0	0		1	3.9	0	
7 I found offenders were very much like any ordinary young men.	11	42.3	10	38.5	2	7.7	2	7.7	1	3.9
8 These meetings are more useful for offenders than for victims.	2	7.7	3	11.5	13	50.0	7	26.9	1	3.9
9 I have found the offenders to be unfriendly.	1	3.9	0		0		9	34.6	16	61.5
10 I have found it interesting to listen to the offenders' 'side of the story'.	11	42.3	15	57.7	0		0		0	

taking part in such a scheme. Offenders were all very cynical about their own motives if given the chance to 'win' a lighter sentence by 'selling' themselves to their victims. One offender explained why he thought it would be quite easy to get the victim 'on his side'.

> My friends have all got a lot of chat and you learn it from them. It comes naturally half the time. If you were shy it might be more difficult, but if you are confident in yourself, it would be easy to bring them in your confidence. It depends what the victim was like. If you have an old lady you would try and win her over not so much by the reasons you have done it, but by talking to her and making her feel at home with you. If it was a younger person you would talk to them and make them see the reasons why you have done it hoping they would understand, plus bring a lot of bluff with it.

It should be borne in mind, however, firstly that these offenders did not have experience of one-to-one meetings with their 'own' victims, and secondly that not all mediation schemes are structured in a way which makes it appear likely, or even possible, that the sentence will be affected.

Maybe not surprisingly, since they were all VOIC volunteers, victims liked the idea of meeting their offenders. However, they took the traditional view (expressed for example in 1985 by the politician Enoch Powell) that a criminal offence is committed primarily against the rules of society and that it is up to society and its criminal justice system to decide on the consequences. They clearly had confidence in this process and did not think it was appropriate that they, as victims, should be involved in it.

Research on VOIC

The evaluation of VOIC has taken place in two phases. The results of phase I, completed at the end of 1984, are reported in Launay (1987) and summarized below. Phase I consisted of the administration of questionnaires to victim and offender participants before and after the meetings. The questionnaires administered to the offenders were also administered to a control group of offenders who took part in meetings run by a representative of VSS. They discussed the same issues as in the 'experimental group' i.e. crime and its consequences, but did not meet victims. No such control group was set up for the victims.

The results of the evaluation show that victims rate themselves as being less anxious and angry after the meetings and that they rate burglars more positively, in particular as being more friendly and likeable. Offenders similarly rate victims more positively after the meetings and are then better at predicting both the attitude of victims towards burglars, and the impact of a burglary on its victim. For instance, the percentage of offenders who believed that victims complain more about 'having a stranger in the house' than 'losing property' increased from 22 per cent before the meetings to 57 per cent after the meetings. No such increase took place in the control group. This result is taken as an indication that the comments of the victim participants, who often argued that the loss of property was secondary to the invasion of privacy, are accepted and remembered by the offenders.

Phase II of the evaluation is in progress at the time of writing. It benefits from an improved methodology (including use of a control group for victims) and the use of specialized attitude scales. Attitude change in the victim participants resulting from meeting the offenders is now assessed using the Melvin scale (Melvin et al., 1985), which measures the attitude of the general public towards offenders. Attitude change among offenders is assessed by a new scale which has been especially constructed to measure the extent to which people are willing to accept excuses or justifications for crime, the JUDEX scale (JUstifications, DEnials, and EXcuses). The scale items are based on comments made by offenders during the meetings. The items include such excuses as 'In some neighbourhoods you have to break the law to survive', and 'You can't blame a drug addict who steals when desperate for drugs.' The justification items include such statements as 'People who wear valuable jewellery in public are asking for trouble', and 'It is understandable that someone should steal from a shopkeeper who overcharges his customers.'

Validation research has shown that offenders obtain a much higher JUDEX score (that is, they accept more excuses or justifications) than non-offenders – matched for age and socio-economic group (Larkin, 1986). The JUDEX scale is also positively correlated with the psychoticism scale of the Eysenck Personality Inventory which measures criminality, cruelty, lack of feelings, or empathy (Eysenck et al., 1985), and is negatively correlated with Gudjonsson's guilt scale (Gudjonsson, 1984), which suggests that the making of excuses for crime may be an efficient way of reducing guilt.

These results suggest that the scales mentioned above could be used to predict the offenders' reactions to the encounter and also to pre-select the offenders most likely to benefit from the scheme. Offenders with high JUDEX scores (i.e. showing a high degree of rationalizations) would clearly be prime targets. However, offenders who also have a high psychoticism score may well lack the empathy required to benefit from meeting victims. Offenders with a low psychoticism score and a high guilt score may benefit from meetings, in as much as the meetings might give them the opportunity to assuage their guilt. (Indeed some offenders are very keen to help and reassure victims by giving them advice on how to protect their homes or by helping to challenge their more criminal peers.)

What makes VOIC work?

Having noted that VOIC occupies a particular position in the framework of victim/offender schemes, and that research has established that it works in practice, an exploration of the link between these two facts may be helpful to practitioners considering the setting up of a victim/offender scheme. Basically, what advantages accrue from operating at the post-sentencing stage and using groups, and why?

The prime overriding advantage of operating post-sentencing (stage 3 in Table 8.1) is that there the process of conciliation is independent of the decisions of the criminal justice process, such as the decision to impose a custodial sentence. At this stage the protagonists are completely powerless to decide the outcome of their conflict, as this has already been decided. A similar argument may be applied to those schemes operating *before* criminal justice involvement (stage 0) although, there, the independence is due to the power vested in the protagonists to decide the outcome of their conflict. In contrast, for schemes operating pre-conviction and pre-sentencing (stages 1 and 2) there is an interdependence between the conciliatory process and the decision of the criminal justice system, most notably for those schemes operating at stage 2, where the final disposal of the offender is still to be made by the court.

The use of group techniques has a number of advantages over one-to-one work (p. 121 above). However, what is lost is a high degree of participant psychological involvement (PPI). The degree of PPI diminishes from type A schemes (one-to-one) through to type C schemes (community). It is highest in type A because the actual victim and offender involved in a particular conflict take part. It is less in type B schemes (groups) because the victims and offenders, although matched, are unrelated. In type C schemes the degree of PPI is least of all because the offender does not meet a personal victim. The degree of PPI a practitioner would wish to achieve will have a strong bearing on the type of scheme chosen.

In using the framework to decide which type of scheme they should operate, practitioners need to be aware of their aims and objectives on the two dimensions defined in Table 8.3. Those

Table 8.3 *Conciliation and the criminal justice process: a two-dimensional model*

Type of scheme	Stages in the CJP					Primary aim of scheme	
	0	1	2	3a	3b		
A						Resolution of conflict	Increasing
B						Mutual understanding	participant
C						Reconciliation of individual with community	psychological involvement

←

Increasing power of participants to decide the outcome of their conflict

wishing to achieve a high degree of PPI, and to remain independent of the decisions of the criminal justice system, might by reference to the framework set up a type A scheme at stage 3. If, however, they are not concerned with achieving such a high degree of PPI in those taking part, and also believe that such schemes should exist outside of the criminal justice process, then they might prefer being involved in a type B scheme at stage 0.

Conclusion and summary

In this chapter we have presented evidence to show that bringing together unrelated victims and offenders (not, that is, related by the same offence) can promote positive attitude change and a better understanding among participants. We have argued that the ideal conditions for this to happen are firstly that victims and offenders should meet as a group, secondly that they should be well matched for type of crime, and finally that offenders should already have been sentenced so that they have nothing to gain or lose from the outcome of the meeting. Some attempt has been made to generalize these arguments to other types of victim/offender meetings.

Note

1   Since this chapter was written, Rochester Youth Custody Centre has become a prison for adults, and the VOIC project has been transferred to the Probation Service.

References

Akerstrom, M. (1985) *Crooks and Squares: Lifestyles of Thieves and Addicts in Comparison to Conventional People*. Oxford: Transaction Books.

Annis, L.V., L.G. Mathers and C.A. Baker (1984) 'Victim workers as therapists for incarcerated sex offenders', *Victimology*, 9: 426–35.

Blagg, H. (1985) 'Reparation and justice for juveniles: the Corby experience', *British Journal of Criminology*, 25: 267–79.

Brody, S. (1976) *The Effectiveness of Sentencing*, Home Office Research Study 35. London: HMSO.

Davis, G., J. Boucherat and D. Watson (1987) *A Preliminary Study of Victim/ Offender Mediation and Reparation Schemes in England and Wales*. London: Home Office.

Eysenck, S.B.G., H.J. Eysenck and P. Barrett (1985) 'A revised version of the Psychoticism scale', *Personality and Individual Differences*, 6: 21–30.

Gadsby, J. and K. Thompson (1985) 'Working with incest: an alternative to custody', *Probation Journal*, 32: 143–5.

Garrett, C.J. (1985) 'Effects of residential treatment on adjudicated delinquents: a meta-analysis', *Journal of Research in Crime and Delinquency*, 22 (4): 287–308.

Goldwyn, E. (1986) 'The thick skin of white racism', *Listener*, 9 January 1986, 7–9.

Graham, J. (1986) 'Preventing football hooliganism: multi-agency intervention and community schemes', *Home Office Research Bulletin*, 20: 9–12.

Gudjonsson, G.H. (1984) 'Attribution of blame for criminal acts and its relationship with personality', *Personality and Individual Differences*, 5: 53–8.

Hawkins, H. (1986) 'The treatment of rapists: groups and victims', *NASPO News*, 6 (3): 6–7.

Hough, M. (1985) 'The impact of victimisation: findings from the 1984 British Crime Survey', *Victimology*, 10: 488–97.

Hough, M. and P. Mayhew (1985) *Taking Account of Crime: Key Findings from the 1984 British Crime Survey*, Home Office Research Study 85. London: HMSO.

Landau, S.F. (1974) 'The offender's perception of the victim', in I. Drapkin and E. Viano (eds), *Victimology: A New Focus*, vol. I. Lexington, Mass.: Lexington Books. pp. 137–54.

Larkin, T. (1986) 'The development of an attitude scale to measure the willingness to accept excuses for crimes', unpublished thesis, Brunel University.

Launay, G. (1985) 'Bringing victims and offenders together: a comparison of two models', *Howard Journal*, 24: 200–12.

Launay, G. (1987) 'Victim offender conciliation', in B. McGurk, D. Thornton and M. Williams (eds), *Applying Psychology to Imprisonment: Theory and Practice*. London: HMSO. pp. 273–302.

Maguire, M. (1982) *Burglary in a Dwelling: The Offender, the Offence and the Victim*. London: Heinemann.

Maguire, M. and C. Corbett (1987) *The Effects of Crime and the Work of Victims Support Schemes*. Aldershot: Gower.

Marshall, T. (1984) *Reparation, Conciliation and Mediation*, Home Office Research and Planning Unit Paper 27. London: HMSO.

Marshall, T. and M. Walpole (1985) *Bringing People Together: Mediation and Reparation Projects in Great Britain*, Home Office Research and Planning Unit Paper 33. London: HMSO.

Martinson, R. (1974) 'What works: questions and answers about prison reform', *Public Interest*, 35: 25–54.

McGuire, J. and P. Priestley (1985) *Offending Behaviour: Skills and Stratagems for Going Straight*. London: Batsford Academic and Educational.

McWhirter, E. (1985) 'An evaluation study of Protestant–Catholic workshops', paper presented at the British Psychological Society conference 'Contact and the reconciliation of conflict', 7 March 1985, Stranmillis College, Belfast.

Melvin, K.B., L.K. Gramlin and W.M. Gardner (1985) 'A scale to measure attitudes towards prisoners', *Criminal Justice and Behaviour*, 12: 241–53.

Pease, K. (1985) 'Community service orders', in M. Tonry and N. Morris (eds), *Crime and Justice: An Annual Review of Research*, vol. 6. Chicago: University of Chicago Press.

Powell, E. (1985) *The Times*, 21 October.

Priest, T. and J. McGrath (1970) 'Techniques of neutralisation: young marijuana smokers', *Criminology*, 8: 679–86.

Reich, B. and C. Addock (1976) *Values, Attitudes and Behaviour Change*. London: Methuen and Co.

Rogers, J.W. (1977) *Why are you not a Criminal?* Englewood Cliffs, NJ: Prentice-Hall.

Scully, D. and J. Marolla (1984) 'Convicted rapists' vocabulary of motives: excuses and justifications', *Social Problems*, 31: 530–44.

Shapland, J., J. Willmore and P. Duff (1985) *Victims in the Criminal Justice System*. Aldershot: Gower.

Smith, D., H. Blagg and N. Derricourt (1985) 'Does mediation work in practice?', *Probation Journal*, 32 (4): 135–8.

Sykes, G.M. and D. Matza (1957) 'Techniques of neutralization: a theory of delinquency', *American Sociological Review*, 22: 664–70.

Thornton, D. (1987) 'Treatment effects on recidivism: a reappraisal of the "Nothing works" doctrine', in B.J. McGurk, D. Thornton and M. Williams (eds), *Applying Psychology to Imprisonment: Theory and Practice*. London: HMSO. pp. 181–90.

Thorpe, D.H. et al. (1980) *Out of Care: The Community Support of Juvenile Offenders*. London: Allen and Unwin.

Velarde, A.J. (1978) 'Do delinquents really drift?', *British Journal of Criminology*, 18: 23–39.

Wall, R. and J. Hopkinson (1987) 'The Avon probation service victim–offender group'. Unpublished paper.

9

Mediating Adolescent/Parent Conflicts

Margaret Shaw

The Children's Aid Society's PINS (Persons in Need of Supervision) Mediation Project was established in 1981 and offers mediation as an alternative to the court for 'status offender' cases throughout New York City. The PINS Mediation Project accepts more than 500 referrals a year and is primarily a court-based programme, although referrals also come from the community, schools, and police. The project's volunteer mediators meet with families during the day or evening at one of the project's mediation centres located in the community.

The project was developed as a family court alternative because of the widespread conviction that the court system is inappropriate and ineffective in these 'status offender' cases, that is, ones involving truants, runaways and youth beyond their parents' control (excluding those involved with drugs or chemicals). The court's adversarial process pits child against parent and parent against child, and focuses exclusively on the juvenile for problems which are usually family ones. The court can do little other than order placement in a non-secure facility, from which the child is then free to abscond. As a result, staff in the court system feel an overwhelming sense of frustration with these cases, which also distract from the handling of more serious and violent offenders. More importantly, perhaps, the families who petition the court for help in controlling their children do not receive the kind of help they really need.

The mediation process

Participation in this mediation project is voluntary for all parties. Thus all the family members involved must agree to participate before mediation will occur. Intake workers are located in each of the family court buildings in the city to accept referrals from the department of probation before a PINS petition has been filed; once the court process has been initiated, referrals are also accepted from the parent's or the child's lawyer. Since its inception in 1981 the project has involved over 600 families in mediation.

The intake worker explains mediation to the referred family; if all of the family members agree to participate, he or she conducts a preliminary assessment to determine the nature and extent of the problem, and assigns a mediator. The family may also be referred to a project social worker if there is an immediate crisis or some other need is present.

Mediators are lay volunteers trained in mediation skills and techniques. They act as third-party neutrals, encouraging parents and children to communicate with each other, and helping them reframe the issues and explore solutions which, if mutually agreeable, will be reduced to writing and monitored from week to week. Written agreements are reached with about 73 per cent of the families.

Mediators meet families for up to four sessions, scheduled a week apart. More than one session is needed to reach a comprehensive agreement covering a large number of family problems. The emphasis in the first session is on re-establishing communication between the parent and child and on reaching agreement on a small specific item for which a high probability of compliance can be expected. Subsequent sessions build upon the first, and the agreement is strengthened and broadened as additional problem areas are addressed.

At any time the family may secure additional help in the form of mental health counselling, medical services, recreational and educational programmes, or other supportive services. These services are offered either directly by the project's social work staff or through referral to outside agencies with which the project has developed relationships. Follow-ups are done with families for two to three months after the last mediation session to determine whether mediation has been successful and whether further services are needed.

Specific issues

In addition to the use of a multi-session model, mediation between parents and children differs from other kinds of mediation in several respects. First and most obvious is the disparity in power between the mediating parties. Parents often say at intake, 'Are you telling me I am going to have to compromise with my child?' Both the mediator and the parties themselves must recognize that the mediator's task is not to rebalance power in the parent/child relationship; the parent's role as an appropriate authority is not called into question. At the same time, the mediator takes care to accord both parent and child equal dignity in the mediation process and equal input into resolution of the conflict. In the case of 'status offenders' parents have the power to file a court petition asking that their child be adjudicated a status offender. This places the focus on the child and the child's behaviour, not on problems within the family that may have caused the behaviour. While it is important to reframe the issue in neutral terms, redressing the imbalance can become a delicate matter in parent/child mediation, because the upset parent usually resists considering his or her own contribution to the problem and fears being blamed. Thus, issues are reframed in terms of goals and future satisfaction of the family as a whole so that all parties feel engaged rather than threatened.

Parent/child mediation programmes also usually include a strong social service component. Mediation often uncovers long-standing needs, such as alcohol treatment, mental health counselling, medical services, educational advocacy, and the like. Mediation is often a good first step toward preparing family members to accept and benefit from additional services. Agreement to obtain services is usually made a provision of the contract reached in mediation.

Mediating between parents and children can be quite difficult, perhaps because the relationship itself is the client. A parent/child mediator is not dealing with one particular dispute, although particular incidents are always involved, nor is he or she dealing with one particular aspect of a relationship, such as how two employees can structure their working relationship in order to get the job done or how two business entities can structure their contractual relationship. Rather, the mediator is dealing with the troubled relationship between two people who will continue to live together closely on a day-to-day basis and who will continue to be related throughout the rest of their lives.

One case the programme handled, for example, involved a child and a parent who had been undergoing family therapy for a number of years. The therapist reported that one obstacle to the family's making any progress was the child's failure to participate in the therapy process. Finally, the mother took the child to family court on a status offender charge. The family was then referred to mediation. The child sat through the first mediation session staring out the window, arms folded, refusing any kind of verbal communication. The mediator tried everything she could think of to encourage the child to talk. She asked about sports, told a few jokes, tried talking to the child on his own; nothing worked. Finally, in exasperation, she said 'Isn't there anything you want?' In response, the child mumbled that he wanted his mother to make him something. As the session wore on, the mother volunteered that one of her son's favourite foods was sweet potato pie and that she would make him one that week. In the interest of balance, the mediator encouraged the child to address one of his mother's concerns, and he agreed not to exercise with his barbells in the living room on Sundays. An agreement by a mother to make her son a sweet potato pie may not seem to go very far to address the problems involved in a troubled relationship. However, when the family returned the following week, the mother had made the pie as promised, and the child began to participate, very slowly at first, but increasingly during the next few sessions. At the conclusion of the mediation, the family was referred back to the family therapist, who reported on follow-up that the family was finally beginning to make progress. As this example illustrates, simple task-orientated agreements may have deeper implications for relationships as a whole. They can also get a family started in a positive direction, and the process can serve as a model for the handling of conflict and crisis in the future. But reasonable expectations must also be set from the outset; mediation will not resolve all a family's problems.

How then, should issues in a parent/child dispute be defined and dealt with in the context of the mediation process? Addressing a curfew dispute by defining the issue as what time the child will come home or how late the parent will allow the child to stay out is not enough. A mediator should explore why the child is staying out and why the parent wants the child home earlier. One child was staying out late because his parents were Seventh-Day Adventists who would not allow him to play music at home. An agreement around this issue is likely to be far more effective than an agreement that only addresses the hour by which the child is to return home. By the same token, if a child is staying out late and school performance is suffering because she feels the parent is preoccupied with a handicapped sibling, an agreement which simply addressed curfew and homework will be less effective than an agreement relating to the amount of time this parent and child will spend together, and the ways in which they will spend that time. Addressing issues in parent/child disputes too broadly, however, may also be risky. While the mediator should be sensitive to dynamics underlying family relationships and help to bring some of these issues to the surface, mediation must remain a time-limited, task-oriented process. The mediator's job is to guide the parties toward their own written agreements on specific behaviours in problem areas. A restructuring of family relationships may be a result of the mediation process, but it is not the mediator's goal.

Mediation outcomes

Parent/child mediators believe that it is the process of mediation itself, rather than whether the family reaches agreements and adheres to them, which is most important. Mediation addresses conflicts as the problem of both parties. It looks not to the past to attach blame or assign wrong but to the future to explore options for behavioural and attitudinal changes. Participants are encouraged to communicate with each other, to see the situation from the other's point of view, and are empowered to take ownership of the resolution. Mediation can both help to resolve the problems at hand and educate participants about dealing constructively with future conflicts.

To test success empirically, however, the PINS Mediation Project undertook research both to determine whether mediation between parents and children was working and to identify critical components of the process (Morris, 1983). The study included an intake interview to collect demographic and family background information, a telephone interview for families who had left the programme before attending mediation sessions, and a follow-up telephone interview of each family two months after the last mediation session to assess the quality of the family's mediation experience. Data were also collected from the project's case files and from department of probation computer records on recidivism.

The research looked beyond whether the parties appeared for and took part in the scheduled number of mediation sessions, or whether the agreements were achieved. How were the parties doing several months after mediation? What criteria could be used to determine success from that viewpoint? Participating families were contacted two months after their last mediation session and data secured for five factors.

1   Did the parent think that mediation had been helpful?
2   Did he or she think the child was now more manageable?
3   Had the presenting problems been resolved?
4   Did the family complete mediation (attend all the sessions scheduled for them)?
5   Had the child returned to court in the eight months after beginning mediation?

Positive results for each of these five factors were added up, producing a score ranging from zero to five. Results were assessed conservatively. For example, manageability was considered positive only if the parent reported that the child was more manageable (a report that the child was the same was considered negative).

Whether the problems were resolved was considered positive only if the parent specifically reported such at follow-up (lack of response to these factors was considered negative). Mediation was considered to have been of little or no success if none or one of the five factors was reported positive, of moderate success if two or three were reported positive, and highly successful if four or five of the factors were reported positive. Seventy-seven per cent of the families had been moderately (55.5 per cent) or highly (21.8 per cent) successful. Of the 23 per cent in the category of little or no success, the majority reported one factor as positive.

There was no significant difference between families who completed mediation and families that terminated prematurely in terms of age, sex, type or number of allegations, prior court history, and social service history. These family characteristics were also unrelated to the likelihood of a family's reaching a contract in mediation, to the nature of the contract reached, or to the family's response at follow-up. These findings suggest that the mediation approach is adaptable to many different kinds of families and family situations.

Earlier research focused on the first six months of project operations and compared families that chose mediation after seeking help from the family court with a control group of families that continued with the normal court process (Block, 1982). Nearly one-third of the petitioners contacted at follow-up (exactly half of those who reported that mediation had been helpful) mentioned on their own initiative that communication within the family had improved as a result of mediation. The research also found interesting differences between families referred to mediation at the probation intake level (before the parent had drawn up a formal petition or complaint against the child) and families referred to mediation after their first appearance in court. Families that were diverted to mediation at the pre-petition stage were significantly more likely to report satisfaction with mediation than families diverted at the post-petition stage. These families were similar in terms of prior court involvement, runaway history, or placement history, and the problems they were facing were probably no less severe. This finding suggests that the court's adversarial procedures may serve to exacerbate family conflict; the further a family proceeds in the court system, the more difficult it may become to effect a reconciliation through the mediation process.

Finally, important lessons were learned with respect to engaging the child in the mediation process. The project's first research study (Block, 1982) found that when the mediator described the child as uninterested in the mediation process, the family was less likely to arrive at a written agreement and was also less likely to complete the mediation process. As a result, project court liaison workers and mediators were more intensively trained in techniques of engaging the child, assuring both parties neutrality in the mediation setting, and explaining the possible benefits of mediation. This training appears to have been effective. Not only did the vast majority of families in the second study (Morris, 1983) reach contracts, but the rate of completion reported in the second study was higher than the rate reported in the first.

These findings highlight the advantage of mediation as a method of addressing parent/child conflicts. A child's perception of being brought to court by a parent can reaffirm the child's notion that the adult world is conspiring against him or her. The cards may seem to have been stacked against the child, which can substantially diminish the child's investment in the process. In contrast, mediation gives equal weight to the child's concerns, and he or she is accorded equal input into resolution of the conflict. This can lead both parties to make a greater investment in the process, and increase the chances that the outcome will be self-sustaining.

Families whose first appointment for mediation was scheduled within three days of intake were more likely to complete mediation than families whose first appointment was scheduled later. Families who were most successful in mediation (as measured by completion of mediation and by responses at follow-up) were more likely than those who were not successful to have arrived at two or more contracts including modifications of the first agreement (rather than one) during the mediation process. This finding confirms the view that a multi-session model is important for mediation between parents and children.

The subject-matter of contract provisions was generally unrelated to the success of mediation, but one exception involved contracts that addressed the subject of peers and lovers (for example, telephone calls with friends, or the involvement of third parties in family members' arguments). Families whose contracts addressed this subject were significantly more likely to report at follow-up that their children were more manageable. Finally, and not surprisingly, the research showed that families that reached balanced contracts – contracts containing a comparable number of concessions by each party – were more likely to report at follow-up that both parties were adhering to their agreements than families that did not.

Conclusions and recommendations

What are the implications of this experience? One of the most obvious implications is that mediation between parents and children can work for many different types of families and family situations, even for a difficult 'status offender' population. The findings also suggest that divorce mediators should give more thought to ways of including children in the divorce mediation process. Children do very well in mediation; their involvement can be productive, and should be encouraged.

The programme and research also offer important directions for those interested in developing parent/child mediation programmes. The multi-session model is preferable, and families should be diverted to mediation early in the juvenile justice process. Techniques for engaging the child, approaches to contract development and modification, and inquiries into the extent to which peers and lovers contribute to the parent/child conflict are all important.

But many questions are unanswered. For example, how do different mediation styles influence the success of mediation? Does a more directive and interventionist mediator do better than a more passive mediator? Should mediators and clients be matched in terms of race or sex? To what extent do results depend on the characteristics of the parties? What mediator qualities do the parties consider to be the most important? These are all fruitful areas for research. As knowledge of the process increases, efforts to address parent/child conflicts in the context of mediation will become increasingly responsive and responsible.

References

Block, Joyce (1982) *Mediation: An Alternative for PINS*. New York: Children's Aid Society, 105 East 22nd Street, New York, NY10010.

Morris, Marlene (1983) *Parent Child Mediation: An Alternative that Works*. New York: Children's Aid Society.

10

Ideals and Reality in Community Mediation

Martti Grönfors

Finland's first community mediation project began in 1983 in the city of Vantaa, near the capital, Helsinki. The impetus for the project came principally from a Scandinavian–North American conference on dispute handling, organized in Norway in 1980 by Nils Christie. First funds were given to the project in 1982 for planning. The project 'proper' received funds and support from five prime sources: the Academy of Finland (main supporter); city of Vantaa; Ministry of Justice; Vantaa Lutheran Parishes; and the Workers' Adult Education College of Vantaa. As the impetus for the project came from the academic world, the idea had to be sold to local authorities. After initial reluctance to start something so different, the authorities remained supportive throughout the project. However, although initially playing the role of a receiving party, and a somewhat subservient one, once it became clear that the mediations would be established on a permanent basis, the local authorities became more directive. This shift naturally affected the operation of the project, which towards the end of the experimental period in 1985 became more bureaucratic and authoritative, as will be shown. The organization of the project can be seen in Figure 10.1.

The area within which the project operated has a total population of about 50,000 people, which means that it is not accurate to talk about 'community' mediation in the true sense of the term; rather it is based on a geographical area. The communality is expressed through the selection of mediators and cases from within the area which the service covers. During the autumn of 1983 the first eight voluntary mediators were trained, and the office with two paid employees established. The mediations started at the beginning of 1984, and the experimental period was to last two years. Further training of new volunteers took place annually and there are now 35 active trained mediators. The project accepts both criminal and civil cases, either directly from the public or from the authorities. In most of the criminal cases the disputants (or offender and victim) are not known to each other, whereas in most of the civil disputes

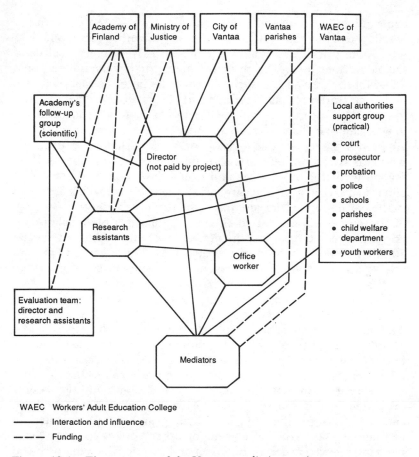

WAEC   Workers' Adult Education College
———————   Interaction and influence
— — —   Funding

Figure 10.1   *The structure of the Vantaa mediation project*

the disputants know each other or are related to one another. With a couple of exceptions, the participants in mediations have come from the same district.

Most of the cases which come from the authorities are referred by the police or the prosecutor; a few come from the Child Welfare Department. It is not known exactly how they select the cases, but the analysis of these cases, which during the second half of the year of operation consisted of over half of all cases, indicates that they involved either petty offences or complex, unclear disputes or human factors. The usual case referral procedure is as follows. A member of the public or an authority either telephones or visits the mediation office, explains the case in brief, and what his or her expectations are in relation to it. The office worker notes down the details, including the name and address of the other party. She then selects the principal mediator for the case, who in turn selects a secondary mediator. The principal mediator has overall responsibility for the case and he or she contacts the parties either by letter, phone, or (rarely) in person. Each party is first given an opportunity to state their case alone, which gives the mediators a chance to see how urgent or difficult the case is. A mediation hearing is set only if all parties agree; on the division of work, usually the principal mediator is responsible for the main line of negotiation and the second mediator only assists and keeps the mediation notes. The aim is to arrive at a written agreement, the copies of which are given to the parties, and if the case has come from the authorities, a copy of the agreement is sent to them. In situations of imbalance of power between the parties, the mediators are trained to pay special attention to the support of the weaker party. They can also play an active part in the negotiations, even suggest suitable solutions, if the parties themselves have difficulties in this respect.

The finance for the project has come mainly from public sources, and right from the beginning research on all possible aspects of mediation has been incorporated into the project. The experimental period ended at the end of 1985, although mediations continue as before, but now as part of the city's general social services. The effects of this transfer of management are referred to below.

The year 1986 was the year of evaluation, and the results presented in this chapter relate to research which has just been completed. Approximately 50 people who have participated in mediations – as parties to a crime or other kind of conflict – have been interviewed in depth. Eighteen of the 22 active mediators, who mediated cases during 1984–5, have also been interviewed; the remaining four have moved out of the district.

Theoretical background

The general theoretical guidelines came from three prime sources: from my work on traditional justice (Grönfors, 1977; 1979; 1986); from the experience of other similar projects, mainly those operating in California which were visited on three different occasions; and from the recent critique of the official justice system (Christie, 1977; 1981) and abolitionist discussion (Hulsman, 1979).

This broad framework can be expressed by the following general assumptions. Firstly, the problems which arise within a neighbourhood can, by and large, be handled by the community itself without referring them to the faceless official system. Secondly, in most problems the mediative help from ordinary community members is sufficient for finding an adequate solution. Such help relies on the everyday communicative skills of the people. Thirdly, the possibility of two-way discussion between the participants in the conflict gives a certain amount of satisfaction to the participants, as does the effort of finding a mutually satisfactory solution. Fourthly, participants in the conflict, especially in criminal conflict, often have quite different background and life experiences. The process of mediation makes it possible to understand varying motives for action which broadens the general level of understanding in the community. Fifthly, mediation in itself is positive in that it activates local people to tackle their own problems, and gives some of the power and responsibilities about their own destinies back to the people themselves. Sixthly, mediation, as an alternative to the official system, offers a chance for a critical examination of the operation of the official justice system. People, rather than being the objects of action, become active subjects in broader societal affairs.

Mediators and their training

In mediation the broad life experiences of people are utilized, and the formal training is based on that; the differences of personality and life experience are acknowledged and made use of in the training. The training is seen as a process which continues as long as people work as mediators, the influence of which, it is hoped, will extend to other spheres of their lives.

The purpose of mediators is not to judge or reform, but to facilitate communication between the participants in the conflict. The desired attitude toward mediation should be one of understanding and empathy. Formal schooling does not necessarily have anything to do with practical mediation skills, but when people have a suitable training, the special abilities which they may have gained through it can be utilized. The prime characteristics which people are made aware of and which are put into use in practical situations are found in people's personality, their life experience, and their willingness to work for and with other people.

Of the 22 active mediators during the experimental period, 18 were women, which is a common situation with most voluntary work. The median age is approximately 35 years, and the range is from 18 to 65. The level of basic education is higher than among the general population. An active effort has been made to activate men, younger people, and those of working-class background, but success has been limited. It is believed that differences in the personal background of the mediators add a positive dimension to practical mediation work.

The training of mediators has taken place on three different levels. Initially there was a 30-hour introductory course, in which the candidates were given some basic information about mediation, about various aspects of the working of the official justice system, and about the various social services found in the area. Practical mediation skills have been taught in live-in seminars, which were held three times a year, two days at a time. The secondary purpose of these seminars has been to provide the mediators with a chance to get to know each other and strengthen the feeling of solidarity and mutual friendship – i.e. the feeling of belonging to the same community. The third form of training was individual and group counselling. When an individual mediator felt that there were some problems which required counselling help, either in relation to certain individual cases of mediation, or some more general problems relating to the principles of mediation and his or her own relationship to those, he or she was able to call upon a counsellor. In comparison to the first mediation scheme in Scandinavia, started in the rural district of Lier in Norway in 1981 (Stangeland, 1985), where the mediators only received one day of training, the training of the mediators in Finland has been reasonably thorough.

In terms of motives, the mediators can roughly be divided into three main groups. One group of people have a critical view of established society and especially of its official justice system, and see mediation as a way to put their beliefs actively into practice. Another group of mediators see mediation as an inherent part of established society, and of the official justice system; they enter mediation with the aim of aiding society to function more effectively and more humanely. The largest group is somewhere in between these two; mediation is seen as their personal contribution to community activities without necessarily any deeper analysis of its place in the larger context of society. It is natural that the way in which people view their own participation affects their practical approach to mediation cases. While the 'critical group' tends to work consciously with strategies which are very different to those of the official system, the 'conservative group' tends to identify and work more closely with the local authorities. Both groups are interested in the broader issues of principle and are active in developing the mediation programme. The group which sees mediation largely in terms of helping people in difficulties tends to concentrate primarily on the actual mediation work and not participate in discussions about organizational matters.

Those who saw mediation in terms of the conventional justice model included all the male mediators and the research assistant – also male. They, more than alternative justice model mediators, were able to assert their influence in the day-to-day development of the service, in that they were 'rewarded' for their compliance by representing the mediators in the main decision-making body, the support group. Those opposing this development were kept out of decision-making.

This diversity of approach has both positive and negative effects on the day-to-day working of mediation. One clear positive effect is the fact that mediation cannot easily become routine work, but is continuously evaluated, discussed, and developed. Here again the Finnish scheme is different from that in Lier, Norway, where the mediators tend to work in isolation without attempts to influence the principles of mediation (Stangeland, 1985: 8). It also means that it is possible for mediators to take cases which best suit their particular approach. Since in this project the cases can come either directly from the public or from the authorities (mainly police and prosecutor), the solutions do not need to follow the same line in each case. One of the most important negative effects is the fact that there are quite clear opposing cliques, and much time has been spent in non-constructive arguments and even quarrelling. Perhaps the biggest negative influence has been the disproportionate influence which the 'conservative' group has been able to exert in the organizational aspects of mediation, mainly because one member of the paid staff had this view. That has been possible because of the close cooperation with the authorities forming the support group, whose role in this particular project has been very active. (The composition of this group is given in the next section.) Hence in certain respects – as will be seen later – some of the original principles of mediation have been lost sight of. With the mediators, though, notwithstanding the previous comments, one important goal has been achieved. People who originally were unknown to each other, although drawn from the same community, have formed a fairly solid mutual friendship network; they also cooperate with each other outside the project. So, through mediation a small section of the local population has been activated to a cooperative way of living and a feeling of collective responsibility.

The authorities and mediation

The project had a paid staff of two people in addition to its unpaid director (myself). The city of Vantaa paid for the general office worker, whose task – in addition to general office duties – was the allocation and follow-up of the mediation cases. The Academy of Finland paid for the research assistant, whose general task was the practical implementation (together with the director) of the project.

Representatives of the various local authorities, who came into contact with offenders in their work, or who were interested in rehabilitation of offenders, formed an advisory body. In addition there was a scientific follow-up group, consisting of three members of Finland's Academy. After the completion of the experimental period, at the end of 1985, the city also paid the salary of the general coordinator of the project, and Finland's Academy the salary of one full-time and one part-time research assistant.

The role which the local authorities have played has been very important right from the beginning. As it is a pioneer programme, many issues of principle had to be cleared with the authorities before the project could begin. The main influence has been exerted through the initially *ad hoc* support group of the authorities, which has now become an official governing body. The representatives of local judges, prosecution, probation service, police, child welfare, school authority, Lutheran church, and the youth bureau have been the active members of this group.

This close cooperation has had both positive and negative effects on mediation, when its original aims are examined. Having to adjust their thinking around mediation, the horizons of the authorities must have been widened. Another positive effect comes from the fact that for the first time the area's authorities, who all come into contact with offenders in the area, are examining the issues around the same table.

The most serious problem, though, arises from the fact that the way in which they view offending and the treatment of offenders can be in sharp contrast to the ideas of mediation. It has been quite difficult to make some authorities understand the basic principles of mediation as a non-judgemental, non-moralizing citizen activity. Another negative aspect comes from the authorities' excessive opportunities to influence the day-to-day working of mediation. This arose from the fact that a very close working relationship existed between the authorities and the practical coordinator of mediation, and has led to the result that a great part of the cases referred for mediation come from the authorities. In order to secure those cases, the authorities have had to be kept satisfied, and even courted. Most clearly its effect is seen in mediation agreements, which towards the end of the experimental period emphasized primarily the compensation in cash of the victims of offences, the human relationship between the participants receiving less and less attention. Now that the project is part of the social services which the city provides, it is no longer even considered an experiment in alternative justice, but as a support service to the official justice system.

As the situation stands today, it is clear that the original aims have to a large extent been lost sight of, and this claim is supported by both the quantitative and the qualitative research material about the way in which the mediation has developed in Vantaa.

Evaluation of mediation in 1984–5

During 1984 73 cases came into mediation. Of those, 57 were criminal matters and the rest other kinds of conflict, mainly civil quarrels. The largest category of crimes were petty property offences (24), violence against the person being the next (15). Civil cases consisted of quarrels about debts, housing, neighbourhood complaints of disturbance, conflicts about inheritance, and problems relating to division of property after a divorce.

As seems to be the case elsewhere, an overwhelming proportion of cases mediated end up in agreement. The mere fact that people agree to mediation ensures that nine cases out of ten end satisfactorily. This figure corresponds to those experienced in Norway (Stangeland, 1985: 8).

In 1985 the total number of cases doubled (142). However, looking at the development more closely, the shift towards the official system had already started showing in the figures. Of the 142 cases in 1985 only 5 were non-criminal matters. While in 1984 only 10 per cent of the cases came from the authorities, in 1985 over half (80) came either from the police or from the prosecutor. The shift towards monetary compensation is seen from the fact that while in 1984 a quarter of all agreements included compensation by work for the victim, in 1985 only two such agreements were made.

The personal interviews support the figures, and especially the fact that participants see mediation as part of the official system. They, especially the young offenders, more often than not did not know that their participation in mediation was voluntary, and only a few understood mediation as being outside the official justice system. However, when their attitude towards mediation was examined, almost without exception it was positive. An often-heard comment was that the offenders felt that for the first time in their lives they were regarded as human beings by people handling their offending. Some of these offenders (who were referred to mediation by authorities) expressed their disappointment when they discovered that a successful mediation did not necessarily end the matter, and some were angry when they were given a punishment at court as well.[1]

In relation to the attitude of the victims of crime towards the mediation they have undergone, it can be said that it is also mainly positive. Even in those few cases where the agreement has not been kept, it is surprising that many have retained a positive attitude.[2] This is at least partly explained by two things. Firstly, the offenders are in the main quite young, usually just over the age of legal responsibility (15 in Finland). Secondly, the offences are quite minor, and the offenders either still at school or unemployed, and the victims have made a correct assumption that had the case gone through the legal system they would not have had an order of restitution imposed against the offender there either. However, prospects for community mediation in general do seem promising, in that, contrary to the often-heard claim that the general public is quite punitive in its attitudes towards offenders, this does not appear to be the case when the relatively minor offences of young people are in question.[3] (See also Wright, Chapter 18 this volume.)

Some tentative conclusions

It is clear that over the two-year experimental period mediation changed its focus from being a conflict resolution process to being one aiding the official legal system in deciding on compensation. Therefore, rather than being an *alternative* way of handling conflicts in the community, it has become primarily an addition to the formal system. Its supporters would defend its activity, even in its altered form, if further sanctions were not imposed on the young offenders after a successful mediation. Sanctions are, however, avoided only in very rare cases. Now that the scheme is being extended to some other major cities in Finland, this aspect should receive serious attention if they are to have any concrete effect. Otherwise it would be accurate to say that there was a net-strengthening effect, whereby even unemployed and penniless young offenders commit themselves through informal procedures to paying restitution and compensation which no court would have ordered against them. This cannot be a proper use of mediation.

It is also reasonably clear that if the local authorities can have a concrete influence on the way in which the mediation works, the scheme will evolve as a support service to the official system, and not as an alternative to it. If a true alternative scheme is attempted, then attention should be paid to the ways in which the scheme gets its cases – directly from the public, or as referrals from the authorities, or both. The administration and control of the mediation service will have an effect on the way in which the emphasis of the scheme will develop. Funding arrangements will similarly affect its direction. If the major source of funds is the state or local administration, it is clear that they will attempt to retain the final say in the way in which such money is spent, and that will also dictate how the mediation scheme functions.

It has to be noted that the trained community mediators, even when they are dealing with criminal matters referred to them by the authorities, are still at their best when they deal with the human matters between the participants in mediation. An undue emphasis on legalistic and quasi-legalistic matters, such as are involved in fixing compensation, concentrates on the guilt of the offender (and thus does not differ all that much from the official system's way of handling the cases), and places responsibilities on the shoulders of the mediators which – taking into account the demands of equality before the law and the legal protection of the offenders – might be better handled by the due process model.

From the experience gained from the experiment in Finland, the following decisions need to be made in considering setting up a mediation scheme.

1   Is the scheme attempting to be a true alternative to the official system, or to support the official system?
2   What kinds of cases will the scheme handle, e.g. will the scheme handle *only* non-criminal conflicts or *only* crimes, and if so what categories, or both?
3   Will cases be accepted only when they come directly from the public, or will officially referred cases also be handled?
4   What kinds of issues can be handled by mediation, and should mediators for example handle questions of compensation (what kinds of compensation)?
5   Who is responsible for the mediation and who can influence its principles and day-to-day working procedures?
6   Above all, there should be clear agreement among those who are responsible for setting up a mediation scheme about its objectives. Should mediation concentrate on interpersonal relationships (whether or not the dispute has led to a crime), or should it help the official justice system to function more efficiently (for example by diverting cases out of the system or by fixing the compensation before the case comes to court)? These two main directions cannot be married in a satisfactory way.

All in all, the qualitative analysis of the experiences of the Finnish scheme seems to point towards the importance of interpersonal matters. The most interesting results of successful mediations were obtained in the first year of the experiment, when it still attempted to keep to the original aims. The enthusiasm with which the young offenders related their experiences when they had had to compensate the victims with their own work was remarkable. It is of course more demanding to search for imaginative solutions to conflicts, but if mediation is to provide anything new into the way in which conflicts and crimes are being handled, spending the effort needed to develop it further seems to be well worth it. An overemphasis on monetary ways of resolving conflicts will only add to the inequality of offenders before the law; those who are able to compensate with money have a clear advantage over those who cannot.

Notes

1   In Finland crimes are divided into two categories, those where the victim can stop prosecution at any stage of the process, and those where the victim cannot do so whether he or she desires it or not. With the first category of crimes, which includes for example the common assault and family violence (and even rape), the effect of a successful mediation is clear. The matter does not proceed in the official system, even when the case was referred to mediation by the authorities. With the second group of offences – when they are referred to mediation by authorities – the situation is more complex. The police have some limited powers *not* to refer a successfully mediated case to the prosecutor, but they seldom exercise this right. The prosecutor, likewise, has a power not to prosecute in some very minor offences committed by people under 18, and occasionally the prosecutor has exercised this right. At court the judge has a similar power of not convicting even where the case is found to be proved; he or she could use this power after a successful mediation, but in practice seldom does so. The court in the experimental area has indicated by its actions that it prefers to reduce the intended sentence rather than resorting to an outright dismissal of the case. This creates much confusion in the minds of the offenders, for whom it is of little consequence if the fine is reduced from 2,000 marks to 1,500 marks, or a term of conditional imprisonment is reduced from six months to three months.

2   Of those interviewed at least 80–90 per cent have retained a positive attitude towards mediation, whether or not the agreement was kept. The Finnish word for 'mediation', when translated into English, is associated with 'making peace', and hence is a very positive word. That could also affect the way in which people's perception is directed, as it predisposes people to have a positive attitude.

3   In Finland issues of law and order do not have a high political profile, and seldom assume any importance in elections. Criminal policy and criminal law drafting is done mainly in the law-drafting section of the Ministry of Justice, with little outside influence.

References

Christie, Nils (1977) 'Conflicts as property', *British Journal of Criminology*, 17 (1): 1–15.

Christie, Nils (1981) *Limits to Pain*. Oslo: Universitetsforlaget. Also Oxford: Martin Robertson, 1982.

Grönfors, Martti (1977) *Blood Feuding among Finnish Gypsies*, University of Helsinki Department of Sociology Research Report 213. Helsinki: University of Helsinki.

Grönfors, Martti (1979) *Ethnic Minorities and Deviance: The Relationship between*

Finnish Gypsies and the Police, University of Helsinki Sociology of Law Series 1. Helsinki: University of Helsinki.

Grönfors, Martti (1986) 'Social control and law in the Finnish gypsy community: blood feuding as a system of justice', *Journal of Legal Pluralism*, 24: 101–25.

Hulsman, L.H.C. (1979) 'An abolitionist perspective on criminal justice systems and a scheme to organise approaches to "problematic situations"'. Paper presented at the international colloquium organized for the fifteenth anniversary of the École de Criminologie, Louvan-la-Neuve, 22–6 May 1979.

Stangeland, Per (1985) 'Informal modes of conflict resolution: the Norwegian experience', unpublished research paper.

11

Law and Practice of Victim/Offender Agreements

Frieder Dünkel and Dieter Rössner

The concept of reparation and conflict-resolving victim/offender mediation has made significant advances over the past few years, encouraged by a generally more focused recognition, especially in West Germany, of victims' needs, of their unsatisfactory position within the criminal justice system, and of the practical possibilities of victim/offender mediation.[1] This chapter will look at the scope for victim/offender mediation under existing criminal law, opportunities within justice-based social services, and, in the final section, examples of active projects, in the Federal Republic of Germany, Austria, and Switzerland.

Several schools of thought in criminal policy support the idea of victim/offender mediation. At the top end of the scale are those subscribing to the abolitionist ideas of Nils Christie and other advocates of the suppression of existing criminal law in favour of a civil law approach to resolving conflicts ('return of conflicts appropriated by the state'). These ideas have found support, particularly in West Germany and Austria.[2]

The overwhelming majority, however, sees victim/offender mediation as remaining within the system, in the form of a more 'victim-oriented criminal justice system' (Rössner and Wulf, 1984). Besides improving the legal status of the victim during legal proceedings,[3] the main concern here is to modify the punitive response in favour of conflict-resolving and peace-restoring ones, and in certain circumstances to do away with it altogether in cases of minor and moderate gravity. The ground for this approach is prepared mainly in the West German law of criminal procedure, in the shape of extensive restrictions on the principle of mandatory prosecution (see below).

The diversion movement has been expanding since the late seventies.[4] From the beginning it was characterized by projects based on community service (which can be seen as symbolic reparation towards society), as a substantial element of reform within the existing framework of juvenile criminal law (Pfeiffer,

1983: 117 ff.). Central to this approach was the replacement of custodial sanctions such as youth custody (six months to five years in general) or detention (placement in custody at weekends or for up to four weeks) by more rehabilitative alternatives.[5] It was therefore logical for the diversion movement to adopt, in the early 1980s, the idea of reparation and face-to-face victim/offender mediation.[6] There is also increasing interest among justice-based social workers (in probation, prison welfare, etc.) who see victim/offender mediation as being, additionally, an important element in the rehabilitation of offenders (see the overview by Dünkel, 1986b: 141 ff.).

In this context, efforts are being made to steer criminal law in the direction of reconciliatory conflict resolution, while the basic rule of section 46 of the West German Penal Code, on the purposes of punishment, is to be extended to include this dimension (Rössner and Wulf, 1984: 124). The existing law (section 46(2) of the West German Penal Code) already stresses that when sentencing, the efforts of the offender to make good the damage and 'to reach an agreement with the injured party'[7] are expressly relevant in selecting the type and amount of the sanctions imposed. Thus the principles of reparation and victim/offender mediation are already inherent in current criminal law, especially in West Germany. Ways of increasing the relatively limited initiatives (see below) are under discussion. This involves a theory of criminal law based on restoring peace instead of encouraging the retributive tendency, and on promoting the assumption of accountability through constructive negotiation over the conflict rather than treating the offender as pathological (Kuhn and Rössner, 1987). The emphasis which victim/offender mediation projects place on the interests of the victim in no way contradicts efforts at rehabilitating the offender. The agreement of both parties is essential for the success of such endeavours; this ensures that the desired direct conflict resolution, and in some cases a personal meeting between offender and victim, does not become unduly stressful for those concerned. Procedural safeguards for victim and offender must also be observed.

Possibilities for victim/offender mediation under criminal law, and its practical application

Pre-trial mediation
Findings on reporting of offences by victims (see the overview by Kaiser, 1985a: 109 ff.; 1985b: 27 ff.; Sessar, 1986: 383 ff.) show that out-of-court conflict resolution takes place more often than not,[8] even in incidents which could be regarded as criminal, particularly with offences involving little damage (Sessar, 1983: 157; Pilgram

and Steinert, 1986: 205 ff.).[9] Although, even when the offender is known, this seldom results in a completely satisfactory settlement, victims mostly still consider the state reaction, prosecution, to be either unpromising or contrary to their own interests.

Although the police in continental Europe have no discretion as regards criminal prosecution, research shows, especially in West Germany, that *de facto* discretionary selection is exercised: crimes reported are not always proceeded with, especially with offences, such as assault, by people known or related to each other (Kürzinger, 1978: 206, 217), and when the state 'redefines' the dispute as 'private'.

The state prosecution service therefore becomes particularly significant for the analysis of the legal criteria for pre-court victim/ offender mediation. First the distinction must be made between rules of criminal procedure based on the principle of mandatory prosecution, and those where the prosecution can be stopped at the discretion of the state prosecution service (the principle of discretionary prosecution).

In West Germany, the principle of mandatory prosecution applies (section 152(2) of the Code of Criminal Procedure), but the law provides extensive exceptions, allowing the exercise of discretion. Thus the state prosecution service can discontinue the prosecution in any case of a property offence involving minor damage, and it can do so subject to the court's agreement in other cases involving a small degree of offender culpability (section 153(1), Code of Criminal Procedure). Discontinuing the prosecution in this way is considered particularly if the offender has made good the damage.

Austrian criminal law goes much further. Section 167 provides that 'active repentance' is a separate ground for not imposing a penalty if the offender has made good the damage before the law enforcement agencies become aware of the incident, or has made a binding undertaking to do so (Driendl, 1981: 403 ff.). The difference from West Germany is that when the damage is voluntarily made good, the liability to punishment must be dropped. When civil liability has been made good the victim has no further entitlement to compensation, and society no longer requires a punishment since the offender has returned to legality (Driendl, 1981: 404). The Austrian provision, however, often seems to be circumvented since the law enforcement authorities are informed immediately, so that the offender has no opportunity for active repentance (see Driendl, 1981: 411, with further references on practical problems). Since the state prosecution service is subject to a strict principle of mandatory prosecution (section 34, Austrian Code of Criminal Procedure), this prevents victim/offender mediation projects such as those in West

Germany at the prosecutor's level. The judge alone can discontinue the case on grounds of minor culpability or minor consequences of the offence (section 42, Austrian Code of Criminal Procedure).[10]

In Switzerland a reform proposal by Schultz (1985: 186 ff.) would go further: where there had been a 'special effort at financial restitution', prosecution or punishment would no longer be required.

At the prosecution level in West Germany, however, section 153a of the Code of Criminal Procedure, introduced in 1975, is particularly important for pre-court victim/offender mediation. This allows the prosecution, with the agreement of the court, to refrain from proceeding with formal charges in cases of low culpability, and at the same time to require the accused:

1 to make a specific contribution to make amends for the damage caused by the offence;
2 to pay a sum of money to a voluntary organization or the State;
3 to perform other service for the community; or
4 to pay a specified amount of maintenance
if thereby the public interest in criminal prosecution would be removed.
(section 153a(1), West German Code of Criminal Procedure)

Although restitution is listed first, in practice it has been of small significance, and has even declined since 1977. In 1983, 98 per cent of the requirements involved financial payments, only 0.5 per cent restitution, and 1.1 per cent community service (Riess, 1985: 213).

The situation in Switzerland is somewhat complicated, as each of the 25 cantons has its own law of criminal procedure. It may be summarized by saying that in most of the cantons the strict principle of mandatory prosecution applies, while in the French-speaking cantons influenced by French law the discretionary principle is in force. Individual cantons, however, provide for exceptions to the mandatory principle in relation to particular offences or offenders (as with the low culpability or immediate restitution in the West German code) (Driendl and Marty, 1979: 391 ff.).

In all three countries there is an important limitation of the requirement to prosecute in what are known as private prosecution offences. In West Germany a state prosecution of offences such as trespass, slander, bodily injury, property damage, and others (section 374, West German Code of Criminal Procedure) is only permissible if this is in the public interest (section 376); otherwise injured parties must bring their own proceedings. They can do so only after an attempt at reconciliation has been made without success (section 380). For this purpose a reconciliation procedure is available in some Federal *Länder* such as Hesse and North-Rhine Westphalia, using special voluntary conciliators known as *Schieds-*

männer (who are also available for civil dispute resolution, although this service is little used). These conciliators achieve an acceptable resolution of the conflict in about half the cases.[11]

Similar provisions exist in some Swiss cantons (Driendl and Marty, 1979: 393, with further references). In Austria the range of private prosecution offences (in which the state prosecution cannot act) is essentially limited to cases involving slander (for details see Kodek and Germ, 1984: 23 f.). Threats, trespass, and minor property offences, however, can only be prosecuted on the application of the injured party.[12] In certain cases an attempt at an out-of-court settlement is required, but only in the private prosecution offences first mentioned above.[13]

These regulations all apply to adult accused aged at least 18. There are, however, special procedures giving wider opportunities for victim/offender mediation for 14–17-year-olds in Austria and West Germany, and for 15–17-year-olds in Switzerland. In West Germany the corresponding provisions of the Juvenile Court Law also apply for 18–20-year-olds in so far as their maturity is considered comparable to that of a juvenile (section 109(2) taken with section 105).[14]

Under section 45(2) of the same law the prosecutor can discontinue the proceedings without the consent of the judge, if a rehabilitative measure has already been ordered which renders a punishment by the judge unnecessary. Such measures could include, especially, efforts on the part of the juvenile offender to make good the damage. Community service, and possibly even direct service to the victim, come under this category.[15] In the Brunswick pilot project, for example, juvenile offenders with no money are required to undertake work of benefit to the community, which is paid for by money from a victim fund, financed by administrative fines. Compensation for the victim is drawn from the wages paid, from this fund, for the work performed (details in Staeter, 1984, and below). The juvenile prosecutor can also propose to the juvenile court that juveniles who admit guilt can be ordered to work, take a course of driving instruction, or be given a warning. If the juvenile fulfils these conditions, the proceedings must be dropped (section 45(1), West German Juvenile Court Law). When the charge has been laid in the juvenile court the judge can still discontinue the proceedings under section 45 (cf. section 47). Wide-ranging possibilities of diversion are given with this in West Germany, i.e. avoidance of prosecution or sentencing of young offenders; these expressly include possibilities of making good damage caused, or victim/offender mediation. In 1985, proceedings against juveniles or young adults were discontinued under sections

45 and 47 of the Juvenile Court Law in 48 per cent of cases, although only rarely in conjunction with a restitution requirement (see below).

Similarly, the Austrian state prosecution service can, under section 12 of the Austrian Juvenile Court Law, depart from the strict principle of mandatory prosecution applicable to adults, and discontinue the proceedings in juvenile cases when offences or expected sanctions are minor (Schroll et al., 1986: 98 ff.). The conflict resolution projects mentioned below make use of this provision.

In Switzerland – also subject to variations between cantons – wider provisions are also made for juvenile prosecutors and comparable agencies to discontinue proceedings for educative reasons against juvenile defendants who admit their guilt (for example section 384 of the Code of Criminal Procedure of Zürich canton; Heine and Locher, 1985: 205). In minor cases in summary proceedings, juvenile prosecutors normally have the power to impose non-institutional rehabilitative measures (Heine and Locher, 1985: 32 ff.). These can consist of a simple reprimand or caution, but can also expressly include restitution of damage and a requirement to apologize.

Victim/offender mediation and restitution of damage – apart from the pilot projects described below – have until now generally played a subordinate role in the three countries. A representative survey showed that 58 per cent of the 'requirements' imposed under section 45 of the West German Juvenile Court Law involved financial reparation, 29 per cent community service, and 9 per cent taking a driving course (Heinz, 1986: 557; Rössner, 1984: 337). Directives to make good the damage are seldom used, although 'special rehabilitative value' is attributed to them in the guidelines issued to courts.[16]

Mediation within criminal procedure

As already stated, efforts by the offender to make good the damage are very significant in sentencing (section 46, West German Penal Code). In Switzerland the judge can reduce the sentence if 'the defendant shows sincere and active repentance, namely, has restored the damage as far as can reasonably be expected of him' (article 64, Swiss Penal Code). In Austria, a sincere attempt to restore the damage constitutes a special reason to reduce the sentence (section 34(15), Austrian Penal Code).

Restitution as a sole sanction (as in the English compensation order since 1982) does not exist within the adult criminal law as such in any of the three countries. It is, however, provided as a requirement or educative directive combined with a suspended sentence with probation. In West Germany, custodial sentences of up to one year (in special cases two years) can be suspended with probation, with the imposition of either restitution of damage, payment to a voluntary organization, or community service (section 56 with 56b, West German Penal Code). In contrast to sanctions affecting the conduct of the offender (section 56c), these requirements are intended to have a more restorative function.[17] In Switzerland, custodial sentences of up to 18 months can be suspended if the offender restores the damage as far as can be expected (article 41, Swiss Penal Code). Restitution can also be ordered as an 'educative directive', combined with a suspended sentence. Similarly, under Austrian criminal law, suspended custodial sentences of up to one year (or two years in special cases) can be combined with educative directives for the offender to make good the damage as far as he or she can (sections 43, 51(2), Austrian Penal Code).

Comparable provisions relating to suspended sentences with probation are made in all three countries with regard to juvenile offenders (section 21, 23, West German Juvenile Court Law; section 11, Austrian Juvenile Court Law taken with section 43, Austrian Penal Code; article 96, Swiss Penal Code). In addition, each country has forms of a genuine conditional sentence comparable to the English probation (section 27, West German Juvenile Court Law; section 13, Austrian Juvenile Court Law; article 97, Swiss Penal Code). In West Germany it is mandatory (section 24, Juvenile Court Law), and in Austria and Switzerland it is usual, for juvenile offenders to be placed on probation (section 17, Austrian Juvenile Courts Law; article 96, Swiss Penal Code). This provides a setting in which the juvenile offender's efforts to make good the damage, do community service work, etc., can be supported effectively.

West German criminal law includes a unique provision with regard to victim/offender mediation, in that the injunction to make good the damage, or to apologize personally to the victim (besides payment of financial reparation to a voluntary organization) can be used as a sanction in its own right (section 15, West German Juvenile Court Law). Such requirements should be preferred to more repressive sanctions such as juvenile detention or youth custody. But these requirements to make good or apologize have as yet hardly been used.

In 1985 only 1.5 per cent of sanctions imposed on juveniles and young adults under juvenile criminal law included a requirement for reparation (1.4 per cent) or apology (0.1 per cent).[18] Despite repeated criticism (e.g. Rössner, 1984: 377 f.; Dünkel, 1985a: 88 f.)

these percentages have in recent years gone down (Dünkel, 1985a: 236), although this may be partly because of experiments in reparation at the pre-court stage, after which most cases do not reach a formal adjudication. It must also be remembered that victims have less interest in reparation if the loss is covered by insurance. But further opportunities are still being missed, as is shown by a current West German study: in 97 of a representative sample of 482 juvenile cases (mainly criminal damage and the like) a loss was still outstanding at the time of sentence, but only seven requirements under section 15 of the West German Juvenile Courts Act were imposed (Heinz and Hügel, 1986: 35 ff.).

Material compensation is often stymied by the offender's lack of means. Hence in Austria the possibility of suspending fines – which may be combined with a directive to make reparation – is of special significance (section 43, Austrian Penal Code). There are no similar provisions in West German or Swiss substantive law. In West Germany a fine can only be suspended in exceptional circumstances, usually with first offenders (section 59, West German Penal Code); in 1985 this was done in only 0.02 per cent of sentences under adult criminal law (whereas the total proportion of fines was 81.3 per cent!).[19] Swiss criminal law, however, allows the judge to make the fine paid by the offender payable to the victim if the latter has fallen into needy circumstances (article 60(2), Swiss Penal Code). In West Germany, the reform passed at the end of 1986, already mentioned, gives the state prosecutor power to authorize easier payments of fines and costs, by postponement or instalments, if otherwise compensation would be 'substantially jeopardized' (section 459a, German Criminal Procedure Code).[20]

For the sake of completeness it may be mentioned that all three countries make legal provision for property confiscated from the offender to be returned to the victim (section 111k, West German Criminal Procedure Code; article 60(1), Swiss Penal Code; section 367, Austrian Criminal Procedure Code).

Rapid and comprehensive arrangements for material reparation can be introduced through special procedures such as the adhesion procedure, as it is called, in which civil claims for restitution are joined to the criminal process (sections 403 ff., West German Code of Criminal Procedure; sections 365 ff., Austrian Code of Criminal Procedure). In Switzerland there are once again different systems in the cantons. Where the criminal procedure is influenced by French law, civil claims on the *action civile* model are more widely available than in the German-speaking cantons.

The German and Austrian situation has in the past been criticized for being in practice a dead letter (e.g. Riess, 1984: 35 ff.). In West

Germany the legislature has now reacted, at the end of 1986, by extending the provisions of criminal law in relation to civil law claims.[21] The judges' reluctance in the past was mainly due to the often long-winded determination of the extent of the loss. It remains to be seen whether the reform which took effect in April 1987 will lead to more and faster compensation for victims.

Mediation in prison
The legal criteria for custodial sentences for juveniles and adults maintain that the sole aim of imprisonment is the rehabilitation of the prisoner (section 91, West German Juvenile Courts Act; section 2, West German Prisons Act). The basic principles of prison regimes, such as making living conditions as close as possible to those outside or minimizing the damaging effects of imprisonment (section 3(1) and (2), West German Prisons Act) are rightly seen as points of entry for victim/offender mediation (Wulf, 1985: 68). Material restitution of damage is expressly mentioned: prisoners are to be supported when they undertake it by the prison social workers (section 73, West German Prisons Act). One method is the 'Resocialization Fund', which tries in many cases to settle the debts of prisoners before they leave prison (see below). But most such attempts founder on the exceptionally low prisoners' wages in West Germany – averaging only 5 per cent of the average employee's wage (section 43 taken with section 200, West German Prisons Act). A prisoner earns an average of only 100 to 200 DM per month, and on release possesses an average of 590 to 1,250 DM. Average debts, however, are 45,000 DM among adult prisoners and 10,000 DM for juveniles. It is not surprising that debt regulation is introduced or completed in only 10 per cent of cases (Klotz, 1983: 21 ff.). Conditions are more favourable in open prisons, where many prisoners work outside the prison for full pay. But on a given day only 15 to 20 per cent of prisoners are in open prisons (Dünkel and Rosner, 1982: 42 ff.; latest figures in Dünkel, 1987: 30, 46).

In West Germany the attempt to find reconciliation (which may be only symbolic) between victims and offenders, as in the juvenile institution at Hameln (see below) is otherwise mainly found in social therapy institutions. At present there are 11 institutions or units, mostly small, with a total of about 700 places (about 2 per cent of custodial capacity in West Germany, Kaiser et al., 1982; Egg, 1983). The aim in social therapy is to work through the guilt using social/practical training and individual or group therapy, which can, at least in theory, include face-to-face discussion with the victim.[22]

Only a few basic principles apply to prisons throughout Switzerland (article 36 ff., Swiss Penal Code); otherwise the laws and regulations of the cantons apply. The educative function of imprisonment is especially stressed (article 37). In Austria, which has had a separate prison law since 1970, the primacy of the rehabilitative goal is also largely unquestioned (Kaiser, 1984: 33; on Switzerland, see 41 ff.). Prison pay in Austria and Switzerland seems just as unrealistic in relation to reparation as in West Germany (Kaiser, 1984: 38). But in the Swiss institution at Saxerriet and in the canton of Zürich social service department there is an interesting scheme for debt regulation at the earliest possible moment; at Saxerriet a personal meeting and reconciliation between victim and offender is also possible (see below).

Finally, there is a place for victim/offender agreement in the context of parole. The prisoner's conduct in prison is an express criterion, in West Germany, for suspension of the last third of the sentence (or the last half for first-time prisoners with sentences up to two years or under other special circumstances (section 57, West German Penal Code)). For juveniles sentenced to more than a year, release after only one-third is possible (section 88, Juvenile Court Law). These decisions are made by the court, but the views of the institutions are given considerable significance (Dünkel and Ganz, 1985, with further references). Parole can be granted in Austria after two-thirds with a favourable prognosis, and after one-half with special indications of future good behaviour (section 46, Austrian Penal Code). Unlike West Germany, Austria allows general deterrent considerations in the court's parole decision. In both Austria and West Germany early release can be combined with directives such as restitution, which is mentioned expressly in article 38 of the Swiss Penal Code. Switzerland allows release after two-thirds, but the decision rests with the prison authorities.

Thus there are clearly legal opportunities for victim/offender agreements in the prison context. Recently there have been efforts in West Germany to strengthen this concept substantially by new provisions in the West German Prisons Act. Section 3, for example, makes the prison regime more specific by requiring the management to work towards 'a greater depth of insight on the part of the prisoner into the act and its consequences, especially for the victim, by suitable measures for conciliation'.[23]

Opportunities for the social workers in the justice system

It is clear from the pilot projects (described below) that victim/ offender mediation and reparation can as a rule only be effectively organized with the involvement of the social workers in the criminal

162 162   Frieder Dünkel and Dieter Rössner

justice system. This applies also to community service, which has been successfully extended in West Germany in recent years.[24] Many new studies and publications indicate that social workers are changing their orientation in the direction of conflict resolution (e.g. Janssen and Kerner, 1985; Müller and Otto, 1986; Wulf, 1986). A survey of probation officers in West Germany showed, for example, that material reparation in the context of debt regulation programmes is a task traditionally accepted by probation officers (Rössner and Wulf, 1984: 96). The probation officers, however, were mostly concerned only with the material problem of clearing the debt, rather than with resolving the conflict with the victim. The average probationer in Baden-Württemberg, for example, was in 1982 liable for over 7,000 DM, but although about half of probation cases have an individual victim, there are often difficulties in motivating offenders towards having personal contact with the victim as well; they seem to feel that they have paid for the offence enough already.

Resistance to more frequent use of victim/offender mediation in prison sometimes arises from the social workers' traditional understanding of their role as having an obligation to the offender unilaterally. The victim's perspective has also long been obscured by the close statutory links of the court assistance service to the prosecutor, and of the probation service to the court. Probation officers also have a role conflict (see Spiess and Johnson, 1980) between the probationer's interest in rehabilitation, and control as the long arm of the court (laid down for example in section 56d, West German Penal Code); involvement of the victim resolves this only to a limited extent. Thus although in surveys probation officers express their unambiguous commitment to the rehabilitative goal, rather than to deterrent or retributive aims of punishment (Kerner et al., 1984: 57 ff.), this means in practice that for example when a probationer re-offends, informal conflict resolution, which would undoubtedly be in the interest of the probationer (because of the threatened alternative of recall to court), cannot be reconciled with the duty to report to the court. Contrary to theoretical assumptions derived from the labelling approach, studies of German probation have shown that probation officers are more inclined to de-dramatize the offences of their probationers, and this can often involve direct reparation (Bieker, 1980; 1982).

Debt regulation programmes are, as mentioned, an integral part of court-based social work, especially for probationers and parolees, often with the help of 'resocialization funds'. These are central foundations, mostly covering a *Land* (Baden-Württemberg, Berlin, Hesse, or Lower Saxony), but sometimes based on a regional probation association or voluntary open-door centre for offenders (*Anlaufstelle*) (e.g. Best, 1982: 221 ff.; Rössner and Wulf, 1984: 29 f.). The basic idea is to contact all the various creditors and reach a complete settlement of all the debts; the creditors are asked to remit a proportion of their financial claims, so that the offender owes only to the fund. The debt regulation schemes have worked very successfully in the last few years and make possible an appropriate settlement between victim and offender. These schemes, however, are in practice limited to offenders with a reasonably good prognosis. From the victims' point of view it could be problematic that they are asked to forgo on average more than 70 per cent of their claims; but since most large creditors are banks, insurance companies and other organizations with large resources, this seems generally acceptable. Clearly a material victim/offender agreement must always take account of the limits of the offender's ability to pay. As with offences having no known or convicted offender, the question is therefore raised of improving the help to individual victims, especially of violence, through state compensation programmes.[25]

Justice-based social services in West Germany are, for historical reasons, organized differently from those in Britain (see overview in Dünkel 1984; 1986b). The social workers of the court assistance service work in the context of the preliminary hearing and in the enforcement of certain sanctions (sections 160(3), 453d, West German Code of Criminal Procedure); they are separate from the probation officers and prison social workers. In Austria and Switzerland too, the tasks and organizational structure of justice-based social work are separate, corresponding to the stages of the criminal process (Dünkel, 1986b: 132 f., with further references). But very recently, the introduction of the concept of victim/offender mediation (and community service) has increasingly brought their field of work closer (Dünkel, 1986b: 141 ff.). Together with this there are models for continuous care for offenders, beginning in pre-trial custody and the preliminary hearing generally, and continuing where necessary through imprisonment to parole and after-care. The example of the Zürich social service and the New Start association in Basle show that at least the material reparation (debt regulation) can be better integrated in this framework (Dünkel, 1986b: 135 ff.). But so far there are only proposals, on the lines of the Dutch early rehabilitation scheme (Tigges and Nuijten-Edelbroek, 1983) to cultivate the idea of victim/offender mediation in the context of avoiding or reducing pre-trial custody.[26]

Overall there is an increasing tendency in justice-based social work, especially the probation and court assistance services, to

164   *Frieder Dünkel and Dieter Rössner*

incorporate reparation and in suitable cases personal conflict resolution between victims and offenders, in the interests of the offender's rehabilitation. There is however a gap, as far as West Germany is concerned, in that there are only a few victim aid centres which would assist collaboration, for example in contacting victims.[27]

Victim/offender mediation projects

It was only in the 1980s that the *Länder* considered here not only began to think about victim/offender mediation as a social control sanction, but also tried to introduce it in the practice of criminal justice. In view of the especially marked state monopoly of power in German criminal law, practical implementation meets many more difficulties here than in the more pragmatic Anglo-American system. Consequently the conceptual considerations of social control through criminal law are of great importance in all practical projects.

Against this background, the projects have developed first in the context of the juvenile system, which lends itself more to innovation,[28] and has traditionally played the pioneering role in criminal policy in West Germany. This is reflected in the following accounts.

Police scheme in Schleswig-Holstein
An official model of victim/offender mediation in the juvenile justice system has been set up in the *Land* Schleswig-Holstein. A decree of the Ministry of Home Affairs in 1984 provides that the police officer in the case can recommend or conduct restitution of damage, an apology, or a similar measure to restore the peace between victim and offender. This creates the preconditions for the public prosecutor to discontinue proceedings immediately. The use of victim/offender mediation early in the procedure and the strategy of diversion are commendable, but the scheme is open to criticism for the fact that it applies only to petty offences by juvenile first offenders who admit guilt and show insight (Kube, 1986: 124).

The Brunswick Scheme
The project in Brunswick, an initiative of the state juvenile court assistance service, is a diversion project, aiming to avoid a criminal sentence by a previous agreement between victim and offender (Hilse and Schalk, 1983). The scheme is linked to the justice process, using the prosecutor's ability to discontinue proceedings (see above; also Staeter, 1984: 498 ff.).

The procedure is as follows: in the normal pre-trial report for the juvenile court, the social worker also considers the reparation of symbolic and material harm and the settlement of any conflict observed between victim and offender. In suitable cases, there is direct discussion between victim and offender. This is at the centre of the reconciliation attempt, and concerns both the personal effect on the victim and the offender's coming to terms with the victim's suffering. In this respect the juvenile court assistance service sees itself as a conflict resolution service. Important aims of the project include diversion, relieving pressure on courts, taking account of the victim's perspective, and the removal of prejudices against juvenile delinquents (Hilse and Schalk, 1983; Schultze, 1984; Staeter, 1984). There is a possibility for young people with no money to make amends to the victim through community service. The project's problem lies in its close association with the justice system.

The 'Scales' in Cologne
The project *Die Waage*, started in 1986, is run by an association independent of the justice system, and employs a psychologist and two social workers. The aim is conflict resolution between victims and offenders, which should normally make punitive reactions unnecessary. The conflict resolution is centred on joint discussion, after separate contacts with victim and offender, leading to a reparation agreement (Herz et al., 1986).

The 'Handshake' project in Reutlingen
The *Handschlag* project is also run by an independent agency. The aim is the avoidance of unnecessary criminalization by resolving social conflicts of juveniles and young adults. The project accepts offences in which there is a personal or at least clearly identifiable victim and the offender admits his or her action. Petty offences are excluded. After separate contacts with offender and victim the characteristic mediation between the offender and the injured party takes place, in which the different perspectives of victim and offender are expressed and, in successful cases, reparation is negotiated. The performance of agreements is supervised by the project and finally a report to the public prosecutor prepared.

A first interim evaluation of 73 cases (Kuhn and Rössner, 1987) showed that in 70 per cent of cases referred to the project a victim/ offender mediation could be carried out which led to discontinuance of prosecution. The conflict resolution involved a wide spectrum of offences from theft through bodily harm to robbery and sexual assault. Contrary to expectations, both offenders and victims showed a surprisingly high willingness to make an agreement. Only twice was a victim not willing to take part in mediation. Throughout, the victims indicated that in reporting the offence they were not concerned with penal sanctioning of the offender, but with restitution of the harm. The injured parties therefore consistently welcomed the project's work. The restitution concentrated on five forms: joint discussion ending with an apology; work for the injured party; work whose financial proceeds benefit the victim; joint actions by the victims and the offenders; and presents as symbolic gestures of reconciliation. This area offers a challenge to the creativity of the social workers.

The STOP Programme of INTEG in Mönchengladbach

The diversionary model of INTEG – another independent agency – is well known in West Germany and particularly controversial, because it concentrates exclusively on one category which is in the middle of the cross-fire of diversion policy versus possible widening of social control: young first-time shoplifters who admit guilt. They receive a home visit from a project worker, to encourage the family's involvement. The actual reparation aspect with the 'victim', which is normally here an impersonal large store, takes the form of a visit by the offender to the injured party, represented by a senior executive of the store, for a discussion of the consequences of shoplifting (Kirchhoff, 1983). Despite the misgivings, the project claims legitimation from the fact that in Mönchengladbach shoplifting by first offenders formerly always led to prosecution, but this now happens only in every tenth case (Kirchhoff, 1985).

The Tübingen adult court assistance project

A first attempt to implement conflict resolution in adult criminal law is being undertaken by the court assistance service in Tübingen. The court assistant, in the course of normal work, talks with the offender and the victim, individually or more often in joint discussion; he or she tries to discover the conditions for reparation and if possible to arrange it. That meets the criteria for discontinuing prosecution under section 153a of the West German Code of Criminal Procedure. The first 50 cases show a similar picture to that in the Handshake project above, so there is no reason not to pursue similar efforts under adult criminal law.

In serious crimes of violence, especially rape, which are hardly suitable for direct victim/offender contact, the victim's perspective is brought into the trial through a victim report by the court assistance service. If the victim so wishes, he or she finds in the court assistant a trustworthy listener for all the anxieties and uncertainties in relation to the trial, and help in resolving personal difficulties. For the prosecutor and the court the report serves as the basis for a fair trial from the point of view of the victim/witness too. It can also form the starting-point for discussion with the offender of the pain experienced by the victim, in the interests of rehabilitation (Hering and Rössner, 1984: 23i ff.).

Victim-related therapy for sexual offenders in Hameln prison

The prison psychologists in Hameln prison have initiated a 'sexual role seminar', carried out largely with voluntary female non-professional therapists. The aim is 'to lead young rapists to sexuality experienced as a partnership, in which the female partner does not have to fulfil the function of an object'. The course consists of a therapy programme with more than 20 individual themes, aiming particularly at respect for female sexual self-determination. A major aspect is confronting the offender, by means of tapes or of the lay helpers, most of whom come from the women's movement; in exceptional cases the offender can meet his own victim. In this way the rapist is intended to experience the effect of his action on the total life of the victim, and to develop inhibitions against repetition. In the observation period of three and a half years so far there has been no recidivism among participants in the programme (Gers et al., 1986; Tügel and Heilemann, 1987).

The conflict resolution project of the Austrian Association for Probation and Social Work

The project for conflict resolution in juvenile justice has operated since 1985 in the cities of Vienna, Linz, and Salzburg. It has especial significance for criminal policy, because it is supported by the government as a pilot project in the light of the reform of the Juvenile Court Act currently being discussed in Austria.[29] In its name – conflict resolution instead of victim/offender mediation – and in its content, the project has emancipated itself more than any other from the criminal law with its dogma of retribution and denunciation of guilt. Foremost in its approach is the conflict which has come to light in the criminal offence and the context of the actions concerned – rather than the offender as an individual. In addition, the autonomy of the social worker in relation to the court in the actual conflict regulation phase is stressed; conflict resolution is even seen as a concept by which conflicts are dealt with beyond considerations of guilt and punishment (Pelikan, 1986).

Justice and educative social work cooperate on remarkably equal terms; this rests on the way in which a conflict resolution affects the legal consequences. The probation officer requires an active contribution of the offender towards reparation, and this can be offset against the harm caused by the offence to a point where prosecution can be discontinued under section 12(1) of the Austrian Juvenile Court Law (see above, and Schroll et al., 1986: 101 ff.). This legal decision, however, remains with the justice system. The probation officer, to whom the prosecutor has entrusted the task of conflict resolution, has to ensure that the juvenile makes up for the harm which his or her act caused to the social environment. Thus the social-educational concept includes three phases: making the juvenile recognize the wrong, accept responsibility, and finally make reparation for it.

Although it has been running only a short time, the project can point to clear achievements. In one year nearly 300 cases were 'conflict regulated'.[30] The success rate in terms of decriminalization through mediation is very high, at over 90 per cent. Also, there was a predominantly positive response from the victims (Schroll et al., 1986: 125).

Debt regulation with social services in Zürich and the Newstart project in Basle
In Switzerland the focus of projects of this kind is on debt regulation between victim and offender. The state social services of Zürich canton maintain their own debt-clearance department with a specialized team of four people, arranging debt regulation mainly through out-of-court negotiation with creditors and an interest-free loan to the offender. The client is expected to tackle his or her debts comprehensively, and to possess a secure income and perseverance (Höhener, 1984: 61 ff.).

Newstart is the initiative of an independent association in Basle, trying to develop alternatives to state help for offenders using voluntary probation officers. The concept is centred on clearing debts with the help of a credit fund. Debt regulation with the help of a project worker is seen as a means of social integration, enabling the offender to start a new phase of his or her life in economically sound circumstances. Both victims and offenders benefit (Hämmerle, 1980).

Mediation in prison: the Saxerriet project in Switzerland
Saxerriet open prison for first-time prisoners (with 100 places) includes in its rehabilitative efforts both debt regulation and contacts with victims with the aim of reconciliation. Social workers find out, in relation to all inmates, whether reparation is worth attempting. The workers caring for victims initiate contacts between victim and offender, carefully and with empathy. Here too the

victims are, more often than expected, ready to take a reconciling attitude. At least as important as material reparation is the discussion of the offence by victim and offender. The victim/offender contacts, described as positive from the viewpoint of both parties, appear all the more remarkable since the average prison term is 4.5 years, so these are not petty offenders (Brenzikofer, 1982, 1986; Dünkel, 1985b: 313).

Prospects

The reorientation of the theory of criminal law in the countries we have been considering, and the first practical experiences, raise the question: what are the chances, in criminal policy, of a new constructive criminal law culture, based on working through the offence? The opposite – retribution for the harm done, as the basic model for the criminal justice response – is still a bastion of the traditional understanding of criminal law. Constructively working through the offence at least offers a way out of the present dilemma of criminal policy between retribution and deterrence, between the abandonment of rehabilitative ideals and the extension of retributive sentencing. Formalized work with the feelings and the offence, including the victim/offender relationship, not only promotes peace, but ensures that sentencing avoids both yielding to the primitive initial feelings of retribution, and employing compulsory personality-changing therapeutic measures for minor offences.

These experiences show above all that the often asserted 'need to punish' among the general public exists more in the heads of lawyers than in society. Victims show surprisingly high acceptance and willingness to co-operate in conflict resolution. Desire for punishment among the public has a totally subordinate place, and there is remarkable appreciation of reparation in the context of victim/offender mediation: this is clear from the data of a large-scale study in Hamburg (Sessar, 1986: 387 ff.; Sessar et al., 1986: 91 ff.).

Criminal cases dealt with in a spirit of conflict resolution have a positive outcome for all concerned: the offender has confronted the harm suffered by the injured party, the victim frees himself or herself of anxieties in relation to the offender by meeting him or her as a 'human being'; there is also job satisfaction for the 'conflict workers'.

It is of course not conceivable at present to renounce completely the rigour of criminal law enforcement; the range of behaviour to which criminal law must react is too various, from simple theft through economic and environmental crimes to murder. A large part of everyday crime, from offences against property and money through threats and abusive behaviour to bodily injuries, is, however, basically suitable for processing through dialogue, because here norms can be upheld in a constructive way, without detriment to the general or individual deterrent aims of the criminal law. Constructive processing of offences comes a good step nearer the old ordinance of St Augustine, that the response to wrongdoing should always take account of humanity. The experiences reported here give cause for hope that the new perspectives of handling criminal offences through victim/offender mediation in a spirit of dialogue and dispute settlement, reconciliation and peacemaking, will show the way for the criminal law of the twenty-first century (see Galaway, 1985: 490 f.).

Notes

This chapter was translated by Martin Wright and Sophie Wright.

1 A major contribution has been made by the discussions and resolutions of the 55th German Jurists' Conference 1984 (*Deutscher Juristentag*) (reprinted in *Neue Juristische Wochenschrift*, 37 (1984), 2671–85; see also the comprehensive preparatory review by Riess (1984)). This is the largest and most influential forum for German academic and practising lawyers, which meets annually to discuss fundamental questions of reform, and makes generally substantial proposals for law reform.

2 See e.g. Hanak, 1980, 1982; Feltes, 1985; Pilgram and Steinert, 1986. On the constitutional legal problems of private, autonomous initiatives there have been various references from the other point of view, e.g. Müller-Dietz, 1985: 29; see also the summary and critique by Kaiser, 1987: 1027 ff., 1035 ff. (with further refs).

3 This question has been considered in many West German publications; following the recommendations of the 55th German Jurists' Conference 1984, a first 'Law to improve the position of the injured party in criminal procedure' was passed at the end of 1986, which came into effect in April 1987.

4 On diversion and individual projects in the Federal Republic of Germany see Pfeiffer, 1983, and the overviews of Kury and Lerchenmüller, 1981; Kerner, 1983; Walter and Koop, 1984; Brusten et al., 1985.

5 The widespread criticism concerns the sentencing practice of juvenile justice, always too punitive in its orientation, while the educative concept, which theoretically had priority, was delivered in short measure (Pfeiffer, 1983: 55 ff.).

6 See the pilot projects described below.

7 Later variants concentrating on non-material mediation were not incorporated until the law reform mentioned in note 3.

8 However, offences are often not proceeded with because the offender is unknown and the police are felt to have little chance of success; for this there is in West Germany and Austria – in addition to private property insurance – within narrow limits state compensation for victims of violent crimes; see survey by Dünkel, 1985b.

9 A striking observation of the 'normality' of private conflict regulation in rural Bavaria is contained in Todd, 1978: 86 ff., esp. 101 ff., 107 ff. On the handling of crimes of defamation there, and dispute settlement practices in and out of court, see Steffen, 1986.

10 For a summary of the principle of mandatory prosecution in Austria, and breaches of it in practice, see Driendl, 1979: 252 ff.; on the obligation to prosecute and conditions for halting prosecution, see a recent comparative study by Tak, 1986.

11 See Riess, 1984: 23 f. with further refs.; according to him there are in West Germany at least 25,000 successful conciliation proceedings a year, which exceed the number of private prosecutions in the ratio 5:2.

12 The Austrian law of criminal procedure still differentiates offences which can only be privately prosecuted and those prosecuted by the state, but only on the application of the injured party, which must be made at latest before the main court proceedings begin. Austrian Code of Criminal Procedure, sec. 2(4 and 5).

13 And only in places where a special community conciliation office has been established (Foregger and Serini, 1982: 79 with further refs). In Austria, unlike West Germany, offences involving bodily injury can be prosecuted without an application from the injured person.

14 At present more than 60 per cent of young adults (aged 18 to 21) are sentenced according to juvenile criminal law, with correspondingly less severe punishments; with serious crimes involving violence, as many as 90 per cent (Dünkel, 1985a: 85 f.).

15 Community service has become very significant in West Germany in the context of numerous diversion projects; see references under note 4, and especially Schädler, 1985a: 186 ff.

16 See Guideline no. 1 to sec. 45 taken with Guideline no. 1 to sec. 15 of the German Juvenile Courts Law, reprinted by Eisenberg, 1985: 809, 821.

17 'Requirements (*Auflagen*) are measures similar to punishment, aiming to provide satisfaction for the wrong committed'; see Lackner, 1985: 329 (marginal note 1 to sec. 56b of the West German Penal Code).

18 Calculated from Federal Statistical Office (*Statistisches Bundesamt*), series 10, group 3: *Sentences imposed 1985 (Strafverfolgung 1985)*, Wiesbaden 1986, pp. 98 f.

19 Calculated from Federal Statistical Office, 1986: 72 f.

20 Proposals of the Social Democratic Party went further: they would have given the state prosecutor more discretion to stop a prosecution when restitution had been made, and would have allowed fines to be suspended; but they were not adopted.

21 In particular a criminal court can now (unlike previously) make an immediate decision at the time of sentencing on an (undisputed) part of the claim under property law (sec. 406, Code of Criminal Procedure; for further details see the draft law of the Federal Government with explanatory justification, in *Bundesratsdrucks*, 51/86).

22 Direct contacts between victims and offenders seem however to take place only exceptionally, according to reports of experience so far.

23 As decided by the prisons committee of the *Länder* in a special session on changing the West German Prisons Act in February 1987, with only one contrary vote.

24 See summary by Albrecht and Schädler, 1986, including European comparisons, and note 15 above.

25 On the preconditions for use in practice in West Germany, with European comparisons, see Dünkel, 1985b.

26 In West Germany there are meanwhile several corresponding projects for avoiding pre-trial detention: Dünkel, 1986b: 142 f. with further refs.

27 On the first open-door centre for victims in West Germany, in Hanau, see Schädler, 1985b; the largest organization for assistance to victims, the *Weisser Ring*, is less appropriate for arranging contacts of this kind, because in its practical work it concerns itself only with victims, often in conjunction with demands for harsher punishment of offenders.

28 A helpful contribution for the planned projects was the decision of the 55th German Jurists' Conference in Autumn 1984 to conduct, and support financially, experimental projects to gain experience in the field of victim/offender mediation – mainly with juvenile offenders; see *Neue Juristische Wochenschrift*, 37 (1984), 2682, and note 1 above.

29 See the extremely positive statements of the federal ministries for justice and family, youth and health, in *SUB* (organ of the Austrian Association for Probation and Social Work), 1986, no. 3.

30 See *SUB* (note 29), 3.

References

Albrecht, H.J. and W. Schädler (eds) (1986): *Community Service: A New Option in Punishing Offenders in Europe*. Freiburg.

Best, P. (1982) '"Resozialisierungsfonds" in Niedersachsen: Entschuldungshilfe für Straffällige' ('Resocialization funds' in Lower Saxony: help in debt clearance for offenders), in H.-D. Schwind and G. Steinhilper (eds), *Modelle zur Kriminalitätsvorbeugung und Resozialisierung (Models for crime prevention and rehabilitation)*. Heidelberg. pp. 221–64.

Bieker, R. (1980) 'Bewährungshelfer und Labeling' (Probation officers and labelling), *Bewährungshilfe*, 27: 261–78.

Bieker, R. (1982) 'Uber die Schwierigkeit von Bewährungshelfern, mit Richtern zusammenzuarbeiten: Ergebnisse einer explorativen Studie über Handlungsprobleme von Sozialarbeitern in der Strafjustiz' (On probation officers' difficulty in working with judges: results of an exploratory study of practice problems of social workers in criminal justice), *Neue Praxis*, 12: 372–83.

Brenzikofer, P. (1982) 'Bemühungen um Opfer von Verbrechern in der Schweiz' ('Efforts for victims of crime in Switzerland'), in H.-J. Schneider (ed.), *Das Verbrechensopfer in der Strafrechtspflege (The victim of crime in criminal justice)*. New York. pp. 367–73.

Brenzikofer, P. (1986) 'Offender and victim contacts: an experience in Switzerland', in Permanent European Conference on Probation and Aftercare (ed.), *The Victim, the Offender and the Probation Service*. 's-Hertogenbosch. pp. 47–50.

Brusten, M. et al. (eds) (1985) *Entkriminalisierung (Decriminalization)*. Opladen.

Driendl, J. (1979) 'Landesbericht Österreich' (National report on Austria), in H.-H. Jescheck and R. Leibinger (eds), *Funktion und Tätigkeit der Anklagebehörde im ausländischen Recht (Function and work of the private prosecution authority in foreign law)*. Baden-Baden. pp. 191–327.

Driendl, J. (1981) 'Alternative Kriminalpolitik in Österreich und der Schweiz' (Alternative criminal policy in Austria and Switzerland), in H. Kury and H. Lerchenmüller (eds), *Diversion*. Bochum. vol. 2, pp. 389–513.

Driendl, J. and D.F. Marty (1979) 'Landesbericht Schweiz' (National report on Switzerland), in H.-H. Jescheck and R. Leibinger (eds), *Funktion und Tätigkeit der Anklagebehörde im ausländischen Recht (Function and work of the private prosecution authority in foreign law)*. Baden-Baden. pp. 329–484.

Dünkel, F. (1984) 'Neuere Entwicklungen im Bereich der Bewährungshilfe und -aufsicht im internationalen Vergleich' (Recent developments in probation assistance and supervision: an international comparison), *Bewährungshilfe*, 31: 162–84.

Dünkel, F. (1985a) 'Situation und Reform von Jugendstrafe, Jugendstrafvollzug und anderen freiheitsentziehenden Sanktionen gegenüber jugendlichen Rechts-brechern in der Bundesrepublik Deutschland' (Current position and reform of juvenile sanctions, youth custody and other custodial penalties for juvenile offenders in the Federal Republic of Germany), in F. Dünkel and K. Meyer (eds), *Jugendstrafe und Jugendstrafvollzug: Stationäre Maßnahmen der Jugend-kriminalrechtspflege im internationalen Vergleich* (*Youth sanctions and youth custody: an international comparison of institutional measures in juvenile criminal law*). Freiburg. Vol. I, pp. 45–256

Dünkel, F. (1985b) 'Victim compensation and offender restitution in the Federal Republic of Germany: a Western-European comparative perspective', *Inter-national Journal of Comparative and Applied Criminal Justice*, 9: 29–39.

Dünkel, F. (1986a) 'Reparation and victim-offender conciliation and aspects of the legal position of the victim in criminal procedures in a Western-European perspective', in H.-J. Kerner et al. (eds), *European and North-American Juvenile Justice Systems: Aspects and Tendencies*. Munich. pp. 303–27.

Dünkel, F. (1986b) 'Möglichkeiten der Fortentwicklung der Sozialen Dienste in der Justiz: eine international vergleichende Betrachtung zu Aufgabenstellungen und Organisationsstruktur' (Possibilities for the future development of justice-related social services: an international comparative consideration of tasks and organiza-tional structure), *Bewährungshilfe*, 33: 129–58.

Dünkel, F. (1987) *Die Herausforderung der geburtenschwachen Jahrgänge: Aspekte der Kosten-Nutzen-Analyse in der Kriminalpolitik* (*The challenge of the low-birth-rate years: aspects of cost/benefit analysis in criminal policy*). Freiburg.

Dünkel, F. and G. Ganz (1985) 'Kriterien der richterlichen Entscheidung bei der Strafrestaussetzung nach s. 57 StGB' (Criteria for judicial decisions in suspending the remainder of prison sentences under section 57 of the Penal Code), *Monatsschrift für Kriminologie*, 68: 157–75.

Dünkel, F. and A. Rosner (1982) *Die Entwicklung des Strafvollzugs in der Bundesrepublik Deutschland seit 1970* (*The development of imprisonment in the Federal Republic of Germany since 1970*), 2nd edn. Freiburg.

Egg, R. (1983) 'Social therapy treatment of criminal offenders: a survey of pilot institutions', *International Journal of Comparative and Applied Criminal Justice*, 7: 49–60.

Eisenberg, U. (1985) *Jugendgerichtsgesetz mit Erläuterungen* (*Juvenile courts law, with annotations*), 2nd edn. Munich.

Feltes, T. (1985) 'Konfliktbereinigung zwischen Täter under Opfer: Institutional-isierung oder Privatisierung' (Conflict settlement between offenders and victims: institutionalization or privatization), in H. Janssen and H.-J. Kerner (eds), *Verbrechensopfer, Sozialarbeit und Justiz* (*Victims of crime, social work and justice*). Bonn. pp. 407–36.

Foregger, E. and E. Serini (1982) *Die österreichische Strafprozeßordnung: Kurz-kommentar* (*The Austrian Code of Criminal Procedure: short commentary*), 3rd edn. Vienna.

Galaway, B. (1985) 'Restitutive Justiz' (Restitutive justice), in H. Janssen and H.-J. Kerner, (eds), *Verbrechensopfer, Sozialarbeit und Justiz* (*Victims of crime, social work and justice*). Bonn. pp. 471–94.

Gers, A. et al. (1986) 'Frauen therapieren Vergewaltiger' (Women give therapy to rapists), *Psychologie Heute*, 52–5.

Hämmerle, A. (1980) *'Neustart': Ein Modellversuch der Straffälligenhilfe* (*'New Start': A Demonstration Project for Prisoners' Aftercare*). Aarau.

174   *Frieder Dünkel and Dieter Rössner*

Hanak, G. (1980) 'Die Vermittlung als Alternative zur strafrechtlichen Konfliktregelung' (Mediation as an alternative to resolving conflicts through the criminal
law), *Kriminalsoziologische Bibliographie*, 7(28/29): 5–47.
Hanak, G. (1982) 'Diversion und Konfliktregelung' (Diversion and conflict resolution), *Kriminalsoziologische Bibliographie*, 9(35): 1-39.
Heine, G. and J. Locher (1985) *Jugendstrafrechtspflege in der Schweiz (Juvenile
justice in Switzerland)*. Freiburg.
Heinz, W. (1986) 'Jugendgerichtsbarkeit in der Bundesrepublik Deutschland:
Empirische Bestandsaufnahme der Sanktionspraxis, gegenwärtige legislative
Reformtendenzen und Perspektiven für die innere Reform' (Juvenile justice in
the Federal Republic of Germany: an empirical account of sentencing practice,
current trends in legislative reform and perspectives for internal reform), in H.-J.
Kerner, B. Galaway and H. Janssen (eds), *Jugendgerichtsbarkeit in Europa und
Nordamerika: Aspekte und Tendenzen (Juvenile Justice in Europe and North
America: Aspects and Trends)*. Munich. pp. 527–641.
Heinz, W. and C. Hügel (1986) *Erzieherische Maßnahmen im deutschen Jugendstraf-
recht (Educational measures in German juvenile criminal law)*. Bonn: Federal
Ministry of Justice.
Hering, R.-D. and D. Rössner (1984) 'Die Opferperspektive in der Gerichtshilfe'
(The victim's perspective in probation), *Bewährungshilfe*, 31: 220–39.
Herz, R. et al. (1986) 'Täter-Opfer-Ausgleich' (Victim/offender mediation), *Bewäh-
rungshilfe*, 33: 185–7.
Hilse, J. and K. Schalk (1983) 'Modellprojekt jugendgerichtshilfe Braunschweig'
(Brunswick demonstration project for juvenile court assistance), in H. Kury and
E. Zimmermann (eds), *Das Kriminologische Forschungsinstitut Niedersachsen
(The Lower Saxony Criminological Research Institute)*. Cologne. pp. 44–51.
Höhener, M. (1984) 'Entwicklungen und Perspektiven ambulanter Straffälligenhilfe
in der Schweiz' (Developments and perspectives for non-custodial aid to
offenders in Switzerland), in B. Maelicke et al. (eds), *Ambulante Straffälligen-
hilfe: Internationale Ansätze und Kriminalpolitik (Non-custodial aid to offenders:
international efforts and criminal policy)*. Frankfurt am Main: Institut für
Sozialarbeit und Sozialpädagogik. pp. 49–66.
Janssen, H. and H.-J. Kerner (ed.) (1985) *Verbrechensopfer, Sozialarbeit und Justiz
(Victims of crime, social work and justice)*. Bonn.
Kaiser, G. (1984) *Prison Systems and Correctional Laws: Europe, the United States
and Japan. A Comparative Analysis*. New York.
Kaiser, G. (1985a) *Kriminologie (Criminology)*, 7th edn. Heidelberg.
Kaiser, G. (1985b) 'Die Rolle des Opfers als Initiator der Verbrechenskontrolle'
(The role of the victim as initiator of the control of crime), in H. Janssen and H.-
J. Kerner (eds), *Verbrechensopfer, Sozialarbeit und Justiz (Victims of crime,
social work and justice)*. Bonn. pp. 25–43.
Kaiser, G. (1987), 'Abolitionismus: Alternative zum Strafrecht?' (Abolitionism:
alternative to criminal law?), in W. Küper et al. (eds): *Festschrift für K. Lackner*.
Berlin/New York. pp. 1027–46.
Kaiser, G. et al. (1982) 'Die sozialtherapeutische Anstalt: Das Ende einer Reform?'
(The social-therapeutic institution: the end of a reform?), *Zeitschrift für
Rechtspolitik*, 15: 198–207.
Kerner, H.-J. (ed.) (1983) *Diversion statt Strafe? Probleme und Gefahren einer neuen
Strategie strafrechtlicher Sozialkontrolle (Diversion instead of punishment?
Problems and dangers of a new strategy for social control through criminal law)*.
Heidelberg.

Kerner, H.-J. et al. (1984) *Straf(rest)aussetzung und Bewährungshilfe* (*Suspension of (remainder of) sentence and probation*), Working papers from the Institute of Criminology, 3. Heidelberg.

Kirchhoff, G.F. (1983) 'Diversion im Jugendstrafrecht nach s. 45 JGG: das STOP-Programm der INTEG nach einem Jahr' (Diversion in juvenile criminal law under section 45 of the Juvenile Courts Law: the STOP programme of INTEG after one year), in H.-J. Kerner, H. Kury, and K. Sessar (eds), *Deutsche Forschungen zur Kriminalitätsentstehung und Kriminalitätskontrolle* (*German research on the origins and control of crime*). Cologne. vol. 6/2, pp. 956–85.

Kirchhoff, G.F. (1985) 'Diversion im Jugendstrafrecht: Das STOP-Programm der INTEG nach zwei Jahren' (Diversion in juvenile criminal law: the STOP programme after two years), in H. Kury (ed.), *Kriminologische Forschung in der Diskussion: Berichte, Standpunkte, Analysen* (*Discussions of criminological research: reports, viewpoints, analyses*). Cologne. pp. 341–69.

Klotz, W. (1983) 'Die Situation entlassener Strafgefangener in Baden-Württemberg' (The situation of discharged prisoners in Baden-Württemberg), in *Hilfen zur Reintegration von Strafentlassenen durch Kirchen und Vereine* (*How churches and voluntary organizations can help the re-integration of discharged prisoners*), Protokolldienst 19/83. Evangelische Akademie Bad Boll. pp. 5–31.

Kodek, G. and H. Germ (1984) *Strafprozeßordnung 1975* (*The Code of Criminal Procedure 1975*), 3rd edn. Vienna.

Kube, E. (1986) 'Täter-Opfer-Ausgleich. Wunschtraum oder Wirklichkeit?' (Victim/offender mediation: dream or reality?), *Deutsche Richterzeitung*, 64: 121–6.

Kürzinger, J. (1978) *Private Strafanzeige und polizeiliche Reaktion* (*Private reporting of crime and police reaction*). Berlin.

Kuhn, A. and D. Rössner (1987) 'Konstruktive Tatverarbeitung im Jugendstrafrecht: "Handschlag" statt Urteil' (Constructive response to offences in juvenile criminal law: 'Handshake' instead of sentence), *Zeitschrift für Rechtspolitik*, 20: 267–70.

Kury, H. and H. Lerchenmüller (eds) (1981) *Diversion: Alternativen zu klassischen Sanktionsformen* (*Diversion: alternatives to classical forms of sanction*). Bochum. vols. 1 and 2.

Lackner, K. (1985) *Strafgesetzbuch mit Erläuterungen* (*Penal code with annotations*), 16th edn. Munich.

Müller, S. and H.-U. Otto (1986) *Damit Erziehung nicht zur Strafe wird. Sozialarbeit als Konfliktschlichtung* (*Preventing education from turning into punishment: social work as conflict resolution*). Bielefeld.

Müller-Dietz, H. (1985) 'Aspekte der Täter-Opfer-Beziehung aus strafrechtlicher Sicht' (Aspects of the victim/offender relationship from the standpoint of criminal law), in Evangelische Akademie Bad Boll (ed.), *Täter, Opfer und Gesellschaft* (*Offenders, victims and society*), Protokolldienst 21/85, Bad Boll. pp. 14–36.

Pelikan, C. (1986) 'Konfliktregelung: etwas ganz anderes als Strafe austeilen' (Conflict resolution: something quite different from punishment), *SUB* (organ of the Austrian Association for Probation and Social Work), 3: 28–30.

Pfeiffer, C. (1983) *Kriminalprävention im Jugendgerichtsverfahren: Jugendrichter-liches Handeln vor dem Hintergrund des Brücke-Projekts* (*Crime prevention in juvenile court practice in the light of the 'Bridge' project*). Cologne.

Pilgrim, A. and H. Steinert (1986) 'Plädoyer für bessere Gründe für die Abschaffung der Gefängnisse und für Besseres als die Abschaffung der Gefängnisse' (A plea for better grounds for abolishing prisons and for something better than abolishing prisons), in H. Ortner (ed.), *Freiheit statt Strafe* (*Freedom instead of punishment*), 2nd edn. Tübingen. pp. 196–217, 241–4.

Riess, P. (1984) 'Die Stellung des Verletzten im Strafverfahren: Gutachten C für den 55. Deutschen Juristentag' (The position of the victim in the criminal process: Working paper C for the 55th German Jurists' Conference), in Ständige Deputation des Deutschen Juristentags (Standing Commission of the German Jurists' Conference) (ed.), *Verhandlungen des fünfundfünfzigsten Deutschen Juristentags Hamburg 1984. (Proceedings of the 55th German Jurists' Conference, Hamburg 1984).* Munich. vol. 1, part C.

Riess, P. (1985) 'Zur weiteren Entwicklungen der Einstellungen nach s. 153a StPO' (On the further development of the halting of prosecutions under section 153a of the Code of Criminal Procedure), *Zeitschrift für Rechtspolitik*, 18: 212–16.

Rössner, D. (1984) 'Konfliktregulierung und Opferperspektive in der jugendstraf-rechtlichen Sozialkontrolle' (Conflict regulation and victims' perspectives in social control through the juvenile criminal law), in Deutsche Vereinigung für Jugendgerichtshilfen e.V. (German Association for Juvenile Courts and Court Assistants) (ed.), *Jugendgerichtsverfahren und Kriminalprävention (Juvenile court procedure and crime prevention).* Munich. pp. 375–86.

Rössner, D. and R. Wulf (1984) *Opferbezogene Strafrechtspflege: Leitgedanken und Handlungsvorschläge für Praxis und Gesetzgebung (Victim-related practice in criminal justice: principles and proposals for action in practice and legislation).* Bonn.

Schädler, W. (1985a) 'Der "weisse Fleck" im Sanktionensystem' (The ray of light in criminal sanctions), *Zeitschrift für Rechtspolitik*, 18: 186–92.

Schädler, W. (1985b): 'Die Hanauer Hilfe: Modell einer effektiven Opfer- und Zeugenhilfe?' (The Hanau assistance project: a model for effective help to victims and witnesses?), *Bewährungshilfe*, 32: 73–83.

Schroll, H.V. et al. (1986) 'Das Linzer Konfliktregelungsmodell' (The Linz model for conflict regulation), *Österreichische Richterzeitung*, 64: 98–104, 124–8.

Schultz, H. (1985) 'Bericht und Vorentwurf zur Revision des Allgemeinen Teils des Schweizerischen Strafgesetzbuches' (Report and preliminary draft for a revision of the General Part of the Swiss Penal Code). Unpublished MS, Bern.

Schultze, W. (1984) 'Der Täter-Opfer-Ausgleich im Jugendstrafrecht' (Victim/offender mediation in juvenile criminal law), in Deutsche Vereinigung für Jugendgerichte und Jugendgerichtshilfen e.V. (German Association for Juvenile Courts and Court Assistants) (ed.), *Jugendgerichtsverfahren und Kriminal prävention (Juvenile court procedure and crime prevention).* Munich. pp. 387–94.

Sessar K. (1983) 'Schadenswiedergutmachung in einer künftigen Kriminalpolitik' (Reparation in a future criminal policy), in H.-J. Kerner et al. (eds), *Festschrift für H. Leferenz.* Heidelberg. pp. 145–61.

Sessar, K. (1986) 'Neue Wege der Kriminologie aus dem Strafrecht' (New directions for criminology outside criminal law), in H.-J. Hirsch et al. (eds), *Gedächtnis-schrift (Memorial collection) für H. Kaufmann.* Berlin/New York. pp. 373–91.

Sessar, K. et al. (1986) 'Wiedergutmachung als Konfliktregelungsparadigma?' (Reparation as paradigm for conflict regulation?), *Kriminologisches Journal*, 18: 86–104.

Spiess, G. and E.H. Johnson (1980) 'Role conflict and the role ambiguity in probation: structural sources and consequences in West Germany', *International Journal of Comparative and Applied Criminal Justice*, 4: 179–89.

Staeter, J. (1984) 'Diversion zwischen Theorie und Praxis' (Diversion: the theory and the practice), *Zentralblatt für Jugendrecht*, 71: 498–507.

Steffen, W. (1986) *'Beleidigungen': Konfliktregelung durch Anzeigeerstattung? ('Defamation': conflict regulation by bringing a private prosecution?).* Munich.

Tak, P.J.P. (1986) *The Legal Scope of Non-Prosecution in Europe*. Helsinki: HEUNI (Helsinki Institute for Crime Prevention and Control, affiliated to the United Nations).

Tigges L.C.M. and E.G.M. Nuijten-Edelbroek (1983) 'Resozialisierungsfrühhilfen in den Niederländen: Praxis und Perspektiven' (First aid in rehabilitation in the Netherlands: practice and perspectives), in F. Dünkel and G. Spiess, *Alternativen zur Freiheitsstrafe* (*Alternatives to custodial penalties*). Freiburg. pp. 355–67.

Todd, H.F. (1978) 'Litigious marginals: character and disputing in a Bavarian village', in L. Nader and H. Todd (eds), *The Disputing Process: Law in Ten Societies*. New York. pp. 86–121.

Tügel, H. and M. Heilemann (eds) (1987) *Frauen verändern Vergewaltiger* (*Women alter Rapists*). Frankfurt.

Walter, M. and G. Koop (eds) (1984) *Die Einstellung des Strafverfahrens im Jugendrecht* (*Discontinuing a prosecution in juvenile law*). Vechta.

Wulf, R. (1985) 'Opferbezogene Vollzugsgestaltung: Grundzüge eines Behandlungsansatzes?' (A victim-related prison régime: principles for an approach to treatment), *Zeitschrift für Strafvollzug*, 34: 67–77.

Wulf, R. (1986) 'Opferperspektive und soziale Arbeit' (Victim perspectives and social work), in M. Salman (ed.), *Soziale Arbeit mit Straffälligen* (*Social work with offenders*). Frankfurt am Main. pp. 26–37.

12

Alternatives to the Judicial Model

Jean-Pierre Bonafé-Schmitt

From the judicial statistics, it would appear that French society is becoming more and more conflict-ridden. But perhaps this conclusion should be qualified, because in the past, a good part of the minor disputes were regulated within the family, the neighbourhood, and other community structures. Today, urbanization and social mobility have undermined these forums for socialization and the regulation of conflicts, and in consequence the state has intervened in these private domains of social life. In such a situation, where society is entirely structured by and around the state, it appears to have fossilized 'into monoliths which can no longer communicate with one another except by constantly asking the State to mediate' (Cohen-Tanugi, 1985: 206).

To cope with the growth of new conflictual situations, the legislature has formed the habit of creating specific jurisdictions superimposed on the existing ones. Although the original primary concern in doing so was to increase the efficacy of the judicial machinery, this proliferation of tribunals has now led to bureaucratization of justice. In general it is easy to see that this model for the operation of the judicial machinery, with all its side-effects (long delays, complex and costly procedure), is no longer adapted to the evolution of society towards greater decentralization, demands for more active participation by citizens, and the search for greater autonomy in relation to state structures. To respond to this type of situation, states have started to develop a number of initiatives with the aim of restructuring these forums of socialization where everyday conflicts could be regulated. This represents a change in the policies of states in matters of social regulation, because until now they have turned to the judicial machinery in their search for more institutionalized ways of conflict regulation.

Mediation: a response to the crisis in the judicial model of dispute regulation?

With the introduction of this policy of diversion from the courts, it is becoming apparent that the problem lies not in malfunctions of the system but in the system itself. The present judicial machinery with its formalism, its cost, its remoteness, cannot effectively handle the complex evolution of social relations.

To respond to this type of situation, states, especially in America, have begun to develop more flexible alternatives to the judicial model, using other techniques of conflict resolution, namely mediation, conciliation, and arbitration. But in parallel to these state initiatives, some community-based experiments have developed, growing out of victim aid associations and neighbour-hood committees; these represent another facet of the movement towards diversion from the courts. These experiments, even if they are still in a minority, reveal the *ambivalence* of the movement, which cannot be reduced to a mere appendage of the judicial machinery, a 'second-class' or 'poor people's' justice.

This contrast between 'state' and 'societal' initiatives should not be pushed too far, because, as we shall see, there are no 'pure' models or 'ideal types', to use Weber's terminology. There are some cases in which the mediation experiments function on the 'judicial model', notably in the civil domain; on the other hand, there are plenty of others where state-supported mediation projects have abandoned this model. Rather than define models, therefore, I have preferred to concentrate on analysing the logical bases underlying the development of mediation experiments, with especial emphasis on the interactions between the state and civilian society.

The management perspective

Another point should be stressed, to highlight the French situation in comparison to experience elsewhere, namely the state's desire to confine experiments in informal justice to the civil domain only. It was not until recently, about 1984–5, that the state, on the initiative of governments of the Left, gave particular attention to the development of mediation experiments in the criminal field; but the dose has been at most a homeopathic one, since there are still fewer than a dozen projects.

In the movement which is experimenting with alternative judicial structures, the first French initiatives, compared with those else-where, seemed to have an underlying logic based on administration or management rather than on an innovative programme modelled on the Dispute Resolution Act adopted by the American Congress in 1980 (McGillis, 1983).

It is in this purely management perspective that one must place the creation of conciliators and the 'P.O. Boxes 5000' (B.P. 5000) created at the end of the seventies. To tackle what has been called

180   *Jean-Pierre Bonafé-Schmitt*

'mass litigation' and a 'clogged up' judicial system, these 'by-passes' were introduced. The introduction of the conciliators (*conciliateurs*), in 1977, originated in an initiative of the Ministry of Justice of the time, which at first limited the experiment to four *départements*. After this experimental phase, considered to be successful, conciliators were appointed throughout France; by 1980 there were 1,000 of them. They are volunteers named by the First Presidents of Courts of Appeal, with the task of trying to find conciliated solutions to petty disputes between individuals. They operate within the framework of the canton, like the former justices of the peace. But the establishment of the conciliators led to some reactions within the judicial world, which feared that a 'parallel system of justice' was being created.

After the victory of the Left in the elections of 1981, the new Minister of Justice, apparently very sensitive to these criticisms, sent a circular to the heads of the Courts of Appeal, indicating that it would be 'desirable not to intensify the recruitment of conciliators'. Without being opposed to the principle of conciliation, the official proposal was to develop it in the framework of the judicial institutions, notably the district court (*tribunal d'instance*). A draft ordinance was presented in 1985 to the Council of State (Conseil d'État), which rejected it on the grounds that the reform should be the subject of legislation.

The P.O. Boxes 5000 had been created a year earlier, in 1976, on the initiative of the then Department of Consumer Affairs. Through them, disputes on consumer affairs can be referred, in writing, to conciliation committees consisting of representatives from the Department of Trade and Consumer Affairs, consumer associations, and professional (manufacturers' and traders') associations. From the start, this initiative met the hostility of the judiciary, who alleged that it trespassed on their field of competence. Similarly, the large consumer organizations were opposed to it. Despite this multiple opposition, the P.O. Boxes 5000 had, on balance, a moderate success, although there were big differences between the *départements*. In 1981 they received altogether 25,000 letters. Like the conciliators, they did not escape the criticism of new ministers after May 1981, who proposed to replace them with a sort of consumers' conciliation board, but this project never saw the light.

The left-wing government was not inactive in the face of this growth of mass litigation. It established a multiplicity of commissions and study groups to make proposals for the reform of justice, both civil and criminal. The best known were the Pesce Commission and the Bonnemaison Commission on crime prevention (Bonnemaison, 1983), not forgetting the most recent, chaired by Senator

Edgar Tailhades, which produced a report with the promising title *The Modernization of Justice* (Tailhades, 1985). This wish to reform the methods of dispute regulation led to concrete results in the shape of a number of more or less experimental initiatives. These included the creation of the commissions for landlord–tenant relations (*commissions des rapports locatifs* – CDRL). These were formed on the labour court model, that is to say they are composed of representatives of landlords and tenants on a basis of parity. Their role is to try to resolve disputes, especially by conciliation.

The social integration perspective
It was only in a second phase, particularly influenced by the Left after its victory in 1981, that some initiatives appeared which aimed not at remedying dysfunctions of the machinery of justice, but rather at seeking better social integration. Their objective was not to promote better access to justice, but to try to reduce social tensions, to build solidarity through greater participation of citizens in the resolution of conflicts, and thus to work towards the improvement of social relations.

This movement marked a break with the type of state interventionism which made it the principal actor in all forms of mediation in social relations. Until this point the basic tendency in social mediation had been to reinforce the role of the state, whether through the judicial or the administrative machinery. By promoting these experiments with 'direct' mediation the State was seeking, not without difficulty, to give impetus to a social dynamic that aimed at making citizens full participants in the resolution of conflicts. In this framework mediation comes closer to action towards reforming social ties than to a mere technique for conflict management.

This search for a better social integration by the state was not, as we shall see, pursued by the dissemination of a unique 'normative model', as in the past, but by promoting or maintaining a number of experiments. These were not developed as the fruit of a rational policy, but were rather the result of a piece-meal approach by various ministries, such as Justice, Social Security, the Interior; or they sprang from initiatives by bodies such as the National Council for Crime Prevention (Conseil National de Prévention de la Déliquance – CNDP) or the National Commission for the Social Development of Neighbourhoods (Commission Nationale pour le Développement Social des Quartiers – CNDSQ).

The experiment of Neighbourhood Councils (*régies de quartier*) is perhaps the most developed manifestation of this social integration model. These councils, established jointly by the National Commission for the Social Development of Neighbourhoods, the Interdepartmental Committee for the Care of Young People in Difficulty (Délégation Interministérielle à l'insertion des jeunes en difficultés), and the CNDP, are not instances of mediation proper, but their work and their activities lead them to play a mediating role. The Neighbourhood Councils are in effect a regrouping, on a 'round-table' basis, of neighbourhood associations and of those bodies (such as the local authority and the low-cost housing associations) whose task is not only to provide local services (small repairs and building maintenance, etc.) but also to promote social regulation. These councils have thus come to play a mediating role between residents and institutions (such as the management of the housing associations, the social services). They are also urged to intervene in 'neighbourhood conflicts, rivalries or animosities between social groups' (*Plan urbain*, 1986). It is difficult to evaluate these experiments in mediation, since the movement is still at the experimental stage and depends on the outcome of three projects: the technical council (*régie technique*) of Alma-Gare in Roubaix, the technical council of Les Flamants in Marseille, the Pierre Collinet Neighbourhood Council in Meaux.

But it is above all the network of victims aid associations, operating with the help of grants from the Ministry of Justice, that forms the most fertile breeding ground for mediation projects (Akermann and Dulong, 1984). Of the three most significant mediation experiments, two belong to this network: the Association SOS Aggression-Conflicts (SOS Agressions-Conflits), in Paris, and the Friendly Association for Co-ordinating Prevention, Rehabilit-ation of Offenders and Aid to Victims (ACCORD), in Strasbourg. Although it is difficult to conduct a complete census, since there has been no follow-up of these experiments, we should add to the three mentioned a number of projects still in the early stages: the Association for Aid to Victims of Acts of Delinquency (AVAD) in Marseille, and the Association for Social Readjustment and Judicial Supervision (ARESCJ) in Bordeaux. At a more advanced stage are the Association for Aid and Information to Victims (AIV) in Grenoble, and the Corrèze Association for the Rehabilitation of Offenders and Aid to Victims (ARAVIC) in Tulle. In other cases, the mediation project has started under one association and continued in another, as at St Étienne, where the project trans-ferred from the Association for Aid to Victims (AIV) to the Probation Committee; or, as at Mende, has never got off the ground because of the opposition of certain members of the judiciary.

With the information available, it is somewhat difficult to construct a typology of mediation projects, but I can provide a summary of different experiments. It should be stressed at the outset that they were conceived within victims aid associations (AVAD and AIV) or judicial supervision associations (ARAVIC, ARESCJ), and often represent the culmination and formalization of mediation techniques operated in the past. In effect, the leaders of these associations, faced with the problems of restoring the harm suffered by victims, or of rehabilitating offenders, have been led more or less spontaneously to maintain or promote conciliation attempts.

Thus for ARAVIC and ARESCJ the project for developing mediation is a form of response to the requests made by persons placed under judicial supervision who express 'the desire to compensate the victims of their crime' (ARESCJ, 1985). A similar initiative, but from the victim's side, led the leaders of AIV to propose setting up a mediation scheme.

If at first the mediation projects did not reflect the social objectives of these associations, the staff in their daily work soon observed the limits of judicial action, which led them to propose the creation 'of a place for negotiation, for mediation between the victim and the offender'. This approach explains why at ARAVIC and AIV the staff donned the mantle of 'mediator'. ARESCJ on the other hand recruited a psychologist to perform the mediating role.

As mentioned, these experiments are only in their first years of operation, so it is difficult to evaluate them. But it can be said that at the AIV in Grenoble between January 1985 and August 1986, for example, there were 78 referrals, of which 62 were dealt with (AIV, 1986). Of these 62: 47 related to minor violence after brawls, assaults, or quarrels between neighbours; 10 to property and belongings; 1 to the enforcement of a judgement; 3 to insults; 1 to non-criminal neighbourhood conflicts (noise). Of all these cases, 25 (about 40 per cent) ended with a conciliated agreement, which is not a negligible proportion, as we shall see, compared with the results of the judicial machinery.

This expansion of initiatives led to the idea of creating a coordinating agency for mediation. It was proposed at the national meeting of the Associations for Aid to Victims, in Marseille in June 1986. The creation of this coordinating body, called the National Institute for Aid to Victims and for Mediation (INAVEM), was, in addition to its specific functions relating to aid to victims, to make it possible to give some coherence to this untidy movement, to create structures for mediation, and thus to promote the development of this form of conflict regulation.

The perspective of empowerment and conflict management

These various experiments in diversion from the courts have

aroused, in America as well as in France, severe criticisms from certain authors, who see them as forms of social control (Abel, 1981). For them the presence of citizens at the core of mediation structures does not prevent power from remaining in the hands of representatives of judicial institutions or the police (Hofrichter, 1982). They stress particularly that the mediation projects have the effect of neutralizing and fragmenting collective action, by individualizing conflicts and detaching them from their social context.

These criticisms, even if not entirely without foundation, do not make clear the reality and the ambivalent nature of the movement for diversion from the courts. Although most of these experiments have been established by the state, particular attention should also be given to initiatives which do not arise from state Machiavellianism, especially those of organizations of consumers, tenants, and districts, offering intervention in the process of conflict regulation. The existence of these different experiments has led me to wonder if there is a resurrection of the concept of the 'community' or primary solidarity, of which civil society had been dispossessed by the 'social state' (Melucci, 1983). The re-creation of this form of 'social community' would, in our view, be facilitated by the evolution of our societies towards complex, very specialized systems which would leave much more autonomy to individuals and social groups, especially in the field that concerns us here, that of conflict management (Melucci, 1983).

This type of experiment, based on a concept of reaffirming people's power to manage their own conflicts, is admittedly still in a small minority – both in France and elsewhere. Of the non-French experiments, the most often cited is the Community Board Program of San Francisco, whose aim is to promote conciliation and mediation techniques by involving the inhabitants of a district with the resolution of conflicts. In France, the mediation project of the Association SOS Aggression-Conflicts in Paris has been largely inspired by the principles developed by the Community Board.

Another experiment deserving attention is the law shops (*boutiques de droit*). These developed mainly in the 1970s, in the Paris region and in some large cities like Lyon, Nantes, Montpellier, Orléans, and Avignon. The originality of the law shops' approach was their desire to associate the people involved with the search for a solution to their own cases, through experimenting with new practices and new methods of conflict resolution. Thus in divorce cases, the law shops in Paris and Lyon formed 'divorce groups' to enable the parties themselves to regulate the consequences of their divorces. Starting from the idea that divorce is not a legal but a social problem, activists of the Lyon law shop proposed to members of the divorce group that they should not let themselves be trapped in a purely judicial perspective. The process of mediation and negotiation appeared to these law shop activists to be the procedure that allowed the greatest involvement of the participants in the settlement of their own cases. Members of the divorce group reorganized their future relationships on a negotiated basis, by determining between themselves the amount of maintenance payments, the details of custody of the children, the division of the household goods, and so on.

On the basis of this experience the members of the Lyon law shop, with two other associations (Social Action Movement, and San Marco), want to develop a mediation project in a district of Lyon. Starting from a community approach, the architects of this project would like to show the ability of the community movement not only to take charge of conflicts but to deal with them before they become violent. Unlike many mediation systems which operate like sub-contractors of the judicial system, the Lyon project aims to regulate disputes before they enter the traditional judicial system.

Mediation: a multiplicity of models

In the criminal domain, plea bargaining on the American pattern is not found in France. French mediation experiments have taken place outside the sphere of criminal justice. But there are 'informal mediations' on the initiative of magistrates or lawyers, which generally lead to a *nolle prosequi*. These informal mediations have not been recognized as part of the system, so that it is difficult to assess their extent. Discussion here will therefore focus on three mediation experiments in the criminal sphere: the projects of the Conciliation Committee of Valence, of the Association SOS Aggression-Conflicts in Paris, and the ACCORD Association in Strasbourg. These projects have been chosen because they have been running for some time, and are well known because they have been accorded exemplary status by such bodies as the National Council for the Prevention of Crime or the Ministry of Justice, rather than on truly scientific criteria. They are not in any way a representative sample of the experiments currently under way in France. Rather than presenting a detailed account of each project, I will analyse them comparatively, giving particular attention to their distinguishing features.

The Valence project
The proposal to set up a mediation project in Valence arose from a

concern among some judges in 1985 about the uncertainty and inadequacy of the judicial model for the resolution of conflicts arising from opposing interests, in the context of disputes involving people with a continuing relationship. The proposal to establish mediation projects in two districts of the town of Valence was supported by the local Council for Crime Prevention (Conseil Communal de Prévention de la Déliquence – CCPD).

In terms of foreign comparisons, the Valence Conciliation Committee is related to the American model of Neighborhood Justice Centers. In broad outline it belongs within a perspective of rebuilding social relationships, in which it is clearly stated that the project's philosophy 'tends to restore the solution of the problem to the community from which it came' (Obrégo and Apap, 1985).

The community roots of the mediation project are evident, especially in the wish to confine the experiment to two districts, and by the methods of selecting mediators. The authors of the project adopted selection criteria in no way connected to any professional or legal qualifications. On the contrary, they put the accent on social factors; the conciliators were chosen 'on the basis of their knowledge of the district and the way they are integrated and accepted into it, or their interest in the problems of everyday life, especially those arising from the coexistence of ethnic groups or of different generations' (Obrégo and Apap, 1985). Among the six men and two women who have been chosen as conciliators, there are representatives of associations (for example of parents and tenants) and one is of Moroccan nationality.

The philosophy of the Valence project is closer to that of the Neighborhood Justice Centers than to the Community Board of San Francisco. The umbilical link between the mediation project and the courts should not be underestimated, and should have a place in any evaluation. The judicial authorities appoint the conciliators, and refer the great majority of cases, thus ensuring the continuance of the project. The National Council for Crime Prevention designates the Valence experiment as an exemplary project, which cannot be without influence in the development of state policies in relation to conflict regulation.

I have already drawn attention to the ambivalent character of these mediation experiments, which seem both to respond to social demands, and at the same time to provide the subject of state research into new ways of conflict management and even preservation of social order. The Valence experiment is not the only one to have received particular attention from the state; the Paris project is in some ways similar.

The Paris project

In the Paris project we also find this idea of using mediation not only to resolve conflicts, but as a means, or tool, for effecting a transformation of social relationships. But unlike Valence, it originated from a voluntary organization, Human Rights and Solidarity (Droits de l'Homme et Solidarité), which has no connection with the judicial system.

This concept led in 1983 to the formation of the Association SOS Aggression-Conflicts, with the double objective of helping victims of crime, but also in cases of conflict to propose a meeting between the two parties, to try to resolve the problem through mediation. The model preferred by the authors of the Paris project is that of the Community Board of San Francisco. Mediation is presented as a means of enabling citizens to regain the power of regulating disputes, and contributing to the creation of new social cohesion by spreading knowledge of mediation, especially through the training of mediators. This emphasis on training is not intended to create professional mediators, but rather to initiate as many people as possible into mediation techniques. In short, it is to make mediation the main form of conflict resolution in all areas of social life: in the workplace, the neighbourhood, the family.

The founders of the Paris association, like their American opposite numbers at the Community Board, see a positive value in the expression of conflicts, in the sense that their resolution can contribute to the improvement of social relations. It is for this reason that they insist that the mediators should be as representative as possible of the background of the two parties in conflict, so as to understand them better. 'For example, if a Moroccan or a Vietnamese is implicated in the conflict, one of the mediators should be Moroccan or Vietnamese' (Morineau, 1985). Consequently, particular attention has been given to the recruitment of mediators in order to have representatives of all social and ethnic categories. Of the panel of twenty mediators trained by SOS Aggression-Conflicts, there are as many women as men, all age groups are represented, a secretary may sit next to a businessman, an unemployed Moroccan with a gendarme, a housewife with a law student, etc.

One point on which the Paris project falls down by comparison with the American model is the referral of cases. The Association SOS Aggression-Conflicts receives most of its cases from the Paris public prosecutor's office (*Parquet*); it is rarely approached by the parties in conflict. The Community Board, by contrast, distinguishes itself from other American projects by its unwillingness to take on any cases except those referred directly from the local communities, without having been previously processed by social services or the courts.

The Strasbourg project

Unlike the two other projects described, the association ACCORD is based on professionalized mediation. This perspective does not merely take the form of the involvement of specialists, whether lawyers or psychologists, but also defines a new field of conflict regulation employing special techniques, formalizing different procedures of the judicial model.

This approach did not arise by chance, but results from the association's conclusion that it is necessary to tackle the crime phenomenon in a cross-sectional and interdisciplinary way. That is to say, the question of victims' aid should not be dissociated from prevention and from the rehabilitation of offenders. This approach has been put into practice through the opening of two reception offices, one for victims' aid and the other for assistance to discharged prisoners (Hellbrunn et al., 1985).

This approach, using 'non-institutional coordination', as the leaders of ACCORD put it, is based on a particular perception of conciliation, seen above all as an 'attitude, a life-style, that is a way of welcoming the other person as a client while trying to comprehend the globality of his problems instead of compartmentalizing them' (Hincker, n.d. 17). The practice of this form of mediation appeals more to psychological than to juridical techniques, in as much as the emphasis is placed on the relational aspect and specifically on communication within interpersonal relationships.

The 'non-institutional' approach, more psychological than juridical, in dealing with conflicts, was not adopted without considering the formalization of mediation procedures. The need to formalize mediation matches the logic of professionalization which aims to mark out a new field of conflict resolution, breaking with the judicial model. According to the authors of the project, this process of formalization tends to fix 'bench-marks' to avoid any 'deviation' from conciliation. They fear that this type of unsupervised practice could lead to illegal 'transactions' involving humiliation or black-mail (Hellbrunn et al., 1985). While refusing to become either 'a parallel justice agency' or an 'annexe' of the court, they advocate a degree of institutionalization of this new mode of dispute resolution, through legislation. This has led them to pose a series of questions on the type of relations they should maintain with the judicial system, and also with those who apply to them (problems of anonymity and professional confidentiality).

The disputes
It is difficult to pin down the nature of the disputes dealt with by mediation projects because many of them do not produce statistics, or do so using vague criteria which give little real information. Each has used its own categories, which makes comparative analysis difficult. Because of this lack of common nomenclature I have been unable to collect comparable data on the socio-professional profile of the parties, the type of case, the solutions. I say this to put in context the data I have collected, and to draw attention to the need for a proper evaluation based on more elaborate methodology.

To start at the quantitative level, the number of cases dealt with by the different mediation projects is still very low if it is based on the number of cases they have recorded. In 18 months, the Parisian Association SOS Aggression-Conflicts received 70 cases from the Paris public prosecutor. The Conciliation Committee in Valence has succeeded in conciliating 36 cases in a year, while ACCORD in Strasbourg has only dealt with a dozen since its creation. The *total* number of cases is below 200, even if numbers referred to other projects are included. At the quantitative level we are thus far from having a tidal wave which threatens to submerge the judicial institution, but qualitatively the results recorded are more significant. From a study in a court in the Paris region it appears that of victims accepted as *partie civile*:[1] 76 per cent did not obtain payment of damages or interest; 12.7 per cent obtained partial payment; 11.3 per cent received total payment of the damages and interest allocated to them (of whom 75 per cent received it after amicable agreement with the author of the damage and 25 per cent thanks to the intervention of the advocate) (Trioux, 1985).

With mediation, it would appear that the results of the Paris experiment are better, since of 55 cases dealt with, the proportion mediated was 35 per cent. The figure reaches 46 per cent if complaints withdrawn in the course of the mediation process are included.

These results have to be analysed with caution, however, since, as I have stressed, the bases of comparison are far from identical. The mediation projects can take on cases with more civil than criminal aspects, such as debtors. Unlike the courts, they are not statutorily limited in their field of competence. Only in the Valence project is there a definition of the areas of intervention of the conciliation committee, such as:

● neighbourhood troubles: late or untimely noise, failure to maintain communal areas, pavements, etc;
● minor damage to property, acts of vandalism;

- minor violence causing no time off work, or time off less than 8 days;
- insults, threats, offensive language, etc.;
- petty thefts, from shop displays, cellars or cars;
- debts, small loans between private individuals, small debts to shops;
- family quarrels. (Obrégo and Apap, 1985: 5)

Techniques of mediation

There are at present not one but several techniques of mediation, because of the diversity of the experiments. But before analysing them, a word is needed on their different referral procedures. At Valence and Paris, the great majority of cases are referred by the judicial authorities; the proportion of direct referrals remains marginal (6 out of 36 at Valence). At Strasbourg, however, there is no institutional link with the judicial services, and most cases come from the Victims Aid Bureau.

A basic principle of mediation is *collective mediation*, not only to avoid personalization of the relationship and perception of the mediator as an arbitrator, but also to increase the 'effectiveness' of mediation. The composition of the group of mediators varies, as mentioned, from one project to another: it is composed of two or three persons, who may be non-professionals (Valence and Paris) or professionals (Strasbourg); particular attention is given to the composition of the mediating panel by the Paris project, which holds that the panel should be as representative as possible of the social categories of the disputants.

The three projects have given particular thought to the course of the mediation process. Without going into details, they observe the following main principles.

The mediators make initial contact with each of the parties separately. At this first meeting they not only tell them about the objectives of the mediation project, and the stages of the procedure, but also explain their own role and the limits of their intervention. In the case of direct referrals the mediators also undertake an obligation to inform each party of his or her rights under the law, and they stress that ultimately judicial action can be taken if there is a stalemate or even if the mediation succeeds (Hellbrunn et al., 1985: 59). On this last point, however, in the case of the Valence project, it is stated that if 'referral to conciliation was made by the court, the public prosecutor undertakes, in the event of conciliation, not to prosecute' (Obrégo and Apap, 1985: 7).

Only after the agreement of both parties has been obtained is their meeting arranged. Those in charge of the various projects stress the importance of this type of meeting, because it gives each party the opportunity to express his or her point of view, feelings, perception of the problem. This face-to-face encounter in some cases allows the (re-)establishment of broken lines of communication between the parties.

The role of the mediators is initially limited to facilitating the confrontation, clarifying the points of view of both parties, and summarizing their positions. Having thus 'cleared the undergrowth', they then explore with the parties the different possibilities for reaching an agreement. When they have identified a basis for agreement, they reformulate its terms and write them down. This process of putting them in writing can take different forms: it can be transcribed into a notebook, or there can be a more formal procedure, as at Valence where the agreement can be the subject of an official conciliation statement at the district court.

Finally, the last phase, but not the least important: the projects all underline the importance of the implementation of the agreement, that is, the mediators must satisfy themselves that the parties carry out their obligations.

In the absence of evaluation, I cannot present very significant results for the measures adopted by mediation schemes. The Valence project proposed the following list, which is not exhaustive:

- apologies made to the 'victim' in the presence of the conciliator, for example in cases of insults or threats;
- monetary reparation;
- direct reparation, such as replacement of a broken window pane;
- indirect reparation: alternative work. For instance, when an elderly person has been subjected to taunts or minor violence, as reparation the offender could go to collect his or her bread for a certain number of days. Or he or she could undertake tasks looking after the lawn, garden, housework, cleaning communal areas of a building, flower beds, etc. (Obrégo and Apap, 1985: 6)

In practice, in cases of fights for example, the participants will in some instances undertake a simple commitment to live peaceably or to ignore each other. In others, however, notably where one party has had to take time off work, financial compensation has been agreed, with sums that can reach 3,000 French francs. Where a sum of money in a handbag was stolen by a relative, conciliation was achieved by the conciliators in Paris without the victim reporting the matter to the police, in return for an undertaking to repay in instalments the amount stolen.

Although the latter case does not *a priori* appear to pose an ethical problem, the same is not true of compensation for time off work. The different projects adopt different practices. The ACCORD Association considers that determination of the amount requires the competence not of conciliators but of lawyers. According to them, if the conciliators involve themselves in the determination of the amount in such a transaction, they are exchanging the role of conciliator for that of arbitrator.

Conclusion

To appreciate fully the importance of this movement of diversion from the judicial system, one must consider that conflict resolution cannot be confined to the management of individual disputes but should be seen as an aspect of the operation of the system of social regulation. This system is in crisis, in as much as the judicial model for resolving conflicts by opposing interests (adversary model) is shown to be inappropriate for the resolution of certain types of conflict, notably those involving parties who are in a continuing relationship, for example in a neighbourhood or family. Traditional justice, because of its formality, its slowness, its cost, its distance, finds more and more difficulty in taking account of the evolution and complexity of social relationships.

We recognize this crisis in the 'rational model' of justice, based on a continuing rationalization of the procedures for regulating conflicts; but we cannot side-step a debate on the emergence of one or more 'new models' for the management of disputes, arising from the movement for diversion from the courts. The existence of these extra-judicial modes of conflict resolution raises the question of the evolution in our societies towards what could be called a 'differentiated society', with sub-systems which generate their own systems of regulation (Teubner, 1983). One cannot be content with analysing the development of these mediation projects as the result simply of poor functioning in the machinery of justice; on the contrary, this process of diversion from the courts should be seen as part of a deeper trend, linked to the evolution of systems of social regulation which have been called judicial pluralism or multi-track justice. The existence of these extra-judicial methods of dispute resolution leads us to re-examine the criterion of 'justiciability'. In fact, as has been pointed out elsewhere, the judicial machinery has never had the monopoly of conflict resolution (Bonafé-Schmitt et al., 1986). It has always been present, in a more or less developed form, which we have called 'informal justice': for example, disciplinary councils in companies, associations, religious congregations; various forms of arbitration, particularly in commercial matters. The question which remains is whether it is necessary to hold to a restrictive concept of judicial pluralism, that is to confine this phenomenon to the field of formal judicial organization (pluralism of jurisdictions or of decision-making), or whether to extend it to all formal and informal forms of conflict resolution. In support of the idea that there is a degree of judicial pluralism, it may be pointed out that these informal methods of dispute resolution do not function in isolation, but are part of a larger system of juridical regulation. This adds up to a social system whose complexity makes it difficult to comprehend; in the light of the movement towards dejudiciarization of the last few years, there does appear to be a need for the concept of 'judicial pluralism.'

Notes

This chapter was translated by Martin Wright.

1 *Partie civile* is a provision in French criminal procedure. The complainant, or victim, can bring a civil action against the accused, claiming compensation. This civil action can be joined to a criminal trial, and the complainant can be legally represented.

References

Abel, R. (1981) 'Règlement formel et informel des conflits: Analyse d'une alternative' (Formal and informal conflict regulation: analysis of an alternative), *Sociologie du Travail*, 1: 32–43.

Akermann, W. and R. Dulong (1984) *L'aide aux victimes: Premières initiatives, premières évaluations* (*Help for victims: first initiatives, first evaluations*). Paris: Maison des Sciences de l'Homme.

AIV (Aide Information aux Victimes) (1986) *Rapport d'activité 1986* (*Report on activities 1986*). Grenoble.

ARESCJ (Association de Réadaptation Sociale et de Controle Social) (1985) *Rapport d'activité, 1985* (*Report on activities, 1985*). Bourdeaux.

Bonafé-Schmitt, J.-P., C. Gérard, D. Picon and P. Porcher (1986) *Les justices du quotidien: Les modes formels et informels de règlement des petits litiges* (*Everyday justice: formal and informal modes of resolving small disputes*). Lyon: GLYSI/ Université Lyon II.

Bonnemaison, G. (1983) *Face à la délinquance: prévention, répression, solidarité* (*Confronting crime: prevention, law enforcement, solidarity*). Paris: La Documentation Française.

Cohen-Tanugi, L. (1985) '*Le droit sans l'Etat': sur la démocratie en France et en Amérique* (*Law without the State: on democracy in France and America*). Paris: PUF.

Hellbrunn, R., C. Lienhard and P. Martin (1985) 'Avant propos' by L. Hincker, *Peut-on aider les victimes?* (*Can we help victims?*). Strasbourg: ACCORD.

Hincker, L. (n.d.) 'Les expériences de conciliation: le Bureau d'Aide aux Victimes de l'Association ACCORD à Strasbourg' (The experience of conciliation: the Victims' Help Bureau of the ACCORD Association in Strasbourg). Strasbourg: unpublished paper.

Hofrichter, R. (1982) 'Neighborhood justice and the social control problem of American capitalism: a perspective', in R. Abel (ed.), *The Politics of Informal Justice*, New York: Academic Press, vol. 1.

McGillis, D. (1983) 'Minor dispute processing: a review of recent developments', in H. Tomasic and M. Feeley (eds), *Neighborhood Justice: Assessment of an Emerging Idea*. New York/London: Longman.

Melucci, A. (1983) 'Nouveaux mouvements sociaux et action collective' (New social movements and collective action), *Revue Internationale d'Action Communautaire*, 50 (10): 31–9.

Morineau, J. (1985) 'Pourquoi la médiation?' (Why mediation?). Paris: unpublished paper.

Obrégo, N. and G. Apap (1985) 'Pour un règlement social des conflits' (The case for social regulation of conflicts). Valence: unpublished paper.

Plan urbain (1986) *Les régies de quartier* (*Neighbourhood councils*). Paris: unpublished.

Tailhades, E. (1985) *La modernisation de la Justice: rapport au Premier Ministre* (*The modernization of justice: report to the Prime Minister*). Paris: La Documentation Française.

Teubner, G. (1983) 'Substantive and reflexive elements in modern law', *Law and Society Review*, 17 (2): 239–85.

Trioux, M. (1985) 'La médiation pénale' (Mediation and crime). Paris: Ministry of Justice: unpublished paper.

PART III

PROBLEMS AND POTENTIAL

13
Confession, Repentance and Absolution

John O. Haley

Criminal justice in Japan operates on two tracks. The first is a
familiar formal process. Although shaped by Japan's particular
cultural environment and institutional needs, the formal system of
criminal justice reflects the pervasive influence of German law and
legal institutions with the addition of American-inspired constitutional protections (Appleton, 1949; Meyers, 1950; Nagashima,
1963; Dando, 1965; Koshi, 1970). One thus encounters few features
unknown to the criminal justice systems of other industrial countries
in the West. Each stage in the process – from the apprehension of
offenders to the determination of guilt and application of punitive
sanctions – is governed by substantive and procedural rules of
special statutes, codes, and constitution common to other modern
industrial states. Each stage also has the familiar roster of special
players: police, prosecutors, defence attorneys, and judges. Even
institutions that may appear at first blush to be uniquely Japanese
innovations are, on examination, often found to be adaptations of
Western models.[1]

Paralleling the formal process, however, is a second track to
which there is no Western analogue. A pattern of confession,
repentance, and absolution dominates each stage of law enforcement in Japan. The players in the process include not only the
authorities in new roles but also the offender and the victim. From
the initial police interrogation to the final judicial hearing on
sentencing, the vast majority of those accused of criminal offences
confess, display repentance, negotiate for their victims' pardon and
submit to the mercy of the authorities. In return they are treated
with extraordinary leniency; they gain at least the prospect of
absolution by being dropped from the formal process altogether
(Haley, 1982: 269–73; Haley, 1986).

Japanese law enforcement statistics tell some of the story. In
1978, for example, the Japanese police cleared 599,302 cases out of

Table 13.1 Disposition of criminal cases by Japanese public prosecutors 1983

	Caseload	Prosecuted cases	Formal trial	Summary proceedings	Suspended prosecution	Closed for insufficient evidence	Closed for other reasons	Transferred to	
								Other prosecutors' office	Family court[a]
Total	4,486,238	2,471,277	140,205	2,331,072	240,211	44,934	15,835	1,096,012	599,262
Criminal Code offences	1,180,598	452,352	88,132	364,229	162,452	39,536	10,141	261,548	250,827
Homicide (art. 199)	2,229	1,097	1,097	—	60	128	752	52	82
Bodily Injury (art. 204)	48,812	20,292	5,042	15,250	3,623	707	220	12,357	11,352
Negligent bodily injury while driving (including death)	739,328	338,229	10,097	328,132	98,410	31,288	1,844	209,850	57,617
Larceny (art. 235)	236,861	42,216	42,216	—	34,085	1,315	1,621	15,670	141,796
Indecency through compulsion (art. 176) and rape (art. 177)	2,914	786	786	—	138	90	274	83	940
Rape or death in course of robbery (art. 241)	968	445	445	—	11	49	47	27	377
Robbery (art. 236)	1,215	676	676	—	49	42	79	36	331
Fraud (art. 246)	20,455	11,025	11,025	—	5,260	1,922	291	890	746
Extortion (art. 249)	12,082	3,344	3,344	—	1,285	472	40	272	6,609
Embezzlement (art. 252) and breach of trust (art. 247)	24,721	1,629	1,511	118	4,212	742	156	1,126	16,729
Motor vehicle violations	3,055,072	1,906,607	11,789	1,894,818	47,650	1,420	4,721	761,563	319,472
Offences under special statutes	250,568	112,318	40,284	72,034	30,109	3,978	973	72,901	28,963

[a] All cases transferred to Family court involve juvenile offenders (aged 14–19).

Source: Ministry of Justice, 1983: 320–1.

1,136,448 known offences (National Police Agency, 1979: 116–17). In so doing, they identified 231,403 offenders who could be subject to prosecution. Of these, however, the police referred only 168,646 to public prosecutors. They released without further process 62,727 offenders (21.12 per cent) pursuant to article 193 of the Code of Criminal Procedure, which gives the police discretion to close 'simple' cases (*bizai shobun*). Citing similar statistics that between 1975 and 1980 an average ratio of 17.6 per cent of non-traffic Criminal Code offences were disposed of in this manner, B.J. George notes that assaults, thefts, fraud, embezzlement, and gambling were the most common types of offence (George, 1984: 51, n. 94). One Japanese source suggests a higher estimate, that in the Tokyo Metropolitan District the police fail to report about 40 per cent of all referrable cases (Shikita, 1982: 37). In similar fashion public prosecutors in Japan generally prosecute in ordinary criminal proceedings about 5 per cent of all prosecutable cases. They allow the vast majority to be adjudicated in uncontested summary proceedings (*rakushiki tetsuzuki*) based on documentary evidence in which the maximum penalty is 200,000 yen (or US $1,000 to 1,350 at prevailing exchange rates).[2] Japanese prosecutors routinely suspend prosecution in the remaining 10 to 15 per cent of all cases and from 30 to 35 per cent of all Criminal Code offences (George, 1984: 56–60). As indicated in Table 13.1, for example, in 1983 Japanese public prosecutors faced a total case-load of 4,486,238 cases, of which 2,717,488 did not involve juveniles and were determined to warrant prosecution. Of these, 2,331,072 (85.8 per cent) were tried in summary proceedings and only 140,205 (5.1 per cent) were prosecuted as ordinary criminal trials. Prosecution was suspended in 240,211 cases, or 9 per cent of all prosecutable cases involving adult offenders.

The ratios of formal prosecution to summary and suspended prosecution vary significantly depending upon the nature of the offence. Summary proceedings are not available for more serious offences for which a fine is not a statutory option.[3] Consequently, in 1983 no homicide cases could be submitted to summary proceedings. During 1983 prosecution was suspended in 11 of 456 or 2.4 per cent of prosecutable homicide cases. Since fraud and extortion do not carry an optional fine as a statutory penalty, summary prosecution was not permitted in these cases as well, but prosecution was suspended in 32 per cent of prosecutable fraud cases and 28 per cent of all prosecutable extortion cases.

Few suspects reported by the police are determined by public prosecutors not to be convictable. Of the total case-load of 4.5 million in 1984, in only 60,769 (1 per cent) were the suspects released for lack of sufficient evidence or on other grounds related to convictability. Those who are prosecuted are nearly always convicted. Conviction rates in Japan consistently hover around 99.5 per cent (Supreme Court of Japan, 1977: 21–3). In 1984 only 67 of 65,502 criminal defendants were acquitted in formal trials in district courts (Supreme Court of Japan, 1984: 242–3). Yet few offenders are subject to more than a minor fine or prison term. In summary proceedings, as noted, the maximum penalty is about 1,350 US dollars at prevailing exchange rates. In practice, however, most offenders pay much less. Of the 2,385,976 defendants in summary proceedings concluded in 1984, only 5,046 (0.2 per cent) were fined the maximum. Over half (1,215,507) were fined over 10,000 yen but less than 30,000 yen ($200). Nearly a quarter (559,719) were fined less than $66 (Supreme Court of Japan, 1984: 238–9).　　　．

Table 13.2　*Sentencing by District Courts in cases involving imprisonment or detention of adult offenders, 1984*

Crime	Convicted	Sentence suspended	Sentenced	Longest term	Shortest term	Median term
All Criminal Code offences	36,712	20,247	16,465	Life (38)	<6 months (585)	1–2 yrs (5,533)
Homicide	975	238	737	Life (13)	1–2 yrs (10)	5–7 yrs (138)
Robbery	470	117	353	7–10 yrs (7)	1–2 yrs (2)	3–5 yrs (181)
Arson	453	163	290	10–20 yrs (2)	6 months–1 yr (2)	3–5 yrs (116)
Rape	339	121	218	7–10 yrs (1)	1–2 yrs (29)	2–3 yrs (101)

Source: Supreme Court, 1984: 210–13.

Even those sentenced to imprisonment or detention rarely serve more than one-year terms. For example, 64,990 persons were sentenced to imprisonment or detention in 1984. However, 56 per cent (36,256) received suspended sentences and less than 13 per cent (8,085) were subjected to prison terms exceeding one year (Supreme Court of Japan, 1984: 210–11). The figures in Table 13.2 provide an indication of Japanese sentencing patterns for serious offences. In 1984 sentences were suspended for nearly 25 per cent of those convicted of homicide, or robbery and 36 per cent of those convicted of arson or rape. Moreover, only about 45 per cent of all imprisoned offenders actually serve a full term. More than 50 per cent are paroled before the expiration of their sentences (Abe, 1963: 334; Ōyama, *c.* 1978: 9).

From these figures it is evident that by almost any standards criminal justice in Japan is extraordinarily lenient. Although identified as offenders by the police, many are never reported. Although convictable, large numbers are released by prosecutors without prosecution. Although prosecution is tantamount to conviction, the overwhelming majority of those convicted receive no more than a minor fine or have their sentences suspended. Combining the figures in Tables 13.2 and 13.3, for example, it appears that formal penalties are imposed on only about 43 per cent of those determined by the police to have committed homicide; 17 per cent, robbery; 29 per cent, arson; and 9 per cent, rape. Moreover, the few who are imprisoned serve relatively short terms.

Table 13.3 *Number of criminal offenders identified by police in selected categories, 1980–4*

Crime	5-year high	5-year low	5-year average
Homicide	1,560 (1980)	1,789 (1983)	1,723.4
Robbery	2,031 (1984)	2,124 (1981)	2,072.0
Arson	948 (1980)	1,023 (1981)	999.6
Rape	1,907 (1984)	2,667 (1981)	2,324.6

Source: National Police Agency, 1985: 267.

A variety of factors go into the decisions by police, prosecutors and judges on how to treat offenders. They include considerations common to most criminal justice systems: the gravity of the offence, the circumstances and nature of the crime, the age and prior record of the offender.[4] Added to this matrix in Japan, however, are additional factors that appear to be missing elsewhere – at least in the West. Not only the attitude of the offender in acknowledging guilt, expressing remorse, and compensating any victim but also the victims' response in expressing willingness to pardon are determinative elements in the decision whether to report, to prosecute and to sentence the offender.

Minoru Shikita, former director of the United Nations Asia and Far East Institute for the Prevention of Crime and Treatment of Offenders (UNAFEI) describes the pattern with respect to the police:

> [T]he police, with the general accord of the chief public prosecutor of a district, need not refer all cases formally to the prosecution, but may report cases in consolidated form monthly, provided the offences are minor property offences, the suspects have shown repentance, restitution has been made, and victims forgive the suspects. (Shikita, 1982: 37)

Even in the cases referred to public prosecutors, Shikita notes, 'the police invariably recommend a lenient disposition, if a suspect has shown sincere repentence about his or her alleged crime and the transgression against a social norm is not particularly serious' (Shikita, 1982: 37). That most suspects do confess to the police is beyond doubt. Walter Ames reports an estimate in Okayama prefecture that 95 per cent of all suspects confess during police interrogation (Ames, 1981: 136). Others report similar percentages (Bayley, 1976: 148).

Similar considerations motivate prosecutors in deciding whether to suspend prosecution. The critical factors include 'the existence of a confession, sincere repentance by the suspect and the forgiveness of the victim' (Parker, 1984: 108). Japanese judges also uniformly confirm that the defendant's acknowledgment of guilt, sincerity in displaying remorse, evidenced in part by compensation of the victim and the victim's forgiving response, are pivotal in their decision on whether to suspend sentence. One senior Japanese judge is said to have refused even after conviction and sentencing to allow defendants to leave the courtroom until they have confessed and expressed remorse.

Typically, the suspect not only confesses, but through family and friends also seeks letters from any victims addressed to the prosecutor or judge that acknowledge restitution and express the victim's sentiment that no further penalty need be imposed. So customary are such letters that most Japanese attorneys have some sense of the amounts usually required.

The victim thus participates in the process. Restitution is ordinarily made and the victim has a voice in the authorities' decisions whether to report, to prosecute, or to sentence the offender. The experience of an American resident of Tokyo is illustrative. His summer house was burned down by a burglar in a clumsy attempt to destroy any incriminating evidence. Once the suspect was apprehended and charged, intermediaries arranged for the suspect's father to meet the American owner. In response to an offer to pay the entire amount of the damage, the American first insisted that this was not necessary because the house was insured. Only after the father prostrated himself, begging to pay some amount in compensation, with the intermediary explaining that some restitution was necessary as a matter of social custom, did the American relent and agree to accept money for the uninsured furniture and other personal belongings destroyed in the fire. In return, he wrote the necessary letter to the authorities explaining that compensation was paid.

In this way the victims participate in the process but do not control it. Ultimately they must defer to the authorities' decision. The burglar-arsonist in the preceding account was in fact prosecuted and convicted, and served some time in prison. The process gives the offender an incentive to make amends and the victim an opportunity to forgive. However, the victim does not assume the role of adversary or prosecutor, nor is he or she enabled to use the formal process vindictively for revenge.

Most studies of the criminal process in Japan note the evidentiary importance of confession but seldom proceed further either to analyse further its implications or to note the victims' role in the process. A few depict the dark side and even more, its cultural underpinnings. Futaba Igarashi, for instance, is among the best-known critics of the use of confessions in the Japanese-criminal process. As an attorney, she has written extensively on the use of torture and threats by police interrogators to coerce confessions from suspects, especially in cases involving violent activities by political dissidents (Igarashi, 1977, 1980, 1984). The English-language studies of the Japanese police have been far more positive. They also focus on the evidentiary value of the confession, but they generally conclude that the Japanese not only share a propensity to confess but also expect lenient treatment explained in large part by child-rearing practices and other cultural phenomena (Bayley, 1976; Ames, 1981; Parker, 1984). Conceding 'the temptation' of the police and procuracy to coerce confessions from seemingly un-repentant suspects, Bayley argues:

> Despite these factors in favor of pressing for a confession, most informed observers – lawyers, criminal reporters, law professors, and prosecutors – contend that instances of abuse of persons in custody are rare. Celebrated cases have occurred but the incidence is small . . . (Bayley, 1976: 152)

Instead, he notes the strength of 'the psychological compulsion to confess' and the 'enormous moral authority' of the Japanese police (Bayley, 1976: 153, 154). 'So,' he concludes, 'guilt is admitted in Japan for a variety of reasons: because it is a moral imperative, but also because it is a *quid pro quo* for leniency' (Bayley, 1976: 150).

Chalmers Johnson (1972) treats the role of confession at some length in his study of the Matsukawa cases. 'It is,' he states, 'the decisive element of proof sought by every procurator before he takes a case into court and the single more important item in determining the reception his efforts are likely to receive from most Japanese judges when he gets there' (Johnson, 1972: 149). Johnson criticizes exclusive emphasis on either the evidentiary value of confession and the consequent resort by the authorities to induce-ment or torture to obtain them, or cultural explanations that stress Japanese behavioural norms that 'predispose prisoners to confess to anything that authorities want them to' (Johnson, 1972: 151). Instead, he argues, both operate to produce the extraordinarily high Japanese rate of confessions and convictions. One should add that both views also suffer from a restrictive ethnocentricity.

The focus on the evidentiary importance of confessions, whether or not elaborated by charges of abusive coercion, is generally premised on Western-derived notions of the primacy of the formal process and the exclusivity of its function to ascertain guilt. Prior to sentencing, the criminal justice system is conceived to have a single overall objective – to identify accurately the offender. This premise inexorably leads to a predominant emphasis on the credibility of evidence of guilt as well as procedural controls to prevent error in the investigatory and trial processes. American observers tend to be particularly sensitive to such concerns, because confessions and plea-bargaining play so significant a role in reducing the burdens on the criminal process in the United States.

No person in Japan is convicted solely by confession. Unlike the United States, the United Kingdom, and other common law jurisdictions, there is no guilty plea in Japan eliminating the need for a trial on guilt. In all cases, even summary proceedings, an evidentiary hearing to determine that a crime has been committed and the guilt of the accused is necessary (Dando, 1965: 196). Moreover, the judge in the trial has the duty to clarify evidence and, as the finder of fact, be convinced of guilt and thus of the reliability of any confession (Dando, 1965: 205–6); although prosecutorial and judicial scrutiny of collaborative evidence is not likely to be as vigorous if the accused has confessed and offers no defence. Nevertheless, such procedural protections may not be as important a control on accuracy as the concern of judges, police, and prosecutors over the 'sincerity' of the confession and demonstrated remorse. The informal, second track includes telling tests of credibility.

The fundamental aim of the criminal process in Japan is correction, not determination of guilt or punishment of the offender. Law enforcement officials at all levels tend to share this objective, in what Shikita (1982) refers to as an 'integrated approach' to criminal justice. Thus their roles are not confined to the formal tasks of apprehending, prosecuting, and adjudicating. Rather, once personally convinced that a suspect is an offender, their concern for evidentiary proof of guilt shifts to a concern over the suspect's attitude and prospects for rehabilitation and reintegration into society, including acceptance of authority. Leniency is considered an appropriate response if the correctional process has begun. The sincerity of confession and remorse therefore becomes a significant factor in deciding whether correction is likely. Since confession and repentance provoke leniency, and most do confess, law enforcement authorities also generally expect offenders to confess and to behave with remorseful submission. For a suspect whom the authorities believe to be guilty, not to confess thus poses a dilemma. Either they have erred and the suspect is not guilty, or he is unrepentant and less correctable. Under these circumstances, it is not surprising – but not, one hastens to add, excusable – that police, prosecutors, and judges are tempted to induce or coerce acknowledgement of guilt. The more convinced the authorities become that the suspect is guilty, the more likely they are to resort to harsh and abusive measures. Yet there is also a mitigating incentive for them to re-examine more carefully the evidence of guilt before attempting to coerce the suspect.

Cultural explanations tend to be equally, albeit more subtly, ethnocentric by quarantining the Japanese experience and denying its relevance outside Japan's peculiar cultural setting. There is no question that history and societal values underpin the pattern of confession, repentance, and absolution in Japan. East Asian legal orders all place emphasis on confession. At least as early as the T'ang dynasty (AD 619–906) codified Chinese law provided for more lenient treatment to those who confessed. If the commission of the crime itself was unknown to the authorities, confession resulted in pardon (Johnson, 1979: 11, 34–6, 201), and for all categories of crime confession gained a reduction in penalty (Johnson, 1979: 34–6). Similar patterns are observed in contemporary China (Cohen, 1968: 26, 30–3, 35, 554). Differentiated from evidence or proof of guilt (Shiga, 1974: 120), confession was a means of insulating the officials from committing error, and of maintaining the legitimacy of their authority. Thus the authorities pressed for confession, and in turn, regulations were imposed on torture and other means of coercion to protect the credibility of confessions as evidence. Hulsewé (1955) notes the existence of an edict restricting the use of torture to assure the accuracy of coerced confessions as early as AD 84 (Hulsewé, 1955: 76). During the era of Mongol domination under the Yüan dynasty (AD 1280–1368) greater emphasis was placed on the victims' restitution and penalties were reduced (Ch'en, 1979: 51–61). Apparently in the succeeding Ming (AD 1368–1644) and Ch'ing (AD 1644–1912) dynasties the severity of penal sanctions was restored, although compensation of the victim continued to be demanded as an additional penalty (Ch'en, 1979: 54–5).

Societal values in Japan do encourage the use of confession, but, more important, they also permit a lenient response. As many have pointed out, repentance and forgiveness is a pervasive theme evident throughout Japanese culture from adaptations of Western fairy tales to conventional social behaviour (Bayley, 1976: 128–40). In this respect the West, not Japan, should be considered remarkable. The moral imperative of forgiveness as a response to repentance is surely as much a part of the Judeo-Christian heritage as the East Asian tradition, as evidenced in the Book of Jonah as well as the parable of the unforgiving servant (Matthew 18: 21–5). Whatever the reason, unlike Japan Western societies failed to develop institutional props for implementing such moral commands. Instead the legal institutions and processes of Western law both reflect and reinforce societal demands for retribution and revenge. This contrast between Japan and the West illustrates all too well the failings of most cultural explanations. Most depict reality in static terms. They offer rationalizations for what exists and miss the critical contrasts between the reinforcement and disintegration of similar values in different societies.

In short, the Japanese experience deserves a closer look. It is not necessarily culture-bound, and there may be something to learn from it.

Japan's success in crime prevention requires little elaboration. The figures in Tables 13.1 and 13.2 on the total number of offences and offenders in a one-year period in Japan are significantly lower in all categories than for any other industrial country. More significant, however, is Japan's achievement in reducing crime. Japan's success is measured less by low crime rates than by the *reduction* of crime in an already relatively crime-free society. Alone among the major industrialized states, Japan's crime rates for all non-traffic offences have steadily fallen during the post-war period, as indicated in Figures 13.1 and 13.2. Whatever merit conventional cultural explanations – from social cohesion or ethnic and cultural homo-geneity to family stability or high rates of literacy and educational achievement – may have in determining Japan's relative lack of crime, unless these cultural variables are conceded to have become increasingly stronger and more pervasive during the past 40 years, they do not explain the reduction of crime in post-war Japan. Not only *is* Japan different, the Japanese must also be *doing* something different. The second track is one possibility.

Unfortunately, little attention has been paid either within Japan or beyond its borders to the implications of confession and compensation in the criminal process. Typical is a study of Tokyo undertaken in the early 1970s by the Citizen's Crime Commission of Philadelphia (1975). Ironically entitled *Tokyo: One City where Crime doesn't Pay*, the study identified two dozen differences

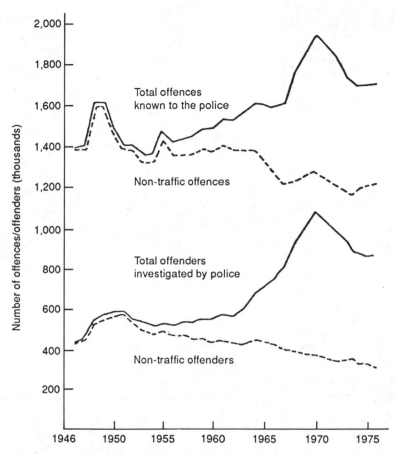

Figure 13.1 *Trends in Japanese Penal Code offences and offenders (Ministry of Justice of Japan, 1977)*

between Japan and the United States that would account for significantly lower crime rates in Japan. Some were purely cultural: Japan's ethnic homogeneity, its insularity, the cohesion of the family unit, a sense of self-discipline, the influence of meditative religions, high literacy rates. Other explanations were more structural or institutional: the accommodation of unskilled workers in the work-force, a unified, national crime control system, an emphasis on counselling and mediation of disputes, police recruitment and training, the family court system. Nowhere, however, did the report mention how offenders or the victims of crime are actually treated within the system. Nor did it explain how crime in Japan has been *reduced*. Apparently no statistics are kept by

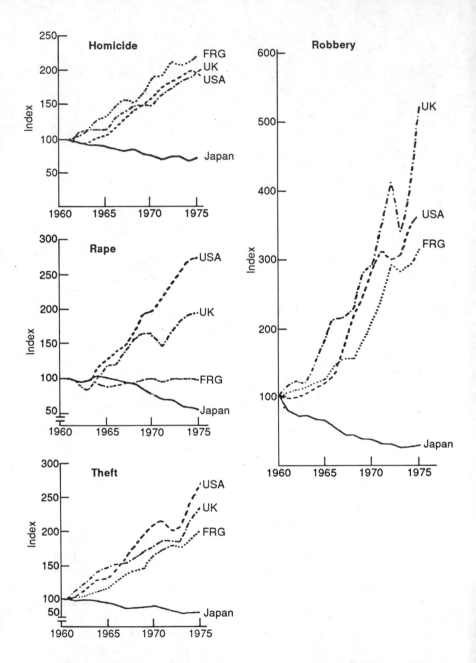

Figure 13.2 *Trends in major crime rates in the United States, the United Kingdom, the Federal Republic of Germany, and Japan, 1960–75 (Ministry of Justice of Japan, 1977)*

The index represents the number of major crimes known to the police per 100,000 population. The year 1960 = 100.

Japanese authorities on confessions or compensation; nor have Japanese criminologists displayed much interest in assessing the positive impact of confession and compensation on either offender or victim. Studies by the principal criminological research programmes in Japan, such as the National Research Institute of Police Science, typically concentrate on the clarification of factors that contribute to criminal behaviour, rather than rehabilitation. One searches their voluminous publications in vain for even a description of the informal process, much less its effects. Academic criminologists and criminal law specialists have also been preoccupied with Western approaches to the neglect of indigenous patterns. Haruo Abe, for example, excoriates judges for being too lenient (Abe, 1963). Others adopt Western concerns and approaches (Miyazawa, 1970). The Japanese no less than their counterparts in the West tend to view Japan's experience in static, cultural terms, seemingly buttressed by the somewhat smug belief that Japan's success is largely the product of a unique cultural identity.

There is, however, evidence to justify the hypothesis that the Japanese pattern – acknowledgment of guilt, expression of remorse including direct negotiation with the victim for restitution and pardon as preconditions for lenient treatment, and sparing resort to long-term imprisonment – does contribute to a reduction in crime. What is lacking is comparative data to validate the hypothesis. The most recent empirical study of recidivism among those released after suspension of prosecution is a 1968 study by the Ministry of Justice Research and Training Institute. Out of a sample of 9,296 of approximately 246,000 persons whose prosecutions for non-traffic offences were suspended in 1946, only 1,243 (13.4 per cent) were identified from fingerprint records kept in the National Police Academy to have committed a new offence before February 1967 (Kawada, *c.* 1978: 19–20). Although the accuracy of this finding has been challenged (Dando, 1970, 527–8), most law-enforcement authorities in Japan consider it to be a reasonably reliable measure of the success of the system of suspension of prosecution as a means of rehabilitation and correction (George, 1984: 59). Recidivism rates for offenders who serve prison terms are apparently considerably higher in Japan than the United States. This is to be expected, since a large number of those imprisoned in Japan compared to the United States are repeat offenders (Bayley, 1976: 140–1).

The Japanese experience also confirms a growing literature on the importance of acknowledgment of guilt and restitution of victims to the psychological rehabilitation of offenders and attitudes of victims toward the offender and the criminal justice system.[5] Studies by Elaine Walster, Ellen Berscheid, and G. William Walster (1967,

1970, 1973) seem especially noteworthy for evaluating the Japanese approach (Macauley and Walster, 1971). They and others (Sykes and Matza, 1957) have found that offenders attempt to relieve distress experienced after committing a crime involving harm to others by justification, derogating the victim and denying responsibility, or restitution. Consequently, there is considerable empirical support for the notion that encouraging remorse and restitution does tend to reduce recidivism.

An arguable added benefit of the Japanese approach is that the emphasis on victim compensation and pardon reduces societal demands for revenge and retribution and thus facilitates efforts by law enforcement authorities to provide effective means for offender rehabilitation. In other words, societal demands for punishment as retribution are reduced and the authorities are then able to respond with greater leniency. Albeit sparse, empirical evidence on victim participation in the legal process in the United States and Canada indicates that victims who have some voice in the process are not only more satisfied with the process itself (Goldstein, 1982) but also, if negotiated restitution is attempted, may be less inclined to view whatever penalty imposed as inadequate. This would also explain why the Japanese are more tolerant of leniency and are more willing to accept whatever punishment the law prescribes (Hamilton and Sanders, 1985).

It is at least arguable therefore that the Japanese second track contributes a process of positive reinforcement in which rehabilitation is more likely both to succeed and to be a more socially acceptable and politically feasible objective. In conclusion, the Japanese leitmotif of confession, repentance, and absolution may provide insights for other industrial societies seeking to establish a more humane and just system of criminal justice, one free from the human and economic costs of overcrowded prisons, increasing crime, and victim alienation. To repeat, it deserves a careful look.

Notes

1 One example is the inquest of prosecution or prosecution review commission (*kensatsu shinsakai*). Established during the Occupation, under the Inquest of Prosecution Law (*Kensatsu shinsakai hō*), Law no. 147 (1948), inquests of prosecution were designed to control the exercise of prosecutorial discretion by means of citizen advisory groups in each district (described with additional references in George, 1984: 64–5). Not mentioned in published accounts of the institution is the contribution of Thomas L. Blakemore, who as a member of the staff of the Law and Courts Division of the Government Section of the Supreme Commander of the Allied Powers (SCAP), devised the institution in order to prevent the imposition of an American-style grand jury system by insistent superiors in the Government Section (comments by Blakemore to author).

2 Code of Criminal Procedure (*Keiji soshō hō*), Law no. 131 (1984), articles 461–70, provide for simplified proceedings by summary courts (*kan'i saibansho*) upon request by the prosecutor (art. 462), and acquiescence in writing by the accused (art. 461–2). Article 7(3) of the Penal Fine Temporary Special Measures Law (*Bakkin tō rinji sochi hō*), law no. 251 (1947), as amended through Law no. 61 (1972), increased the maximum fine from 5,000 yen to 200,000 yen.

3 The 570 summary courts in Japan generally lack jurisdiction over any cases involving an offence not subject to a penal fine at least as an optional penalty: Court Organization Law (*Saibansho hō*), Law 59 (1947), art. 33(2)(i). Excluded from summary proceedings are such serious offences as homicide, burglary, robbery, rape, fraud, and extortion. Summary courts do have express jurisdiction over cases involving habitual gambling, larceny, embezzlement, and accepting or selling stolen property, and authority to impose a sentence of up to three years imprisonment with forced labor in these and certain other special offences under special statutes (Court Organization Law, art. 33(2)(ii)).

As B.J. George notes, similar simplified procedures in which no defence is made are also available under articles 291–2 of the Code of Criminal Procedure in cases favouring offences for which the statutory penalty does not exceed a prison term of one year or less (1984: 57, n. 146). However, in Table 13.1 such cases are included under the 'Formal trial' category. Consequently the number of non-contested cases allowed by the prosecutor in which the penalty is relatively minor is even greater than indicated in Table 13.1.

4 Frase (1980) estimates that US attorneys prosecute 20 to 25 per cent of all new criminal cases; a rate, he believes, considerably lower than state prosecutions. He indicates that, aside from consideration of the convictability of the accused or the availability of a more appropriate means of prosecution, such as state prosecution or civil or administrative proceedings, the decision not to prosecute is based on either the gravity of the offence or such personal characteristics of the accused as age and prior record (Frase, 1980: 264). Apparently neither the attitude of the accused nor the response of the victim is taken into account.

5 I am indebted to Ann Marie Neugebauer, a University of Washington Law graduate, for introducing me to these materials. Ms Neugebauer has been engaged in research on Victim/Offender Reconciliation Programs in an effort to test the hypothesis set out here.

References

Abe, Haruo (1963) 'The accused and society: therapeutic and preventive aspects of criminal justice in Japan', in A. von Mehren (ed.), *Law in Japan: The Legal Order in a Changing Society*. Cambridge: Harvard University Press. pp. 324–63.

Ames, Walter L. (1981) *Police and Community in Japan*. Berkeley: University of California Press.

Appleton, Richard B. (1949) 'Reforms in Japanese criminal procedure under allied occupation', *Washington Law Review*, 24 (4): 491–530.

Bayley, David H. (1976) *Forces of Order: Police Behavior in Japan and the United States*. Berkeley: University of California Press.

Citizen's Crime Commission of Philadelphia (1975) *Tokyo: One City where Crime doesn't Pay*. Philadelphia.

Ch'en, Paul Heng-chao (1979) *Chinese Legal Tradition under the Mongols: The Code of 1291 as Reconstructed*. Princeton: Princeton University Press.

210   *John O. Haley*

Cohen, Jerome Alan (1968) *The Criminal Process in the People's Republic of China: An Introduction.* Cambridge, Mass.: Harvard University Press.

Dando, Shigemitsu (1965) *Japanese Criminal Procedure.* South Hackensack, NJ: Fred B. Rothman (trans. B.J. George).

Dando, Shigemitsu (1970) 'System of discretionary prosecution in Japan', *American Journal of Comparative Law*, 18 (2): 518–31.

Frase, Richard S. (1980) 'The decision to file criminal charges: a quantitative study of prosecutorial discretion', *University of Chicago Law Review*, 47 (2): 246–309.

George, B.J. (1984) 'Discretionary authority of public prosecutors in Japan', *Law in Japan: An Annual*, 17: 42–72.

Goldstein, Abraham S. (1982) 'Refining the role of the victim in criminal prosecution', *Mississippi Law Journal*, 52 (3): 515–61.

Haley, John O. (1982) 'Sheathing the sword of justice in Japan: an essay on law without sanctions', *Journal of Japanese Studies*, 8 (2): 265–81.

Haley, John O. (1986) 'Comment: implications of apology', *Law and Society Review*, 20 (4): 499–507.

Hamilton, V. Lee and Joseph Sanders (1985) 'Accountability, punishment and the self in Japan and the U.S.', unpublished paper delivered at the annual meeting of the Law and Society Association, San Diego.

Hulsewé, A.F.P. (1955) *Remnants of the Han Code.* Leiden: Brill. vol. 1.

Igarashi, Futaba (1977) 'Daiyō kangoku mondai ni tsuite' (Concerning the problem of substitute jails), *Jurisuto*, 637: 116–25.

Igarashi, Futaba (1980) 'Nase 'keiji ryūchijō'ga hitsuyō ka' (Why are 'criminal detention centers' necessary?), *Jurisuto*, 712: 85–91.

Igarashi, Futaba (1984) 'Crime, confession and control in contemporary Japan', *Law in Context*, 2: 1–30 (introduced and trans. by G. McCormick).

Johnson, Chalmers (1972) *Conspiracy at Matsukawa.* Berkeley: University of California Press.

Johnson, Wallace (1979) *The T'ang Code: General Principles.* Princeton: Princeton University Press. vol. 1.

Kawada, Katsuo (*c.* 1978) 'Suspension of prosecution in Japan', unpublished paper prepared for UNAFEI program, Tokyo.

Koshi, George M. (1970) *The Japanese Legal Advisor: Crimes and Punishments.* Rutland and Tokyo: Charles E. Tuttle.

Macauley, Stewart and Elaine Walster (1971) 'Legal structures and restoring equity', *Journal of Social Issues*, 27 (2): 173–95.

Meyers, Howard (1950) 'Revisions of the criminal code of Japan during the occupation', *Washington Law Review*, 25 (1): 104–34.

Ministry of Justice of Japan (Hōemsho) (1977) *Summary of 1977 White Paper on Crime.* Tokyo.

Ministry of Justice of Japan (1983) *Hōmu neuken shōwa 58 nen* (*Yearbook on Administration of Justice 1983*). Tokyo.

Miyazawa, Koichi (ed.) (1970) *Hanzai to higaisha: Nihon no higaishagaku* (Crime and victims: study of victims in Japan). Tokyo: Seibundō.

Nagashima, Atsushi (1963) 'The accused and society: the administration of criminal justice in Japan', in A. von Mehren (ed.), *Law in Japan: The Legal Order in a Changing Society.* Cambridge, Mass.: Harvard University Press. pp. 297–323.

National Police Agency (Keisatsu cho) (1979), *Hanzai tokei shōwa 54 nen* (Crime statistics 1979). Tokyo.

National Police Agency (1985) *Keisatsu hakusho shōwa 60 nen* (*Police white paper, 1985*). Tokyo.

Ōyama, Katsuyoshi (*c.* 1978) 'Criminal justice in Japan IV', unpublished paper prepared for UNAFEI program, Tokyo.

Parker, Craig J. (1984) *The Japanese Police System Today: An American Perspective.* Tokyo: Kodansha International.

Shiga, Shūzō (1974) 'Criminal procedure in the Ch'ing Dynasty', in *Memoirs of the Research Department of the Toyo Bunko*. Tokyo. pp. 1–138.

Shikita, Minoru (1982) 'Integrated approach to effective administration of criminal and juvenile justice', in *Criminal Justice in Asia: The Quest for an Integrated Approach*. Tokyo: UNAFEI. pp. 32–49.

Supreme Court of Japan (1977) *Outline of Criminal Justice in Japan*. Tokyo.

Supreme Court of Japan General Secretariat (Saikō Saibansho Jimu Sō-kyoku) (1984) *Shōwa 59 nen shihō tōkei nenpō: 2 keijihen* (*1984 judicial statistics annual report: vol. 2, criminal cases*). Tokyo.

Sykes, G.M. and D. Matza (1957) 'Techniques of neutralization: a theory of delinquency', *American Sociological Review*, 22 (6): 664–70.

Walster, E. and E. Berscheid (1967) 'When does a harm-doer compensate a victim?', *Journal of Personality and Social Psychology*, 6 (4): 435–41.

Walster, E., E. Berscheid and G.W. Walster (1970) 'The exploited: justice or justification?', in J.P. Macaulay and C. Berkowitz (eds), *Altruism and Helping Behavior*. New York: Academic Press. pp. 179–204.

Walster, E., E. Berscheid and G.W. Walster (1973) 'New directions in equity research', *Journal of Personality and Social Psychology*, 25 (2): 151–76.

14

Reparation for Retributivists

David Watson, Jacky Boucherat
and Gwynn Davis

In 1985–7 we conducted a review of some new initiatives in criminal justice in England and Wales (Davis et al., 1987). The experimental projects we studied were all attempting to promote reparation from offender to victim, although this was not necessarily their core activity. This objective was pursued within, or in conjunction with, a system of criminal justice which is strongly, though not exclusively, retributive in character. Schemes had not responded consistently to this environment and we suspected that this was in part due to the theoretical foundations for reparation not having been sufficiently articulated or understood.

In this chapter we examine the extent to which reparative considerations might be accommodated within a retributive criminal justice system. It will be our contention that efforts to promote reparative justice might be much more effective, and ambitious, than is currently the case. We also review the appropriate status for *mediated* agreements on reparation.

In the course of our discussion we shall comment on the scope for reparation given a *utilitarian* view of criminal justice, in which it is held that what justifies punishment is its effectiveness in achieving reform or deterrence (Acton, 1969). These sections of our discussion have particular relevance for those mediation schemes which are concerned above all to promote offender attitude change.

We begin with a brief description of the thirty or so mediation and reparation schemes included in our study. Many of these were at a very early stage and several have since changed their priorities and mode of operation. Some have folded altogether; others, such as Coventry, have gained further financial support and are continuing to expand (see Ruddick, this volume).

It was clear that the various schemes pursued a range of objectives, and that for some, 'reparation' was a minor part of their activity and one that was, on occasion, viewed with scepticism. This

applied particularly to those schemes working with juvenile
offenders, notably the Northamptonshire Juvenile Liaison Bureaux
and the Exeter Youth Support Team (see Veevers, this volume).
These multi-agency panels were expected to advise on prosecution decisions, and their over-riding objective was to keep
young offenders out of court. 'Reparation' was one means of
achieving this and was employed as an enhancement of a police
caution in cases where the offender appeared at serious risk of
prosecution.

Court-based schemes dealt mainly with adult offenders and were
generally linked to the magistrates court. The Leeds scheme was an
exception in that it was specifically geared to high tariff offenders.
Most of these schemes were run by the probation service, with much
of the work-load being carried by accredited volunteers. With the
exception of Leeds, Coventry, and Wolverhampton, all funded by
the Home Office for an experimental two-year period, only two
schemes (Rochdale and South Yorkshire) had any full-time, paid
members of staff. As a counterpart to pre-court schemes' pursuit of
'diversion', court-based reparation schemes had a mitigatory intent,
although most would deny that this was their first priority. They also
hoped that meeting the victim and discovering what the offence had
meant to them would induce learning and attitude change in
previously indifferent offenders.

Both pre-prosecution and court-based schemes suggested that
victims would also benefit from mediation in that a meeting with the
offender would enable them to challenge stereotypes and overcome
some of the hurt, anger, and fear arising from the offence.
However, the method of selecting cases and the clear focus on the
offender's pending (or threatened) court appearance suggested that
victim needs were in fact secondary.

Selection of cases for mediation was largely determined by the
point on the tariff at which these schemes were operating. The most
common offences were theft, assault, criminal damage, and (more
occasionally) burglary. 'Reparation' might be attempted by means
of a written apology, or through a face-to-face meeting. There
appeared to be very little interest in promoting material reparation,
and many schemes asserted that victims did not want this.

Having given this summary of the kind of mediation and
reparation schemes currently operating in the UK, we now turn to
brief descriptions of 'retributive' and 'reparative' justice. In each
case, more than one account is available in the literature and in
popular usage. In the case of retributive justice, we present an
account which is widely thought to be plausible; in the case of
reparative justice, we argue to establish a conception.

Retribution

Retributivists offer an account of what justifies punishment: they take the view that guilt is both a necessary and a sufficient condition. In order for punishment to be justly imposed, the offender must not only be responsible for an offence, in the sense of having caused it to happen; he or she must also be worthy of blame. At the heart of this conception of justice there lies a belief in the value of personal autonomy. This is interpreted, in modern versions, along individualist lines. For the purposes of a system of criminal justice, we are thought of as members of a moral community which operates within a framework of rights and responsibilities. This framework acknowledges the right of persons to live their own lives, as they wish, provided they do not violate the corresponding right of others (Nozick, 1984: 381).

The work of Immanuel Kant provides us with one answer to the question: why is retribution just? Kant's writings on this subject have been used to develop a distinction between just and unjust enrichment. A summary of his argument is as follows. Through crime, offenders place themselves above others who have obeyed the law, as well as above their victims from whom they have taken certain goods. Not only is it right and fair that offenders be made to disgorge the profits of the crime to the victims, in whatever form, but it is also fitting that offenders be made to pay a price for the undeserved privilege of committing an act against the code. By suffering punishment, they are returned to a place of equality with others (McAnany, 1978; see also Murphy, 1972).

As is apparent from the above account, offences against the person hardly constitute unjust enrichment, but they might be seen as enjoyment of the undeserved privilege of committing an act against the public code, and so to warrant retribution for that reason. It is important to note that this Kantian defence of retribution derives from the same root metaphor as may be employed to support a view of justice expressed in reparative terms. The image presented in each case is that of *justice as balance*.

The individualism which lies at the heart of this view of justice has been under severe academic challenge in recent years (Lukes, 1973), but its influence in social institutions remains strong. The value placed on individual autonomy leads retributivists to regard justice as the imposition of punishment *proportionate to the seriousness of the offence*. Secondly, and again because individual autonomy is valued, offences are ranked as more or less serious *according to the degree to which they reduce the autonomy of others*. Needless to say, this is not a matter which it is always easy to establish.

Belief in the moral significance of individual autonomy pre-supposes individual human beings capable of regulating their own behaviour in accordance with self-imposed standards. Embodying those standards in a system of criminal justice implies that they are shared by other community members. However, there inevitably arises the possibility of a clash between the individual's self-imposed standards and those standards which are required by law. In these circumstances punishment may be viewed as a form of communic-ation, asserting public standards and expressing condemnation of the act in breach. Such communication tends to be one-way. It might, perhaps, be achieved by words alone, but words may be thought an insufficiently powerful form of communication, given the seriousness of the offence.

Where punishment is imposed as a form of communication, retributive justice requires that the suffering be in proportion to that seriousness, although utilitarians might hold that the suffering should reflect the offender's willingness to absorb the message, or the willingness of other potential offenders to be influenced by it. This is relevant to later discussion of what influence an act of reparation might have on the retribution imposed: it seems to us that there are very few 'pure' retributivists around; most will seek to justify punishment, at least in part, on utilitarian grounds; and for the utilitarian, just as much as for practitioners within some 'reparation' schemes, an important objective is to secure the reform of the offender.

Whether or not one wishes to employ these utilitarian consider-ations, it should be recognized that breaches of criminal law will, in all cases of offences against the person, and in many cases of offences against property, also cause suffering to (or restrict the autonomy of) an individual victim. From this point of view, the form of retributive justice imposed by our criminal courts is often unsatisfactorily restricted. The wrong done is conceived as only a breach of public law, and not as wrong also done to an individual victim. The act for which the offender is accountable is described in a way which captures only a part of what was done. Legislation has recently widened opportunities to put this right, at least in those cases where financial compensation to the victim is a realistic possibility.[1]

Reparation

Compensation aims to make amends for harm suffered. It may take a variety of forms and come from a variety of sources (Davis et al., 1987: 6–9). We shall restrict the term 'reparation' to compensation which is provided for the victim *by the offender*. This need not take a material form. Where an offender has the capacity to compensate his or her victim, the offender is under an obligation to make reparation. This obligation is independent of whether or not, in that particular case, retribution, or the utilitarian projects of reform or deterrence, are also thought to be justified. A full defence of this position can be found in MacCormick (1978), but briefly:

> The justifying ground of obligations of reparation, from a moral point of view, is that individuals have as a matter of principle a right to reasonable security in their persons and possessions, and accordingly a right to be compensated when that reasonable security is infringed. (MacCormick, 1978: 177)

It follows that a person has a right of reparation even if the infringement of reasonable security is accidental and not negligent. In these circumstances, of course, retribution would be out of place, because the infringement is not blameworthy, just as it would be inappropriate to pursue reform or deterrence, given that the infringement is not the outcome of bad character or attitudes. But, as a matter of strict liability, reparation is required even when there is no blame.

The obligation to make reparation, and the corresponding right, fall upon offender and victim respectively and upon no one else. Each is attributed as a matter of reparative justice, and it is implied that this is in turn a species of *distributive* justice.

We shall in due course consider what impact reparation undertaken by an offender might properly have upon retribution imposed. But it is worth noting at this point that there is a close correspondence between MacCormick's justification of an independent right to reparation and the framework of rights from which Nozick derives his defence of retribution (1984: 381). The same individualist values which underpin the Nozick arguments lie at the heart of this view of reparation as a species of distributive justice.

On our usage, the term 'reparation' is restricted to what many schemes term *direct* reparation, thus excluding those forms of making amends which involve one offender making good the loss or damage arising from *another* offender's actions. Examples of the latter might include mending the locks of victims of other burglars, or engaging in mediated discussion with those victims. We are reluctant to describe these activities as any kind of reparation because, on so wide a definition, an obligation to make reparation cannot be said to arise from having done the harm in question. If the offender has done no harm to that victim, he or she can hardly be under a personal obligation to make reparation, and the victim can have no corresponding right against that offender, even if he or she has done harm, and harm of a similar kind, to someone else.

Of course, an offender might *make amends* to a victim of someone else's action. We would prefer to describe this as compensation of a non-reparative kind, which anyone might provide out of benevolence, or in acknowledging an obligation in citizenship. An offender might also provide such compensation in order to communicate attitude change, but we shall return to this in discussing the place for apology.

We also exclude from our definition of 'reparation' activities such as community service. Whatever its other merits, community service is 'reparative' only in the sense of suggesting possible attitude change on the part of the offender, thereby, it might be thought, allaying anxiety about future offending. Forms of community service which are undertaken without pressure or inducement may well be persuasive in this regard, but community service ordered by a court will inevitably be less so.

We now turn to a key feature of the kind of event which typically gives rise to thought of reparation: that is, the harm done is never confined to damage to a person's body or property, or to their state of mind; it also involves damage to a social and moral relationship, however tenuous. This arises because victim and offender are related in the sense that they are both citizens, presumed to be law-abiding, in a society in which the victim is acknowledged to have rights in his or her person or possessions. The offence gives the victim good reason for fear for his or her rights in future. Except where the event was accidental and non-negligent, the offender's action implies lack of concern for, perhaps even denial of, the victim's rights. So 'reparation' cannot be solely material; if it is to be adequate, it must include some attempt to make amends for the victim's loss of the presumption of security. The offence has undermined the victim's belief in the existence of moral standards held in common. This means that it has threatened his or her moral relationship with the offender by providing grounds for review of mutual obligations based on trust. The presumption of security and of common values can only be restored by some effort to reassure the victim that his or her rights are now respected; in other words, by some sign of attitude change – or, alternatively, some indication that the offence was 'out of character'.

This point is crucial for discussion of the relationship between reparation and a retributive criminal justice system. We can now see that one component in complete reparation cannot be coerced. Trust that the appropriate moral standards are shared by the offender cannot be restored by a court order requiring the offender to share those standards. If the victim is to be reassured, he or she must believe that the attitude in question is freely expressed. Even then, the victim may reflect that sincere assertion is not always followed by a change in behaviour; given the problems faced by some offenders, further criminal acts need not reflect bad faith.

An apology is the most common expression of remorse in our society. Of course, such an act makes no contribution to the return, repair, or replacement of property, nor does it mend broken bones. Where damage of these kinds has been suffered, an apology, even a sincere apology, followed by behaviour indicating respect for the victim's rights, is incomplete reparation and less than the victim deserves. Even so, such an apology may still be of value to the victim, and in some cases, perhaps those in which victim and offender know one another well, it may be of greater value than the reparation left undone. However, we might add that in a context in which restitution is feasible for the offender, but remains undone, it is difficult to see how an apology could be thought sincere. In the latter case, we imagine, trust would not be restored, nor reconciliation achieved.

The fact that, for whatever reason, even a sincere apology is not always followed by the appropriate change in behaviour has driven some to insist that any other component in reparation which might be fulfilled, must be fulfilled. This is indeed what the victim deserves, but even these additional efforts do not conclusively demonstrate attitude change. Restitution, just as much as an apology, may be made only to avoid a more unpleasant fate, with no intention to respect the victim's rights in future. On the other hand, we should note that restitution made under a court order might be made willingly, where the offender is genuinely remorseful. Of course, in the circumstances of a court appearance, such willingness might be difficult to demonstrate, although not necessarily impossible.

One further point on apology: some reparation schemes refer to it as 'symbolic reparation', apparently because it is thought not to be a component in 'real' reparation, or else to be an inferior component. On our account, provided an apology signifies appropriate attitude change, then it is an actual (not a symbolic) component in reparation. It is different in kind from restitution, but not inferior.

With regard to repair of the moral breach between victim and offender, it should be noted that the relationship to be repaired need be no more extensive than that between one citizen and another under public laws. There need have been no personal relationship between the parties. We might therefore distinguish between: (a) that component in reparation which constitutes restoration of trust in a fellow citizen; and (b) restoration of a pre-existing personal relationship. The latter might be termed 'reconciliation'. In fact, some schemes call both outcomes 'reconciliation', but the difference is significant.

Related to the above point, the social value of an offender's changed attitude is underestimated if it is presented as a change towards the victim personally. It may indeed be as limited as this in a few cases, but that would be disappointing. The rights infringed are possessed by all persons in a particular category. The reparation which reassures the individual victim should also reassure others who possess the same rights – say, in relation to an offence of 'taking and driving away', all owners of a motor vehicle.

This element in reparation bears on the objective (cited by some mediation schemes) of restoring trust between the offender and the community. 'Reassurance' has a broad reach: it provides ground for accepting the offender once more as a trustworthy member of the community, with neither additional responsibilities, nor fewer rights. This is one reason why an individual victim should not have the authority to decide the extent of his or her 'own' offender's obligation to make reparation. The rights threatened are held in common with other citizens, which means that we are all (through the courts) entitled to a voice in that decision.

The proposal that the particular victim should have authority to decide the extent of reparation is sometimes opposed through fear that he or she will have an idiosyncratic view, either too lenient or too harsh in relation to prevailing norms. Against this, it is argued that victims' judgements to date are usually consistent with (or perhaps less punitive than) standards prevailing in our society (Shapland, 1984: 131 ff.). It is indeed important to ensure comparative justice, but there is a further important point of principle, which is that other right-holders are also threatened and should therefore have a voice in determining what ought to reassure.

At the same time, we should not forget that the individual victim experiences something more than this shared harm. It is not enough to say that the offender has transgressed shared social norms; he or she will also have harmed the individual victim in ways not shared by other citizens. It is this fact which invites the conclusion that reparation to the individual victim should form one element in the justice delivered by our courts. What is more, this reparative element cannot easily be determined without reference to the victim. We shall discuss *mediated* reparation in due course, but it is worth noting here that one justification for it is that it opens up the possibility of victim and offender arriving at a form of reparation which reflects the particular circumstances of 'their' case – including, where appropriate, some reference to understandings developed in the course of a prior personal relationship. It is also worth noting that such a procedure is not tantamount to licence. The discretion which might be granted to victim and offender in mediated reparation does not liberate them from public standards of 'rationality, fairness and effectiveness' (Dworkin, 1977: 33). There has to be some limit to the factors deemed relevant: for example, the victim's mother having died shortly prior to the offence is *not* a good reason for requiring additional reparation of the offender, any more than it would be a good reason for imposing additional punishment under a purely retributive system.

Reparation within retribution

We shall now review the scope for incorporating a reparative element within, or otherwise in conjunction with, a retributive system of criminal justice. First, a summary of hopeful signs gleaned from our discussion so far.

1   Both retributive and reparative justice, as described, are species of distributive justice, and both are generally proposed in a form which acknowledges the moral significance of individual autonomy. Both seek to restore the distribution of rights which existed before the offence, so far as this is possible.
2   Current conceptions of retributive justice could be developed in order to acknowledge, more consistently and with greater prominence than at present, that the offences in question also involve wrong done to a victim, for which the offender is also accountable.
3   Reparative justice requires, along with attention to the victim's due, attention to that element in an offence which constitutes a threat to the rights of fellow citizens.

We have also noted one point which suggests that there may be some limit to the accommodation which might be feasible between reparation and any system of criminal justice. This is simply that complete reparation cannot be achieved by means of a court sentence, because trustworthiness cannot be coerced.

Let us now consider the scope for reparative justice within a retributive system, and begin by showing that such an accommodation need not imply either 'net widening' or 'double punishment'.

Reparative justice imposed within a retributive system of criminal justice cannot lead to net widening, in the sense of requiring reparation of individuals *thought likely* to commit, or to have committed, a criminal offence. This is because the court will continue to require a finding of guilt before imposing any penalty on the offender. Equally, reparation which is agreed in a process outside the system of criminal justice cannot lead to net widening in the sense given, because reparation is not *required*. The net of coercion does not spread that far, although, faced with what he or she believes to be the threat of prosecution, the offender may mistake its reach.

Nor can reparation imposed within a retributive system of criminal justice lead to double punishment, in the sense of exacting retribution twice for the same offence. Given that the offence is now seen to include the harm done to the victim, proportionate retribution must be judged in a new way, although it must be recognized that renewed attention to the harm done to the victim might have the effect of increasing overall retribution, if the same incident came to be viewed in a more serious light. This fear has led some mediation schemes, in their reports to court, to emphasize the costs to the offender of the reparation undertaken. It is hoped that this will be taken into account in order that the overall response (in and out of court) remains in proportion to the gravity of the offence, viewed in all its aspects.

It is possible to argue that if the costs of reparation are in proportion to the harm suffered by the victim, there is no reason why any overall proportionality should be put at risk. But in fact, schemes have implicitly joined forces with those who regard the present levels of retribution imposed by courts as too high. Their view would appear to be that just as harm to the individual victim has not been taken seriously enough, so the breaking of a public law generally attracts a penalty that is too great.

As a result of practitioners' fears that an order for reparation may contribute to 'double punishment' of the offender, the rights of victims are currently neglected in the practice of most mediation schemes. Concern lest the offender suffer out of proportion to his or her offence has led some schemes, as a matter of policy, to discourage reparation by first-time offenders. Others have very restrictive offence categories for which they deem reparation to be appropriate. Courts for their part may only be prepared to contemplate reparation in relation to minor offences, or where the offender does not have a long criminal history. Such policies deny relief to victims, making justice as far as they are concerned conditional upon the nature of the offence, or upon the criminal history of the offender. Paradoxically, the more serious the offence, the less interest there appears to be in promoting any measure of reparation to the victim.

We turn now to a discussion of the appropriate impact which

reparation might have on retribution, considering first those reparation agreements arrived at independently of the court. Should meetings between victim and offender and any reparation agreement which follows be permitted to influence the sentence of the court? We think that they should because, on an expanded view of the offence as including wrong done to the victim, justice for the offender (let alone the victim) requires that these matters be given weight. When the wrong to the victim has been put right, in full or in part, the court's sentence, if it is to ensure a proportionate response to the offence as a whole, must reflect that fact. Any compensation order must incorporate the reparation previously agreed, or it must be less than would otherwise have been imposed.

Further, this mediated reparation might justify modification of retribution related to public aspects of the offence. When reparation is thought to indicate renewed respect for other people's rights, the fears of other right-holders should be eased. Part of the public harm is thus put right. It is this insight, we presume, which has encouraged mediation schemes in the belief that reparation agreements negotiated through them should contribute to *diversion* of the offender, either from prosecution entirely, or from a custodial penalty.

However, there are grounds here for caution. Where 'diversion' is a justified response to reparation, it can also become the offender's motive for participating in the negotiation and for agreeing to make reparation. This weakens the basis for our belief that the offender's attitude has changed for the better; the fears of the victim and of other right-holders may have been set aside prematurely.

In addition, we may distinguish between offender-orientated schemes which encourage voluntary (although self-interested) reparation in order that the offender might suffer reduced retribution, and those comparatively few schemes which are concerned to promote the interests of the victim as much as, if not more than, those of the offender. The advantage of voluntary reparation is its contribution to justified restoration of trust. Given the relationship between mediation schemes and the courts, this contribution is seen to be of variable quality, requiring us to consider other details which might clarify the offender's motivation. We can hardly deal with this by denying the offender access to the information that reparation made is likely to reduce the level of retribution imposed by a court. That would be both impracticable and a very paternalistic approach to adopt towards an offender who is supposed to come to share our moral values, including our commitment to individual autonomy.

Still, we must keep this difficulty in perspective. First, any elements in reparation, such as returning property, which *are* made, even when the motive is self-interested, should be taken into account by a court when contemplating the level of retribution to be imposed. This is because such reparation may well have involved *costs* to the offender. One way to encourage pre-sentence reparation would be routinely to ask (or require) courts to adjourn their proceedings in order to permit mediation schemes to explore the possibility of reparation, and, where this was feasible, to give offenders time to undertake it. The Dunpark Committee on Reparation (Dunpark, 1977: 4.05) feared 'that this procedure would be so time-consuming as to impede the administration of criminal justice to an unacceptable extent', although they would tolerate 'its selective use for cases in which the offender appears to have the means and the will to pay'.

Several mediation schemes appear to wish to go further than this, suggesting that, in some cases at least, the court's penalty might be reduced immediately, on the strength of an *undertaking* to make reparation. In that case, of course, some undertakings might not be honoured, in which case the victim would have been denied reparative justice, and have no redress. Victims might be justifiably cautious about any proposal that they should entrust their hopes of reparation to mediation schemes' assessment of the conscientiousness of offenders. Schemes may be expected to press too hard when they are concerned to protect offenders from conventional levels of court-imposed compensation or other retribution which they regard as too harsh.

Given that voluntary reparation should influence orders made by the court, in order that proportionality be maintained, what influence should reparation which is ordered by the court have upon the level of retribution which is imposed by that same court? The short answer is that both elements of the response (reparative and retributive) should be in proportion to the respective harms which the offender has done, providing reparation for the private and retribution for the public wrong. In practice, however, the situation is more complex. This is because, in the absence of any reparative elements, it may be supposed that the retribution imposed by courts is set at a level to take account of the missing component of repair of a private wrong. In other words, the court's penalty is in many cases too severe as a response to *the crime*, because that response, although it is expressed purely retributively, must also take account of (or 'stand for') the suffering of an individual victim. It follows therefore that, to the extent that an individual victim is separately compensated, this over-reaction on the part of courts to the 'public' element in the harm done ought, in the interests of overall proportionality, to cease.

We also recognize that, in certain circumstances, retribution may have to be put aside entirely, if reparative justice towards the victim is to be practicable. As previously noted, our present system of criminal justice gives priority to financial compensation over an appropriate fine where the offender lacks the means to pay both (Criminal Justice Act, 1982: section 67). If a citizen's right to reasonable security of person and possessions is to be restored, in the first instance, from the offender's resources rather than from public funds such as those allocated under our extremely limited Criminal Injuries Compensation scheme,[2] then courts should, whenever possible, give priority to reparation. We say 'whenever possible' because there may be occasions, particularly in relation to some very serious offences, where the scope for reparation is so limited that it would not justify the court's abandoning an appropriate level of retribution (say imprisonment) in order to permit some vestigial element of reparation to be performed. However, this should not be assumed: it is something that we, as researchers, should like to explore.

Mediation in a system of criminal justice

We have so far argued that reparation is an appropriate element within a broader conception of retributive justice, and that justice *ought* to combine both elements. We now turn to consider the status which might be granted to victim/offender mediated agreements on reparation: for example, should victim/offender agreements carry final authority in determining reparation due?

We follow Roberts (1983: 545) in using 'mediation' to describe a possible structure for the process of dispute resolution, namely, that in which there is 'the introduction of a third party who intervenes, in contrast to the partisan, from a position of at least apparent neutrality, with the purpose of helping the disputants towards an agreed outcome'. It is worth noting that this definition is non-committal on the matter of who initiates this third-party intervention. It could be the parties themselves, but it could be someone in authority, such as a judge.

Given that the term 'mediation' is used to describe a *structure* for decision-making, it cannot be reserved for negotiation which is geared to a particular *outcome*. The focus of the negotiation and the possible range of outcomes is in no way circumscribed by the term 'mediation' itself. However, in practice, the term is employed by some mediation schemes to refer to meetings geared towards a particular end, namely, restoration of trust (or 'reconciliation') between victim and offender, rather than material reparation.

Confusion is compounded by some schemes' attempt to distinguish material from non-material reparation by characterizing one as concerned with 'ends' and the other with 'process' (Davis et al., 1987: 5). This is not a distinction between ends and process, but a distinction between two different ends, both of which may need to be pursued in order to achieve complete reparation.

Schemes do not themselves claim that their mediated agreements should have the force of law; they acknowledge that only a court order should be legally binding upon the parties, and that a court may or may not choose to sanction a mediated reparation agreement. The same goes for those, like Nils Christie (1977), who are concerned as much with reform of court procedure as with changes in sentencing, believing that victim and offender should play a more active part in the proceedings. In fact, Christie clearly believes that these two things go together: if justice is to be viewed in reparative terms, greater victim and offender participation is an essential pre-requisite. He also suggests (1981) that if victims and offenders were to play a more active part in legal proceedings, this would contribute to an overall reduction in the level of 'pain' which is delivered to offenders. Courts would be better informed, and thus less punitive.

Christie's arguments remind us that final authority in determining the level of reparation due may be conceded to a court, and yet victim and offender contribute to that decision-making process (exerting influence upon it, rather than control over it) in ways which they are not permitted to do at present.

Let us ask *why* a victim and offender should contribute to decision-making on proposed reparation. After all, the obligation of reparation has been established by the finding (or admission) of guilt, and may therefore appear non-negotiable. This, however, would be a superficial view. The need to apply a particular 'crime' label, so that offending behaviour is described within a highly circumscribed range of legal categories, leads inevitably to an over-simplified and perhaps misleading account of what the offender has actually done. These labels are applied with only limited regard to motive or excuse, and rigorously exclude the possibility of an interactive element. The question then becomes not so much whether victim and offender should have a voice in determining reparation due, but whether they should be encouraged (or, as Christie would have it, required) to furnish the court with a more detailed account of the circumstances surrounding the offence. This would be almost bound to influence the court's assessment of the appropriate penalty, including any reparative element.

This brings us to a second reason why the offender, in particular, should contribute to a discussion of the offence, and thus exert some influence on the level of reparation which is proposed. When victim and offender, or indeed court and offender, are in dispute as to the moral significance of 'the crime', and the offender's view carries no weight, then he or she may be expected to resent reparation coerced, *and not to give that part which cannot be coerced.* (We might also suspect that the part which *can* be coerced is more likely to be delivered if the offender has been granted some voice in the proceedings. The level of non-payment of court-ordered compensation, for example, makes this a real consideration.)

A third reason for involving victim and offender is this: given that reparation is to come from the offender's own resources, he or she is well placed to help frame a realistic proposal; and given that 'reparation' is interpreted literally, which means that the victim is intended to benefit from it, he or she is the person best placed to indicate what actions on the part of the offender, if any, would achieve that end.

It should be clear from the above discussion that we are not proposing that victim and offender should have final authority to determine reparation due. To do so would be at odds with the principle of comparative social justice, which requires that like cases should be treated alike, and different cases differently. An elaborated conception of comparative justice expresses our moral standards; mediated decision-making by victim and offender cannot be granted final authority on reparation, because it need not conform to those standards.

Conclusion

Reparative justice is an infant failing to thrive on the margins of the criminal justice system in England and Wales. It is largely restricted to minor offences, or to disposals in which it might add to the repertoire of means used to achieve other purposes. So, for example, it is admitted that it might contribute to the reform of the offender by teaching him or her about the effects of the offence; or that it might restore a fragile but continuing relationship.

In our view, reparative justice is in part marginalized because we have a retributive criminal justice system which embodies an unjustifiably restricted conception of its remit. (The limited encouragement which courts have been given to order compensation or community service has done little to change this.) If retributivists were to acknowledge that a breach of public law is also wrong done to a victim, reparative justice might be achieved within a framework of retribution. This could be done through present and other forms of compensation order, and by giving reparation priority in all but those cases where 'the crime' is major, and the scope for reparation is found, after careful investigation, to be extremely limited.

When reparation is *voluntarily* made, it should, as a matter of retributive justice in relation to the offender, reduce or make unnecessary any court compensation order (unless, of course, the reparation agreement is incorporated in that order). It should also remind the court that the wrong done to the individual victim has been taken care of, so that the level of retribution imposed as a response to 'the crime' need not also reflect this.

We have reached no firm conclusion as to the contribution which mediation schemes might make to the achievement of offender/ victim reparation, except to say that in order to preserve comparative justice, reparation agreements should be regarded as no more than *proposals*, subject to review by the courts. As to the impact which these agreements might have on court sentencing, much depends on whether, in this context, you believe in a process of incremental change, with courts eventually coming to think reparatively through having experienced the 'drip, drip, drip' of mediation reports being handed in to them. A gloomy view would be that the marginalization of reparation is confirmed and perhaps even reinforced by the development of out-of-court schemes which, as far as we can observe, are treated with varying degrees of condescension by most legal personnel. It is doubtful whether this is the best way to change the practice of courts. Secondly, the pursuit of voluntary (and not self-interested) reparation, which would be the strength of a truly independent mediation scheme, tends to be undermined by the strenuous efforts which *are* made, by schemes themselves, to get courts to take account of whatever reparation has been achieved.

One consequence of this is that mediation schemes, whatever their practice in the course of the meetings which they arrange between victim and offender, are viewed by the court as contributing to the mitigation process. This is hardly surprising given that victims are seldom, if ever, present in court in order to give their account of whether or not a degree of reparation has in fact been achieved.

Notes

In preparing this chapter we have benefited greatly from discussion with our consultant, Adrian Thatcher, and with Ann Warren-Cox.

1 Section 67 of the Criminal Justice Act 1982 modifies section 35 of the Powers of Criminal Courts Act 1973, whereby courts were given power to make a compensa-

tion order in addition to punishing the offender in other ways. Under the 1982 Act, compensation may be imposed as a sole sanction. Where the offender has insufficient means to pay both fine and compensation, 'the court shall give priority to compensation' (see also Criminal Justice (Scotland) Act 1980, part IV).

2 Information about this scheme may be obtained from Criminal Injuries Compensation Board, Whittington House, 19 Alfred Place, London WC1E 7EA.

References

Acton, H.B. (ed.) (1969) *The Philosophy of Punishment*. London: Macmillan.
Christie, N. (1977) 'Conflicts as property', *British Journal of Criminology*, 17 (1): 1–15.
Christie, N. (1981) *Limits to Pain*. Oxford: Martin Robertson.
Davis, G., J. Boucherat and D. Watson (1987) *A Preliminary Study of Victim/Offender Mediation and Reparation Schemes in England and Wales*, Research and Planning Unit Paper 42. London: Home Office.
Dunpark, Lord (1977) *Reparation by the Offender to the Victim in Scotland* (Dunpark Report). Cmnd. 6802. Edinburgh: HMSO.
Dworkin, R. (1977) *Taking Rights Seriously*. London: Duckworth.
Lukes, S. (1973) *Individualism*. Oxford: Basil Blackwell.
MacCormick, D.N. (1978) 'The obligation of reparation', *Proceedings of the Aristotelian Society*, 78: 175–93.
McAnany, P.D. (1978) 'Restitution as idea and practice: the retributive prospect', in B. Galaway and J. Hudson (eds), *Offender Restitution in Theory and Action*. Lexington, Mass.: D.C. Heath. pp. 15–31.
Murphy, J.G. (1972) 'Kant's Theory of Criminal Punishment', in *Proceedings of The Third International Kant Congress*. Dordrecht: D. Reidel. pp. 434–41.
Nozick, R. (1984) *Philosophical Explanations*. Oxford: Clarendon Press.
Roberts, S. (1983) 'Mediation in family disputes', *Modern Law Review*, 46 (5): 537–57.
Shapland, J. (1984) 'Victims, the criminal justice system and compensation', *British Journal of Criminology*, 24: 131–49.

15

The Police Role

Maria R. Volpe

Interest in the study and use of alternative forms of dispute resolution (ADR), especially mediation, has been soaring since the early seventies.[1] For instance, educational institutions from elementary to postgraduate level, particularly law schools, have introduced mediation and related coursework (for examples see ABA, 1983; ABA, 1985; Crohn, 1985; Volpe, 1985; Sander, 1984). Hundreds of community-based dispute resolution programmes have been established throughout the country to handle a wide range of criminal and civil disputes that might otherwise have been sent to the courts (see ABA, 1986). These programmes typically use volunteers who are trained in negotiation, mediation, and, in some instances, arbitration.

Many states have passed legislation recommending, and in some instances requiring, the use of mediation as an alternative to litigation, such as in child custody cases in California (ABA, 1984). In New York State, for example, the criminal procedure law was amended in 1981 so that 'the court may grant an adjournment in contemplation of dismissal on condition that the defendant participate in dispute resolution and comply with any award or settlement resulting therefrom' (Chapter 847 of the Laws of 1981).[2]

On the national level, former Chief Justice Burger of the Supreme Court has strongly encouraged the use of arbitration and mediation (Burger, 1984); the American Bar Association created a Special Committee on Dispute Resolution in 1976; the National Institute for Dispute Resolution has been established as a major foundation; and Congress passed legislation in 1984 which created the United States Institute of Peace to advance the study of conflict resolution education, theory, and practice.

Of what significance are these and other ADR developments for the police in their handling of adult criminal or juvenile delinquency matters? Because the police are expected to handle a wide range of conflicts and are often the first to intervene in disputes, any changes in how disputes are processed by the criminal justice system will have an impact on their work.

Of all of the dispute resolution intervention processes gaining widespread popularity, acceptance, and even becoming a part of the system, mediation raises some of the most significant challenges and concerns for police officers. While the popularization of mediation is relatively new, the use of mediation by police is not. Yet the enormous role played by police in determining how situations involving criminal matters are defined, processed, and handled has not received much attention by students of the mediation process outside police circles (Folberg and Taylor, 1984; Palenski, 1984).

There are two major uses of mediation by police.[3] One involves using mediation skills and techniques as an intervention strategy when handling cases. The other is referring cases to dispute resolution centres. This chapter addresses the potential and problems posed by each of these uses of mediation by police.

Police use of mediation

Police conflict intervention occurs in a context unlike most other conflict intervention. Police usually enter conflict situations when the individuals involved are at the midst of their differences, disputants' reasoning abilities are low, emotions are high, and other people are present. Furthermore, while the police have been called to intervene and to make decisions they have full authority to make, they may also be distrusted, feared, and treated as unwanted intruders. Individuals who have sought out the assistance of police officers or find themselves the reluctant recipients of police intervention frequently try to undermine and sabotage their efforts. People's expectations of police are not always clear when they are handling conflict situations (Bittner, 1970; Niederhoffer and Blumberg, 1970; Lawson, 1977).

Mediation is an intervention process often referred to in police circles. Cox and Fitzgerald (1983: 86) note 'It seems best to view the police, not as officials who prevent community conflict but rather as mediators and managers of such intervention.' Mediation, however, may be a loosely used term in police work, often used interchangeably with giving advice or counselling, both of which are regarded by mediation specialists as quite different.

One of the historically most prominent and frequent uses of police mediation has been the family disturbance call. These calls are also very unpredictable, difficult, and potentially risky for police officers who may be drawn into the disagreement. Through Bard's efforts, among others, police departments throughout the United States have offered crisis intervention training for such calls (Bard,

1975). Rather than taking official action against the offender, police were given the option to defuse the situation and attempt an on-the-scene mediation.

In 1981–2 the relationship between mediation and police work was the subject of a study sponsored by the National Institute of Justice and conducted by the Police Foundation and the Minneapolis Police Department (Sherman and Berk, 1984a; 1984b). When called to misdemeanor-type domestic violence offences, participating officers were given colour-coded report forms specifying one of three responses: arrest, separating disputants for several hours, and mediation. A six-month follow-up survey cautiously concluded that arrest was the most effective intervention strategy in preventing future violence. As a result, numerous police departments have changed their policies to emphasize arrests and de-emphasize mediation for domestic violence.

While this study has had a chilling effect on police mediation, police are called to handle a wide range of other disputes that do not involve domestic violence and lend themselves to the use of mediation skills and techniques. This scenario of a conflict is offered by Klockars:

> I share a property line with my neighbor. About one foot to my side of the property line there stands my horticultural pride and joy: a 25-foot apple tree. (Needless to say, a small portion of this gorgeous tree graces my neighbor's yard.) Though the tree is mine and I am willing to share its bounty with my neighbor, he does not like apples. He likes still less the fact that my apples fall off, rot, and litter his yard. One day he gets fed up with my stinking apples and yells to me that he is going to cut down my tree unless I do. 'No way,' I say. He revs up his chain saw. (Klockars, 1985: 15)

What can a disputant involved in this kind of intervention do? Klockars suggests that in a democratic society one can (a) sue one's neighbour in civil court and attempt to recover damages some time in the distant future or (b) call the police to have them stop the neighbour from cutting down the apple tree. Since the police have the authority to use coercive force, Klockars remarks that 'they can tell my neighbor to stop and if he doesn't, they can use whatever force is necessary to stop him' (1985: 16).

What is evident is that two neighbours are upset with each other. Their threats and counter-threats have the potential to become a very serious matter. Typically, conflict between neighbours has a history, and exchanges between them start long before the police arrive. And, because they will probably continue to be neighbours, they will continue to have a relationship, even if tenuous, long after the police leave. Police intervention in such a situation is problematic. If a situation is not handled effectively, what started out as a routine police intervention may result in serious escalation. It could lead to charges of mishandling, a civilian complaint against the police officer, injuries to the parties and/or the police, feelings of helplessness and frustration by the police, or intervention which requires return appearances and possibly even protracted and embarrassing explanations by police officers to superiors and the public about their actions.

The routine occurrence of similar scenes from coast to coast raises an important question. Is there a place for the gentler arts of dispute resolution in law enforcement work? A simple response would be both yes and no. Yes, because there is potential for mediation. No, because there are problems. A more useful question, however, might be, 'Under what conditions is the use of mediation an appropriate intervention process for police?'

The police as mediator: potential

The potential of mediation for the police has yet to be fully tapped. While they are not in a position to conduct mediation under ideal conditions, mediation skills will enhance police officers' ability to listen carefully, communicate clearly and effectively with all parties as well as with partners, organize ideas logically in order to direct the flow of questioning, reason clearly and make sound judgements, and be alert to the implications of any action taken or questions asked. Mediation skills will also improve their ability to consider alternative courses of action, display resourcefulness and imagination, and establish satisfactory relationships with others by being self-confident, knowledgeable, amenable, decisive, but flexible. Furthermore, mediators know how to clarify underlying facts while keeping arguments and emotions within acceptable limits and to help the parties to save face and lay the groundwork for improved communication in the future.

The effective use of these skills and techniques enable police to defuse potentially difficult situations and demonstrate sensitivity and understanding toward disputants. By facilitating communication between the parties, especially where they have a continuing relationship, agreements may be reached without official legal action, thereby saving police from processing the cases and testifying in court.

Mediation and related skills are more likely to be routinely used in certain types of police work such as handling domestic violence matters or hostage negotiation efforts. Even the negotiator, who is an advocate for a particular side, must learn to intervene using specialized conflict communication skills. In some instances, police officers who intervene in situations involving matters other than family or hostage negotiations have also received mediation and related training as a result of some incident or unrest in the community that warranted police attention. In the Dayton, Ohio, police department, for instance, mediation skills were combined with conflict management skills to help officers on a conflict management team to intervene in particularly sensitive community situations which could have escalated into potentially violent and difficult confrontations. The team was involved in such matters at a labour-management dispute at a city hospital, a drag-racing problem involving teenagers, and landlord–tenant disputes (see Mayhall, 1984: 363–80).

Problems for the police as mediators

The nature of police work may make mediation difficult for police officers. Some of the problems experienced by police are similar to those confronted by mediators in virtually all settings; others are peculiar to police work.

As with other mediators, mediation may not work well when police are confronted with power disparities between disputants. Disputants subjected to instant mediation by police are not inclined to want to work cooperatively, which is a major problem given that mediation works best when the parties engage in the process voluntarily. Further, disputants may be deprived of their legal rights because they are not sent on to court.

For police the problems arising from mediation are compounded by the very nature of police work. Police officers are authorized to use coercive force and are expected to make relatively quick decisions. Although mediation is considered a short-term intervention process, when used in the context of police work it is still time-consuming. Mediators are expected to create a negotiating climate and to deal with substantive matters. In the process of making quick interventions police may impose a decision, which is anathema to mediation.

Furthermore, traditional police work is not organized to reward mediative intervention adequately. Police productivity is usually measured by the number of summonses issued or arrests effected. Take, for example, the case of officers patrolling an area where significant damage has occurred as a result of kids riding dirt bikes on a golf course. The club manager is angry about the ever-increasing damage to the golf course. One afternoon, two of the officers spot a youngster riding a dirt bike, bring him to the club manager's office and then call his parents. When the parents arrive, they express concern and would like to work things out with the club manager. The officers have a choice between taking official action and helping the parties reach an informal agreement. How can the officers' work be recognized if the latter option is chosen? This situation would become more complicated if only one of the officers had been trained in mediation and the other was not understanding or appreciative of the mediation process. The former could have difficulty explaining to his or her colleague why a youngster found red-handed should not be arrested.

Mediation is not very effective when intensive conflict exists (Rubin, 1980) because mediation requires the parties to participate in the negotiation process; this is difficult when their ability to think and communicate is impaired. Intense conflict is a frequent occurrence for police officers. Such conditions disrupt the officer's ability to handle the conflict and if he or she says the wrong thing, the dispute may even be intensified. Bard (1973: 4) notes that 'the incredibly complex role of mediation is anything but mundane and the consequences of incompetent third party intervention may be very serious.'

Mediation assumes that the participants are taking part voluntarily. If the parties do not choose to cooperate, mediation efforts will lose their effectiveness. Police typically interact with disputants who are not agreeing to mediate voluntarily. If disputants do not want to speak or participate in a collaborative problem-solving effort, the police officer does not have the time to try to engage them or enlist their cooperation.

Mediators are trained, neutral, and impartial third parties. Not all police officers will be skilful mediators, and mediation training for police officers has been limited. To complicate matters, police officers are often not seen as impartial and neutral. By virtue of their position, the police have authority to make decisions, to take sides, even to do so coercively. Mediators, on the other hand, are restricted from engaging in any decision-making or even hinting that they may be partial to any side. Finally, mediation is often seen as a soft, non-punitive approach. Police may see themselves as losing control and authority over individuals, or as being indecisive.

Dispute resolution centres as referrals

An increasingly available option for police is the referral of designated cases to dispute resolution centres instead of attempting to mediate cases themselves.[4] This partnership is attractive in the light of the scarce resources available to the criminal justice system.

Dispute resolution centres handle criminal cases that might otherwise be the subject of official police action in the form of summonses or arrests and subsequent court action. Cases sent to these centres are handled by others, usually volunteers, who are trained in mediation and in some instances arbitration (ABA 1986).

These programmes vary in their relationship to the official legal system. For most, the bulk of their cases come from official sources such as the police, prosecutors, and the courts, and the system's needs are uppermost. Others do not maintain any formal ties with the legal system and stress empowerment of the community (Wahrhaftig, 1982; Shonholtz, 1984; Tomasic and Feeley, 1982).

Using dispute resolution centres: potential
The potential of dispute resolution centres for the police has yet to be tapped. Overall, such centres can reduce the amount of time police spend on some disputes. In an article about the police use of a local dispute resolution centre, Schneider (1980: 51) has commented that 'the police have begun to realize the benefits and are referring incidents to the program, as a service to the citizens and to themselves. Every officer should check to see if such a program exists in his area, in hopes of preventing future crimes and recurring neighborhood disturbance calls.'

Mediation conducted by others may be more suitable, since the dispute resolution centre mediators do not have the coercive powers of the police. When the mediation is delayed until a hearing can be held at the dispute resolution centre, the disputants may cool off sufficiently to work through their differences more effectively. Furthermore, the mediation process is informal, private, and held behind closed doors, where the parties can save face in a structured setting. Police work may be reduced if individuals are able to work out their differences and not require repeat police calls. Further, police will not have to prepare cases for booking, court processing, or possible appeals, and the reduced police involvement may even enhance police–community relations.

Problems in using dispute resolution centres
Diverting cases to dispute resolution centres also poses numerous problems and challenges for police departments (Palenski, 1984). A major concern is in rewarding the police department for giving up cases. Police departments' budgets may reflect work-loads; police may have difficulty making a strong case for funding if a significant number of cases are handled by others and police productivity, as measured by arrests and summonses, appears reduced. There may

be little incentive for individual officers to divert a case to mediation unless a procedure is established to reward a diversion.

Finally, dispute resolution centres may not be available. Although widespread, they do not exist in all communities. When these programmes are established, creators need to be careful not to impose themselves on police departments. In their enthusiasm to develop new programmes, programme organizers should not overlook the importance of enlisting the support of the police.

Conclusion

Mediation is not new for the police. By its very nature, police work lends itself to the use of mediation. Police, who are constantly confronted by conflict, may use mediation skills to help guide its resolution. More recently, police in many jurisdictions have been able to refer designated cases to local dispute centres for community mediators to handle.

Several critical concerns are raised by the use of mediation by the police.

1   How can police best assess cases to be mediated in the short time-frame within which they must intervene and then move on?
2   How can the police be prepared to respond to different types of disputes requiring different mediation skills?
3   Can a process that works best informally and behind closed doors work as effectively when disputants are confronted in public, often with interested observers? Who should be included in the negotiations?
4   What provisions can be made to ensure compliance with a mediation agreement?
5   How can the police be rewarded for using the gentler arts of intervening in disputes?
6   How can partnerships between dispute resolution centres and police departments best be developed?

Mediation poses some important challenges for those in police work. For the first time, however, the widespread interest in mediation brings together police and non-police interveners. Each has much to learn from the other, particularly in identifying the potential as well as the problems confronted by those who share a common intervention process.

Notes

1 Other dispute resolution processes used in the United States include conciliation, the use of judges in non-traditional procedures, arbitration, a combination of
mediation and arbitration, an ombudsman, to name a few (see, e.g., Folberg and
Taylor, 1984; Marks et al. 1984; Moore, 1986; Goldberg et al., 1985).

2 The criminal procedure law was further amended in 1986 so that selected
felonies could be referred to dispute resolution centres (Chapter 837 of the Laws of
1986).

3 Other uses include, for example, acting as a disputant in a civilian complaint
process, as a negotiator for a job-related matter such as a contract or grievance issue,
in the role of victim in a post-conviction mediation programme, or as a mediator in a
community-based mediation programme.

4 For example, the New York City police department issued an operations order
on 19 May 1986 (No. 53) providing officers with the option of referring selected
interpersonal disputes under certain conditions to designated dispute resolution
centres, even where the dispute included the following misdemeanours and
violations: assault in the third degree; menacing; reckless endangerment in the
second degree; reckless endangerment of property; misapplication of property;
criminal mischief in the 4th degree; aggravated harassment in the second degree;
harassment; disorderly conduct; trespass; criminal trespass in the second and third
degrees.

References

ABA (American Bar Association) (1983). *Law School Directory*. Washington, DC:
ABA Special Committee on Dispute Resolution.
ABA (American Bar Association) (1984) *Legislation on Dispute Resolution*.
Washington, DC: ABA Special Committee on Dispute Resolution.
ABA (American Bar Association) (1985) *Mediation in the Schools: A Directory,
Report, Bibliography*. Washington, DC: ABA Special Committee on Dispute
Resolution.
ABA (American Bar Association) (1986) *Dispute Resolution Program Directory,
1986–1987*. Washington, DC: ABA Special Committee on Dispute Resolution.
Bard, M. (1973) *Family Crisis Intervention: From Concept to Implementation*.
Washington, DC: US Dept. of Justice.
Bard, M. (1975) *The Function of the Police in Crisis Intervention and Conflict
Management*. Washington, DC: US Dept. of Justice, Law Enforcement Assist-
ance Administration, National Institute of Law Enforcement and Criminal
Justice.
Bittner, E. (1970) *The Functions of the Police in Modern Society*. Rockville, Md:
National Institute of Mental Health.
Burger, W. (1984) 'Isn't there a better way?', *ABA Journal*, 63: 247–77.
Cox, S. and J. Fitzgerald (1983) *Police in Community Relations: Critical Issues*. Iowa:
William C. Brown.
Crohn, M. (1985) 'Dispute resolution and higher education', *Negotiation Journal*, 1:
301–5.
Folberg, J. and A. Taylor (1984) *Mediation: A Comprehensive Guide to Resolving
Conflicts Without Litigation*. San Francisco: Jossey Bass.

Goldberg, S., E. Green and F. Sander (1985) *Dispute Resolution*. Boston: Little, Brown.

Klockars, C. (1985) *The Idea of Police*. Berkeley, Cal.: Sage.

Lawson, P. (1977) 'Solving Somebody Else's Blues: A Study of Police Mediation Activities', Ph.D. dissertation. Ann Arbor: University Microfilms.

Marks, J., E. Johnson, Jr and P. Szanton (1984) *Dispute Resolution in America: Processes in Evolution*. Washington, DC: National Institute for Dispute Resolution.

Mayhall, P. (1984) *Police–Community Relations and the Administration of Justice*, New York: Wiley.

Moore, C. (1986) *The Mediation Process: Practical Strategies for Resolving Conflict*. San Francisco: Jossey Bass.

Niederhoffer, A. and A. Blumberg (1970) *The Ambivalent Force: Perspectives on the Police*. San Francisco: Rinehart Press.

Palenski, J. (1984) 'The use of mediation by police', in J.A. Lemmon (ed.), *Community Mediation*. Special issue, *Mediation Quarterly*, 5. San Francisco: Jossey Bass. pp. 31–8.

Rubin, J. (1980) 'Experimental research on third-party intervention in conflict: toward some generalizations', *Psychological Bulletin*, 87: 379–91.

Sander, F. (1984) 'Alternative dispute resolution in the law school curriculum: opportunities and obstacles', *Journal of Legal Education*, 34: 229–36.

Schneider, W. (1980) 'Dispute resolution', *Police Chief*, 47 (Nov.): 51.

Sherman, L. and R. Berk (1984a) 'The specific deterrent effects of arrest for domestic assault', *American Sociological Review*, 49: 261–72.

Sherman, L. and R. Berk (1984b) 'The Minneapolis domestic violence experiment', Police Foundation Reports, April, Washington, DC.

Shonholtz, R. (1984) 'Neighborhood justice systems: work, structure and guiding principles', in J.A. Lemmon (ed.), *Community Mediation*. Special issue, *Mediation Quarterly*, 5. San Francisco: Jossey Bass, pp. 3–30.

Tomasic, R. and M. Feeley (eds) (1982) *Neighborhood Justice: Assessment of an Emerging Idea*. Longman.

Volpe, M. (1985) 'ADR: the emergence of a new educational landscape', *NIJ Reports*, 14 (July). Washington, DC: National Institute of Justice.

Wahrhaftig, P. (1982) 'An overview of community-oriented citizen dispute resolution programs in the United States', in R. Abel (ed.), *The Politics of Informal Justice*, vol. 1. *The American Experience*. New York: Academic Press. pp. 75–97.

16

Myth and Practice in the Mediation Process

Sally Engle Merry

Despite the promise of mediation, it is important to take a hard look at what mediation really is and can really do. Many of its strengths are not those touted in its myths and many of its weaknesses are ignored. The process is not as benign or free of danger to social justice and individual liberty as its proponents would have us think. The possibility of infringing the rights of weaker parties, the potential for manipulation by mediators, the existence of subtle forms of coercion, the effects of incorporation within institutions, and the possibility of an extension of middle-class control over the working class are nagging questions that cannot be ignored. Mediation can end up a new forum in which the predominantly middle-class helping professions are invited to supervise and control the private lives of the working class.

Without sufficient attention to the practice of mediation, we risk repeating the mistakes of the reformers in the American progressive era at the beginning of this century who, with the best of intentions, uncritically encouraged the extension of government discretion and control over the working class and the poor as they created the juvenile courts and probation, institutions of more informal justice which we now recognize as seriously flawed in their failure to protect individual rights (Rothman, 1981). In this chapter, I will raise some important caveats for the mediation movement, based in part on my own research on mediation programmes in the United States. Most of the discussion will focus on a family mediation programme which handles disputes between parents and their teenage children whom they or others have taken to court and charged as 'status offenders': truants, runaways, or children who behave in a stubborn or incorrigible way. In general, status offenders are minors who have committed acts which would not be considered crimes if they were adults. The programme was established in Cambridge, Massachusetts, in 1980 to replicate the system of Children's Panels established in Scotland in 1968. As far as possible, the Children's Hearings Project in Massachusetts followed its Scottish prototype, but it was unable to replace the juvenile court proceedings fully and, unlike its model, had to function as an adjunct to the court rather than as an alternative.[1]

The problems of inequality

Cross-cultural research on the mediation process indicates that in non-industrial societies, mediation settlements tend to replicate the power relationship between the parties (Merry, 1981). In the absence of a powerful third party, the disputing party who is stronger and has more resources and more effective powers of persuasion will tend to do better. The weaker party argues for the best that he or she thinks she can get, not what he or she thinks is most fair. When the goal is to create any kind of settlement which both parties will accept, the weaker party will take the best deal possible and the stronger party will concede as little as possible. A recent study of labour mediation in the United States indicated that in this context as well, both mediators and parties assume that management is more powerful and that settlements must take into account this power differential (Kolb, 1983). This is an important issue in mediation in many settings. A particularly trenchant example is disputes between spouses, particularly when violence is involved. Many argue that mediation in these situations can only supplement, not replace, the protective role of the law.

Relative power depends not only on resources and powers of persuasion, of course, but also on the situation of conflict: the relative benefits to each party of reaching a settlement or, conversely, the relative pain to each of not settling. For example, a landlord trying to evict an ex-lover tenant whom he allowed into his apartment rent-free is in a weaker position than his tenant who wishes to prolong her inexpensive stay and enjoys taunting the landlord as he struggles to throw her out. Clearly, a person who faces charges in court if he or she fails to reach a mediation agreement is in a weaker position than the person who has filed the charges.

When a mediator asserts a more controlling role, however, he or she may be able to forge settlements that do not entirely coincide with existing power relationships. Since the mediator's role is to encourage the parties to settle themselves, rather than to impose a settlement on them, his or her attempts to direct the settlement process will inevitably be subtle and often unperceived by the parties (Silbey and Merry, 1986). As mediators deal with disputes between unequal parties, they frequently confront the need to intervene in power relationships in order to satisfy their own sense of justice. Yet, given the limitations on the power of mediators, such intervention may take the form of persuading the more compliant party to give up as well as persuading the more insistent party to give in.

The mediation of disputes between parents and their teenage offspring provides a useful setting to examine the problem of inequality, since the children clearly lack the resources of their parents. The court has traditionally taken the side of the parents, seeking to buttress their authority and defining the problem as the misbehaviour of the child rather than the flaws of the parents or the dynamics – or difficulties – of the whole family (Fisher, 1979/80). Moreover, in three-quarters of the fifty-one cases I studied, the parents had taken the child to court. Thus, regardless of the equality of the process itself, the parents began in the more powerful position of plaintiff and the children in the weaker position of defendant, charged with a status offence and vulnerable to legal penalties. The legal context significantly enhanced the position of the parents. On the other hand, the children's enthusiasm for the process was based in part on their realistic observation that through it they had escaped the penalties of the law their parents had attempted to invoke against them.

The results of this two-year study suggest that, overall, teenagers thought the process was fair and balanced almost as often as their parents did, and described themselves as pressured to settle less often than their parents did.[2] Most said that they thought that the mediators were neutral, but of those who felt that the mediators favoured one side, teenagers were more likely than parents to think that the mediators were for them. Few participants felt that the mediators blamed them, but of those who did, parents more often felt blamed than children. Teenagers were slightly more likely to say that mediation is a good process and that the agreement is working than their parents were. Most of the teenagers felt that mediation was fair (84 per cent said so), and over half (57 per cent) of those interviewed after mediation said that they signed the agreement because they thought it was fair, made sense, or gave them what they wanted.

This perception of relatively equal treatment, however, is produced by two unique features of the Children's Hearings Project (CHP): its distinctive ideology and its particular version of the mediation process. The programme was initiated by a child advocacy centre with an interest in the decriminalization of status offenders and the protection of children's rights in the juvenile court. The initial staff all had experience and interest in work with youth. This youth-centred ideology shaped the mediation process at the CHP. It became a detailed negotiation of guidelines for daily life through the extensive use of private sessions. The mediators pressed the family to construct rules about chores, curfews, the child's social life, use of the telephone, and so forth, by discussing them until they could agree on mutually acceptable standards. Since mediators were anxious to avoid rules which they thought the teenagers would probably break, they sometimes urged the parents to be more lenient than they wanted to be. More important, the mediators' requirement that the parents negotiate rules with their children rather than simply impose them immediately shifted the power balance in many families. Many parents had been accustomed to telling their children how to behave or, conversely, to allowing them great freedom because they perceived the children to be beyond control. They found themselves in a new, more equal, bargaining relationship with their children. The intervention of the mediators thus tended to empower the children in relation to their parents, at least temporarily.

Further, the format of many private meetings, in which the mediators talk to each party with the other absent, provided the teenagers with an opportunity to voice their concerns. They were much more likely to raise their own problems and complaints when they were alone with the mediators than when their parents were present. Discussions in which both parents and children were present tended to focus on the parents' complaints about their children's behaviour. Gradually, private meetings (termed 'caucuses' in American usage) came to constitute the bulk of the mediation session.

The first private meeting after the combined initial meeting, was routinely held with the child. This practice increased the bargaining position of the young person. In a mediation session, the person with the first private meeting is in the position to make demands; the person in the second one has the choice to accept or reject these demands. The first party to speak has the advantage of defining the problem in his or her way and establishing conditions for settlement. Any new demands or modifications made by the second party require the mediators to go back to the first party with new demands in an additional private meeting, lengthening the mediation process. Mediators who strive for a short mediation session sometimes seek to keep the process to two private meetings, one with each party. Under these conditions, the second person has a greatly restricted scope for negotiation. A sequence of private meetings somewhat reduces the bargaining advantage of the party who goes first, since the second party can make new demands, suggest modifications, and so forth, but it lengthens the process. The CHP used a process which had, on the average, four private meetings instead of two and lasted an average of 3 hours and 20 minutes. The CHP format provides more room for negotiation than the simpler two-meeting format, but somewhat reduces the advantage to going first.

Although the CHP was able to provide a relatively equal mediation process, it did so in the context of an ideological commitment to the rights of the weaker party and through particular modifications of the mediation process designed to counteract the power advantage of the parents. Under different circumstances, with a different ideology, different programme leadership, or different mediation process, the result could be otherwise.

The potential for manipulation

The mediation process influences the way people think about their problems and the kinds of solutions they create. It has the potential for manipulating their ideas and actions. By manipulation, I mean the ability to affect the way a person thinks about a situation or acts on it in such a way that the person is not aware of the influence.[3] In CHP mediation practice, the mediators did not change the issues the families were concerned about, but did transform them from complaints to solutions, usually through the process of making suggestions. Parents who come to court are desperate for solutions, so the mediation process can involve more advice-giving than the vision of the neutral mediator implies. In the hands of careful and idealistic people, the process has the potential to be very helpful, but it can also be intrusive and controlling.

Although one articulated goal of mediation is to return control of the conflict to the people in dispute, the parents, at least, did not want control over the conflict. They had gone to the court in a desperate, last-resort effort to get someone else to help them. They often wanted the court to straighten out their child. These parents were not searching for greater responsibility, but for someone to provide them with suggestions, direction, and enhanced authority. The children, on the other hand, were typically in mediation because their parents had taken them to court. Whether or not they had freely chosen mediation, they were coerced into court. About one-fifth of those we interviewed said they went to mediation because their parents made them go.

Because the parents were trying to increase their control over their children, they hoped that the mediators would be active in making suggestions or constructing solutions. Parents sometimes wanted the mediators to take on a more authoritarian role than is advocated by the ideology of mediation. The mediators, in interviews, clearly felt ambivalent about how much they should give advice or make suggestions. They seemed to have developed an uneasy compromise in which they made suggestions in terms of hypothetical situations and controlled the process indirectly through shuttle diplomacy. They created a process in which third parties actively pushed families from problems to solutions, from complaints about one another to views of that behaviour placed in a social context, and from arguing and fighting to negotiation. They did so in such a way that the subtle transformation of conflict was not perceived as coercive or experienced as pressure by the family members themselves.

Mediators are expected to be impartial: they are not to make judgements or take sides. This accurately describes mediators' behaviour in so far as they do not take sides between parents and children in ways that either recognizes. Yet the mediators are hardly impartial with regard to values about conflict and family functioning. They clearly view each family situation with a theory of family conflict which advocates parents' setting limits on their children's behaviour and jointly negotiating these limits with their children. Families clearly learn that the mediators think that negotiation is a better way of dealing with conflict than fighting.

Subtle forms of coercion

Mediation risks creating a coercive process under the rhetoric of voluntariness, participation, and community involvement. The problem of coercion in mediation is related to unequal power, since the more unequal the parties, the more serious is the injustice of binding them to an agreement that each finds merely acceptable, the best he or she can do. By coercion I mean the use of force or the threat of its use. A third party exerts coercive power when he or she is able to control the outcome of the process (Taylor, 1982: 15). Courts exercise coercion over defendants once they have determined that these defendants have violated laws. Mediators do not exercise coercive power, in that they cannot impose a decision, but they may convey an impression of coercive power if the disputant is uncertain about the extent and scope of the mediators' power.

The role of coercion is most problematic when the disputant thinks that the mediator is part of the legal process. Mediation programmes, particularly as they become more established and attached to a court, can come to seem to disputants as appendages of the court system rather than as separate institutions. Disputants may believe that the legal system will enforce their mediation agreement. Even when this is not true, this belief subjects them to coercion, in a way. And, as mediation becomes more established, courts may in fact enforce mediation agreements. Even now, there is often ambiguity about the legal status of mediation and its agreement. Disputing parties sometimes agree to mediation in the hope that it will impress the judge, or because they feel that this is a required part of the court process. Some of the disputants I interviewed in various mediation programmes even thought that they had been to court and seen the judge. The initial stages of lower-court processes are typically highly informal, negotiative, and ambiguous, making more likely a disputant's confusion about where the voluntary mediation process ends and the coercive court process begins.

Even in the CHP, with its separate office away from the court, its careful explanation of its programme to potential clients, and its opposition to criminal handling of status offender cases, 10 per cent of the disputants thought they had to go to mediation and about half the teenagers and one-third of the parents thought that the judge could enforce the mediation agreement. In fact, judges were routinely sent copies of the agreements and typically retained oversight over the case, but rarely referred to the agreement in court. In other programmes, I have found that mediators who are having difficulty forging an agreement sometimes resort to claiming their connection to the court or assuring participants that the court will supervise the agreement (Silbey and Merry, 1986). The ambiguity of the relationship of mediation to the court, particularly in the case of a court-annexed and sponsored programme, fosters genuine uncertainty in the minds of disputants about its voluntary nature and may indeed tempt mediators and programme staff to enhance the authority of the mediation process itself by drawing on the legitimacy and power of the court.

The effects of institutionalization and routinization

Can mediation survive institutionalization and routinization? By institutionalization, I mean the incorporation of mediation into an arm of the government such as the court or a social service agency in which the funding, the source of case referrals, and the staffing is controlled by that agency. How will mediation change as it becomes attached to courts and controlled by court administrators? A related question is how mediation will be changed as it becomes routinized; as it begins to handle a high volume of similar cases, as some programmes now do (see Pipkin and Rivkin, 1984). The CHP experience shows that, in the hands of the idealistic, committed, and socially conscious staff and mediator pool which it had during its first two years, the process provided outcomes that many families found helpful and, given the limited expectations that one can have for helping status offender families, was often quite effective. Yet, this study covered the start-up period of the programme, a time when staff and mediator enthusiasm ran high and the commitment to child welfare and to reforming the juvenile justice system flowed strongly. The case coordinators worked intensely with most families. The programme covered a small area and worked closely with two courts. The researcher provided another person who regularly contacted each family. Under these conditions, the CHP provided a process that was considerably more responsive, family-directed, and in many ways more helpful than the court.

But because of its early success, the programme was institutionalized state-wide under the state's department of social services in 1983. It is unclear whether its unique strengths can survive this large-scale institutionalization, funding, and control. The innovative leaders who conceived the project have moved on to other activities or to training and programme development. The new programmes established under the CHP model may not share the same concern with children's rights which served to counterbalance the societal preference for the parents' position. Higher case-loads and smaller staffs will decrease the intensive case-work with each family. The process of case intake and mediation will inevitably become routinized as funders demand lower costs per case and more detailed accounting of time, and as the initial enthusiasm for reform is replaced by the need to deliver an ongoing service. As a result of these pressures, the programme may lose some of its distinctive humanitarian qualities and come to resemble the court more closely.

A comparison of the CHP and the Children's Hearings system in Scotland indicates some of the consequences of establishing a large-scale, government-run mediation programme which replaces, rather than supplements, existing court procedures.[4] The Scottish Children's Hearings system differs from the CHP in that it handles almost all juvenile cases, including delinquency cases, and makes dispositional decisions. However, like the CHP, it uses informal hearings conducted by lay community volunteers. Despite many similarities in the process and content of the discussion in the two settings, the hearings in Scotland tend to be much shorter (an average of 29 minutes, according to one comprehensive study (Martin et al., 1981: 100)) than the CHP mediation sessions, which last an average of three hours and 20 minutes. The nature of the discussion is also different. CHP mediators focus on expressing sympathy and eliciting information, while the Scottish panel members are more likely to tell the child to shape up and do better for the sake of its parents or to avoid getting into trouble with the law. The American juvenile court judge sounds more like the Scottish panel members. American judges engage in a dialogue of threats, exhortations, lectures on the need to do better, and a focus on the precipitating incident, much as the Scottish panel members do. Moreover, American court hearings are also relatively short, like the panel hearings in Scotland.

Both the American juvenile court judge and the Scottish Children's Hearings panel exercise dispositional powers. Both are responsible for the needs of public safety as well as the needs of the child, and both handle juvenile delinquents as well as status offenders. Thus, both hold a mandate to change the child's behaviour to protect society. The CHP mediators, in contrast, are separate from the court process, so do not share the same burden. They are not alone responsible for the child's school attendance, since the judge is also imposing pressure, nor are they concerned with protecting the community from delinquents. In other words, it is precisely because the CHP mediators operate as an adjunct to the criminal justice system, rather than as a substitute, that they are able to focus exclusively on the best interests of the child and to produce a process which is responsive, sympathetic, and successful in improving communication between parents and children. Because the CHP does not replace the court, it does not have the same social control obligations.

The comparison with the Scottish Children's Hearings system suggests how a fully institutionalized informal process can become like the formal system it has replaced. As with any innovation, a new process, even institutionalized and routinized, will not be exactly like the old system. But it will experience pressures to replicate the old system as it takes on its responsibilities and functions. It will combine new features with old practices. Consequently, a full understanding of mediation must examine not only the idealistic start-up phase of the process, but also the well-established, high-volume phase, once it has taken on some of the functions and social control obligations of the legal institutions it has replaced.

Mediation and social class

According to the myths of mediation, disputes should be handled by the disputants' social peers. The rationale for using community volunteers as mediators is the expectation that such people will be like the disputants and share their values and social practices. The

CHP study found that the client families often did not know that the mediators were community volunteers, nor did they think that it was important that they were. Furthermore, in the CHP, as in most other mediation programmes, the mediators are more educated and of a higher social class than the programme clients. A simple listing of the mediator pool in a programme does not necessarily reveal which mediators are actually working; in the programmes I observed, those who were considered 'good' mediators and who mediated most often typically had some college education if not an advanced degree, and had some background in the helping professions. Despite this class difference between mediators and clients, clients report feeling free to define the issues, able to have some input into the solutions, and personally satisfied and often helped.

In this programme, as in many others, mediation provides a forum in which middle-class or professional people teach working-class clients to use negotiation as a form of conflict management and, in accordance with the dominant perspective of human services professionals, to see misbehaviour as a product of social forces rather than an individual's bad character. The process serves, in effect, to train working-class families in the more verbal, negotiative styles of conflict resolution favoured by the middle and upper classes. Whether this transformation of conflict management styles is of overall benefit to working-class families is an important question. Many of the parents have adopted either the stance of strong, unquestioned authority or complete leniency and like the idea of negotiating conflict instead. Family members reported that they were fighting less often after mediation. A significant number said that they had shifted from arguing and fighting to talking about their differences. Family members were generally pleased by this reduced fighting in the home, particularly the children.

But the long-range implications of such social changes are worth considering. Less powerful members of American society have developed a confrontational style of conflict management because it has proved necessary and often helpful (see, for example, Nader, 1980; Merry, 1981; Black, 1983). For some of the situations working-class individuals confront, handling grievances in a confrontational style is critical to defending rights against more powerful adversaries. The history of the labour movement, grassroots political organizing, and civil disobedience and urban violence all suggest that in some situations, a more confrontational strategy has benefited the working classes. Were the powerful more willing to negotiate, they might find less need to deal with these confrontations.

Mediation and social justice

One myth of mediation is that it enhances social justice. Despite the more humane, responsive, and participatory nature of the mediation process in comparison to the court, mediation as practised at the CHP does not have any long-range impact on the distribution of power to control behaviour or on the social and economic pressures which lead these families into the court. It moves the management of working-class family problems from the formal legal system to an informal system staffed and managed by people of approximately similar or higher social status. American communities are not structured to assume the social control functions currently performed by the legal system in a way which would genuinely decentralize control of behaviour.

Consequently, any reform of the legal system, as long as its operation remains an adjunct of the existing criminal justice system, will produce an alternative system, possibly different in process, organization, and working assumptions, but not different in the use of the power of the state as the ultimate source of social control. Ultimately, children must go to court if their parents have charged them with being status offenders, so going to mediation is a choice between that process and the court process. The parents, once they have voluntarily sought the help of the court, must continue to pursue its suggested solutions until the court agrees to dismiss the case. Even though the mediation process is quite different from the court, parents and children usually come to it assuming that it is a service offered by the court, and face real limitations in their ability to reject the service or to ignore its settlements. Within this political framework, mediation can provide a service which facilitates the acquisition of negotiation skills by the working-class clients of the judicial system under the direction of educated, idealistic, middle-class volunteers. As the research on mediation indicates, there are considerable advantages to the use of mediation, but there are also significant pitfalls. More realistic assessments of its strengths and its actual practice, rather than its myths, can only strengthen the process.

Notes

The W.T. Grant Foundation provided generous support for the research described in this paper. The author is grateful to Stanley Fisher and Deborah Kolb for their insightful comments on an earlier draft.

1 This programme is discussed more fully in Merry and Rocheleau, 1985.

2 The study included follow-up interviews with 49 teenagers, 48 mothers, and 17

fathers about one month after their mediation session. These interviews were conducted in person and lasted between 45 and 90 minutes.

3 'Manipulation is the process whereby a person is got to behave or think otherwise than he would have done, in such a way that he is unaware of the source and causes of his new thought and actions (so is unaware that he has been manipulated)' (Taylor, 1982: 24).

4 For more information on the Scottish Children's Hearings System, see the excellent study by Martin et al. (1981). Further discussion of the comparison with the CHP is available in Merry and Rocheleau (1985).

References

Black, Donald (1983) 'Crime as social control', *American Sociological Review*, 48: 34–46.

Fisher, Stanley Z. (1979/80) '"Families with service needs": the newest euphemism?' *Journal of Family Law, University of Louisville School of Law*, 18: 1–79.

Kolb, Deborah (1983) *The Mediators*. Cambridge, Mass.: MIT Press.

Martin, F.M., Sandford J. Fox and Kathleen Murray (1981) *Children out of Court*. Edinburgh: Scottish Academic Press.

Merry, Sally Engle (1981) 'The social organization of mediation in non-industrial societies: implications for informal justice in America', in Richard Abel (ed.), *The Politics of Informal Justice*, vol. 2. New York: Academic Press. pp. 17–45.

Merry, Sally Engle and Ann Marie Rocheleau (1985) *Mediation in Families: A Study of the Children's Hearings Project. Process in Parent/Child Conflicts*. Cambridge, Mass.: Cambridge Children's and Family Services.

Nader, Laura (ed.) (1980) *No Access to Law: Alternatives to the American Judicial System*. New York: Academic Press.

Pipkin, Ronald M. and Janet Rivkin (1984) 'The social organisation in alternative dispute resolution: implications for the professionalization of mediation', *Justice System Journal*, 9 (2): 204–28.

Rothman, David J. (1981) *Conscience and Convenience: The Asylum and its Alternatives in Progressive America*. Boston: Little, Brown.

Silbey, Susan S. and Sally Engle Merry (1986) 'Mediator settlement strategies', *Law and Policy*, 8 (1): 7–32.

Taylor, M. (1982) *Community, Anarchy, and Liberty*. Cambridge, Mass.: Cambridge University Press.

17

An Empirical Assessment

Robert B. Coates and John Gehm

This chapter concentrates on the lessons to be learnt from the Victim/Offender Reconciliation Program (VORP) as it has been practised in the United States. Five central questions guided our assessment:

. 1   How does the VORP process actually function?
2   Who participates and why?
3   How do participants evaluate it?
4   What are the immediate outcomes?
5   To what extent does VORP function as an alternative to incarceration?

These questions reflect the exploratory nature of the study and the emphasis on developing a database which could be useful for guiding further programme development.

The VORP programmes covered in this chapter served seven counties in the state of Indiana and one county in the state of Ohio. Two sets of samples were gathered for analysis. The first is quantitative, based on official records and used to answer questions regarding immediate outcomes and the extent to which VORP is an alternative to incarceration. The second set is qualitative, based on focused interviews (a combination of primarily open-ended questions with some closed-ended questions) with VORP participants to determine who participates, their goals, and their level of satisfaction with the VORP experience.

Three of the VORP programmes were in operation sufficiently long to allow us to generate from programme and court records a sample of offenders who had been referred to VORP in 1983 with a matched sample of offenders who were not referred. The 73 VORP referrals were individually matched with 73 non-VORP referrals on (a) sex, (b) juvenile/adult, (c) race, (d) prior conviction, (e) prior incarceration,[1] and (f) most serious current charge for which convicted.

During 1984, focused interviews were conducted with 37 victims who had participated in face-to-face mediation during the first six months of 1984. For the same time period, telephone interviews were conducted with 26 victims who refused to participate; 23 interviews took place with offenders who participated in VORP, and 22 were held with staff and mediators. Interviews were also completed with 27 probation officers, judges, and prosecutors, and nine face-to-face meetings were observed and recorded.

Who participates in the VORP process and why?

Two-thirds of the meetings in which our 1983 sample of offenders participated were conducted by trained volunteer mediators. Use of community volunteers can save costs, but more importantly, it provides a vested interest in the programme for local citizens while increasing community awareness of alternative ways of dealing with crime.

Seventy-three per cent of the offenders participating in VORP in 1983 were juvenile (under age 18). Over 90 per cent were male and Caucasian. About 20 per cent had had a prior conviction and 17 per cent had served time in a local jail or a state prison. Over half had been convicted for burglary and another quarter for theft. Overall, then, the offenders were mainly young, with little prior criminal justice experience, and in the mid-range of offence seriousness.

Contrary to the rhetoric of VORP staff, which emphasizes the voluntary nature of participation, offenders participate because they believe they must. Most were court-referred or court-ordered to VORP. They did hope that participation would reduce the punishment meted out by the court.

Victims choosing to participate in VORP are quite diverse. Young, middle-aged, and older persons are fairly equally represented. Twenty-four per cent of the victims had not completed high school, 51 per cent had completed twelfth grade or attended some college, and 24 per cent indicated that twelfth grade (approximately age 18) was the highest grade completed. Thirty-two per cent of these people had been victims of burglary, 29 per cent of theft, 21 per cent of vandalism, 13 per cent of fraud, and 3 per cent of assault.

In line with the findings of other chapters, these victims chose to participate in VORP with the hope of recovering their loss, helping the offender, and participating meaningfully in the criminal justice process. Many wanted to 'teach the offender a lesson', to make the offender understand that his or her behaviour had hurt people and that he or she ought to be held accountable.

Victims choosing not to participate indicated that the loss did not merit the perceived hassle of involvement, that they were afraid of meeting the offender, or that they had already worked out a settlement.

Goals of VORP staff and participants

Respondents in this study had varying goals guiding their participation in VORP. For staff and mediators, humanizing the criminal justice process through face-to-face encounters between victim and offender, increasing the offender's personal accountability for behaviour, and providing meaningful roles for victims in the criminal justice process were the highest priorities. For victims, recovering loss, helping offenders stay out of trouble, and participating meaningfully in the criminal justice process were the three highest rated goals. Offender goals were to avoid harsher punishment, to get the whole experience of crime and consequences behind them, and to make things right. Criminal justice officials, responsible for referring offenders in the first place, did so as a way of providing restitution to victims, of encouraging useful involvement of victims in the criminal justice process, and of helping offenders stay out of trouble.

Goals related to increasing victim participation, restitution, and helping the offender have a fairly broad base of support. It is perhaps surprising that two of the goals most often mentioned in VORP programme materials, 'reconciliation' and 'alternative to incarceration', are less accepted by the participants. To obtain an alternative to incarceration was, of course, a primary goal for offenders. These goals, if mentioned at all by other participants, were relegated to lower priority. While they are the rallying flags of programme directors and administrative staff, in practice the more concrete goals of victim involvement and help to the offender receive precedence. The lack of shared priority of goals and the tension between some of them have implications for further programme development.

Participants' assessment of the VORP process

We will begin by looking at responses from the 37 victims and 23 offenders who participated in face-to-face meetings during 1984. Both victims and offenders believed that the programme was initially explained well by mediators. Victims did not feel unduly pressured to participate. Offenders believed that they had little choice but to participate.

Offenders particularly, but also some victims, expressed concern about meeting the other because of possible intense feelings and conflict. However, two-thirds of each group indicated that the meeting was not conflictual. More offenders than victims experienced the meeting as conflictual. Mediators were frequently credited with 'keeping the lid on' while encouraging discussion of feelings.

On the whole, 83 per cent of the offenders and 59 per cent of the victims were satisfied with the VORP experience. Only 11 per cent of the victims expressed some dissatisfaction. Perhaps even more to the point, all but one of the victims indicated that if the occasion arose again they would still choose to participate in VORP. The same number would recommend VORP to other victims of crime. All of the offenders, if they had a choice, said they would choose to participate.

Victims were most satisfied with (a) the opportunity to meet the offender and thereby obtain a better understanding of the crime and the offender's situation; (b) the opportunity to receive restitution for loss; (c) the expression of remorse on the part of the offender; (d) the care and concern of the mediator. Even though the primary motivation for participation was restitution, the most satisfying aspect of the experience was meeting the offender.

These same victims were least satisfied with the lack of follow-up and leverage on the offender to fulfil the agreed contract. They also expressed dissatisfaction with the delay between the crime and the VORP resolution; although over half of the face-to-face meetings occurred within 60 days of referral, a median number of 111 days had elapsed between the crime and conviction. Some victims were also unhappy with the amount of time required to participate in VORP. One victim felt he had given a lot to the process, perhaps too much: 'it's like being hit by a car and having to get out and help the other driver when all you were doing was minding your own business.'

Offenders were most satisfied with: (a) meeting the victim and discovering the victim was willing to listen to him or her; (b) staying out of jail and in some instances not getting a record; (c) the opportunity to work out a realistic schedule for paying back the victim to 'make things right'. Strikingly, what offenders disliked most was, also, meeting the victim. This reflects the tension between, on the one hand, the stress experienced in preparation for meeting the victim, and, on the other hand, the relief of having taken steps 'to make things right'.

Three offenders describe this tension very well. A 16-year-old female comments, 'I did not like the way I felt at first. I was scared. I did not know how he would feel.' And a 19-year-old male: 'It was hard to go to meetings and know some of the victims probably wouldn't understand, because I didn't really understand myself – how could I expect them to.' Another 19-year-old male convicted of battery 'found it hard meeting this person knowing that I was in the wrong. There still might be conflict.'

Part of the philosophy underlying VORP is that bringing victim and offender together will result in attitude change and ultimately reconciliation – victims and offenders will be willing to view each other as people, not merely as objects or stereotypes. In about a third of our cases we were able to establish such attitude change. For those offenders and victims who did express changed views of the other, the common refrain was: 'we now see them as real people.' Some victims were clearly moved by what they believed to be sincere remorse on the part of offenders. Offenders who expressed change were frequently surprised about the meaning attached to the items that they had stolen.

Participants were also asked if their attitudes about crime or criminal justice had changed. Nearly half of each group indicated change. For the victims, change occurred primarily in their understanding of options available to criminal justice officials. Options such as VORP are seen as 'a glimmering light at the end of the tunnel'. Some believed that programmes such as VORP indicated a desire to involve victims more usefully in the criminal justice process. As one woman stated, 'I feel a little better that I've a stake in punishment.' Offender comments primarily focused on changed attitudes about crime – that it doesn't pay and that it is painful not only for the offender but for the victim too. One offender, a 15-year-old, pointed out clearly that the loss to victims lingers on: 'No, I don't think they will forget the fear for awhile – I wasn't thinking about them, I mean as real people.'

Ninety-two per cent of victims interviewed had worked out restitution contracts with the offenders. The remainder did not because stolen items had been returned. Of those with contracts three-quarters felt the contracts represented the amount of restitution expected and 56 per cent indicated that the restitution would account for full recovery of the monetary loss. Ninety-four per cent were satisfied with the contracts.

Given the continuing debate about punishment of criminal and juvenile offenders, we wanted to know whether victims believed that the persons who had committed a crime against them had been punished adequately. Seventy per cent believed that the offender had been punished adequately. Twenty-four per cent indicated that the punishment was too little and 5 per cent felt that it was too much. It seems clear from our interviews and observations that victims see offender participation in VORP as, at least in part, punishment.

Offenders are even clearer that VORP is punishment. For 87 per cent of the offender sample, additional forms of punishment were also received. Sixty-five per cent felt that they were adequately punished; 35 per cent felt that they had received too much punishment. A 41-year-old male stated: 'VORP was fair because I did wrong, but I shouldn't have gone to jail because I'm not a criminal, but VORP did make me responsible to the victim.' Others felt that while meeting the victim and working out a contract was difficult, it had been the right thing to do and a fitting punishment for the wrong that they had done.

In short, was justice done? We asked each person to define justice and then to indicate whether justice was met in their specific case. Definitions of justice were quite diverse, but common themes across these definitions included 'making things right', 'holding the offender accountable for his or her actions', and 'fairness and equality in settling disputes'. Nearly 80 per cent of victims and offenders indicated that justice had been served in their cases.

Immediate outcomes of the VORP process

The descriptive data presented based on interviews with victims and offenders in 1984 focused on participant views and assessments of outcomes. Those interviews also contained data regarding specific outcomes. It is, however, the 1983 matched sample of offenders that offers us the most systematic and representative view of outcomes.

The primary referral point for the 73 offenders referred to VORP was at sentencing. For 80 per cent of the sample, VORP was part of their sentence, usually including probation and sometimes jail. Nineteen per cent were referred as a means of diverting the case from the formal judicial process. The above data suggest that within the three VORP sites being analysed, judges typically use VORP as part of a sentencing package. This use was confirmed by our interviews with judges as well as by our interviews with offenders processed in 1984. Occasionally, VORP is used as a sole sanction, but this is not the norm.

The 73 offenders in our sample were convicted and referred to VORP on 196 offences; 39 offenders were convicted on more than one count or offence.

There are at least two lenses through which one can view outcomes of VORP. The first, which is the common practice in the field, is to look at outcomes based on the number of possible victim/

offender combinations. This reflects most accurately the work-load of staff and provides information useful for programme management. The second is to look at outcomes based on the number of offenders referred to VORP. This perspective is particularly of interest to criminal justice officials, as their primary point of reference in determining outcomes is offender-based. The two ways of looking at outcomes use a different numeric base because, when looking at victim/offender combinations, multiple victims and multiple convictions will increase the number of face-to-face meetings beyond the actual number of offenders. We will report data using both lenses.

The 73 offenders referred to VORP in 1983 had a possible 196 victim/offender meetings, of which 98 (50 per cent) actually occurred. Fourteen per cent of the victim/offender disputes had been settled before VORP contact, and 2 per cent of the potential meetings were pending. Excluding these victim/offender combinations from our total on the premise that it is not realistic to expect victims and offenders to participate in VORP if they have already worked out their difficulties, we have 163 combinations which had the potential for a meeting. Of these possible combinations, 60 per cent resulted in face-to-face meetings; 28 per cent did not occur because victims were unwilling to participate.

There is a very high success rate in obtaining written contracts when face-to-face meetings occur: 98 per cent. In only two instances did offender and victim fail to come to some common agreement. Eighty-seven per cent of these contracts contained some form of restitution. Over half contained contracts with monetary restitution to the victim and a third included some sort of service to the victim. Financial restitution ranged from $3 to $10,000; half of the financial restitution contracts were for $71 or less. Over four-fifths of the 96 contracts were completed at the point of our review of records. The average number of hours of service for the victim was 31; 90 per cent of these contracts had already been completed. In only four cases was there no progress toward contract completion. The data suggest that for the persons who participate in face-to-face meetings there is a very high probability that contracts will be agreed upon *and* successfully completed.

Changing our focus to view outcomes with an offender base, 63 per cent (46) of our offenders participated in at least one face-to-face meeting. We wanted to determine to what extent the occurrence of meetings might be related to selectivity regarding the offender being a juvenile or adult or the nature of the offence. Seventy-eight per cent of the offenders were juvenile. Fifty-four per cent had been convicted of burglary. It is striking that these percentages match those of our entire offender sample, leading us to believe that it is not more likely for meetings to occur for juveniles than adults nor more likely for the less serious offenders in contrast to burglars.

Of the 46 offenders participating in face-to-face meetings, all had at least one contract. Eighty-nine per cent of these offenders had contracts containing restitution agreements; over four-fifths were obligated to make financial restitution and two-fifths to provide service for the victim. About three-quarters of the contracts were complete at the time of our review. Four offenders had made no progress in making restitution.

An alternative to incarceration?

Some proponents of VORP view it as an additional sentencing alternative for judges and hope that VORP might help reduce use of incarceration or length of sentences. We turn to a comparative analysis of our 1983 matched VORP offender and non-VORP offender samples to address this question. The matched offender sample is particularly robust for this purpose as the matched variables include those legal and extra-legal factors most often thought to influence sentencing. Clearly, we cannot control for all possible influences, such as offender's demeanour in court, or the mood of the judge.

Overall, there is little difference between the two samples in terms of the *number of offenders* incarcerated. Approximately 80 per cent of each sample was not incarcerated post-conviction. Combining whether or not the offender was detained prior to conviction with post-conviction incarceration we discover 32 VORP offenders had had a 'taste of jail' compared with 26 non-VORP offenders; this difference is not statistically significant.

Where post-conviction time was served, however, there is a statistical significance. Of the 16 VORP offenders serving time, all did so in a local jail. Of the 15 non-VORP offenders serving time, eight served their time in a local jail and seven in a state institution (four juveniles and three adults). The difference in terms of where time was served between the two total samples is statistically significant. The difference between the two sub-samples, that is, those actually serving time post-conviction, is also statistically significant.

Similarly, there were no statistically significant differences between the two total samples when looking at days served in pre-trial detention or in jail post-conviction. Clearly there was a difference in terms of the number of days served in state institutions.[2] And when using a difference of means *t* test for comparing *total time served post-conviction* (jail and/or state prison) between both total samples a significant difference was found. When comparing the total time served post-conviction of offenders from each sub-sample who were actually incarcerated, a Mann-Whitney *U* of 43 is significant at the 0.001 level. The non-VORP offenders were confined for substantially longer periods of time than the VORP offenders – 3,175 days compared to 613 days.

While VORP referrals were as likely to be incarcerated post-conviction as non-VORP ones, they were statistically less likely to serve time in state institutions, and average length of stay for VORP referrals who were incarcerated was considerably less than that of non-VORP offenders: VORP = 38.3 days; non-VORP = 211.7 days. The cost savings represented by the difference in the number of days served between the samples are substantial. A conservative estimate is $84,500. While we do not conclude that these differences are tied directly to VORP, given the variables that were used to match the samples, the data are suggestive. VORP seems to be used as part of a sentencing package, sometimes including local jail time, resulting in fewer days of incarceration.

As with most reform efforts and innovative ideas, we must remain concerned about unintended consequences. One worry regarding VORP is the common phenomenon among innovative criminal justice programmes of widening the net. Are offenders referred to VORP exposed to more sanctions than they would have been if not referred to VORP? We know that 80 per cent of both matched offender samples did not go to jail after conviction. Does the fact that 80 per cent of the non-VORP sample never went to jail nor were required to participate in VORP mean that they were punished less, and conversely that the VORP offenders were punished more? The offenders would probably respond, 'yes'.

The question of widening the net is not a simple problem. There are trade-offs to make. Some may believe that the relative additional cost to the offender is outweighed by the increased involvement of the victim in the criminal justice process. Or that personal accountability of offender to victim is a good practice from a justice point of view, thereby justifying net-widening. Others may believe that increased involvement of the victim should not be brought about at the expense of offenders. And still others may be more concerned about the equity issue.

Questions of net widening will be enlarged as VORP is used as a diversion programme. To the extent that VORP brings offenders into the system who would normally have had their charges dropped, or leads to further offender penetration into the criminal justice system than otherwise expected, some observers will question its merit and promise (Dittenhoffer and Ericson, 1983).

At this point VORP may be thought to be more of an alternative to incarceration than it is in practice. As more cases are referred and handled between conviction and sentencing, as is now the practice in a number of VORP sites, there may be more opportunity for judges to assess the offenders' experience with VORP before finalizing sentences, and, therefore to be potentially more willing to use VORP as a means for reducing reliance on incarceration.

Implications for VORP and its future linkage with the criminal justice system

Interviews with VORP practitioners and consumers suggest a high level of satisfaction with the VORP process and outcomes. These interviews also make clear the competing goals and philosophies which underpin participation in VORP.

Multiple goals are probably inevitable for any programme dealing with offenders and victims, as the interests of the two groups are not identical. Neither are many of the interests of private reform-minded groups and many county and state criminal justice agencies. Similarly, there is wide range of interest and philosophies represented among VORP practitioners. These differences have implications for how people believe VORP can, and in some instances ought to, relate to the criminal justice system.

From our vantage-point, having analysed the interview data and also being quite familiar with the issues being debated among VORP practitioners, we see four ideal models being posited. Each would intersect the criminal justice system differently. Though they share a common philosophical base and approach, they function on divergent assumptions.

The distinguishing characteristics of VORP are its ultimate goal and philosophical base regarding reconciliation. That goal is operationalized by bringing victim and offender together in a face-to-face meeting to work through feelings and, where appropriate, to design a concrete symbol of reconciliation. In practice this is often some form of restitution.

While the ultimate goal of reconciliation is shared widely by directors of VORP programmes, many differences and resultant tensions are apparent when it comes to juxtaposing VORP with the formal criminal justice system. These differences and tensions will look quite familiar to those who have been close to other community-based reform movements (Coates, 1977; Austin and Krisberg, 1982): which offenders are eligible; what is the relationship with the criminal justice system; at what point in the criminal justice process should VORP be used; what are the appropriate funding auspices; where is the place of punishment; is the net widened?

These are the issues which distinguish the four idealized models: (a) normalized community conflict resolution; (b) diversion from the formal criminal justice system; (c) alternative to incarceration; and (d) justice. We refer to idealized models because with very few exceptions the programmes currently operating represent a mix of models.

The *normalized community conflict resolution model* would work with persons before they are arrested, that is, local residents would bring their conflicts, including acts which would fit legal definitions of criminality, to a VORP programme, which would have no formal relationship with the criminal justice system. Funding would come from private and local non-government sources. Practitioners who favour this model do not want VORP to be seen as a punishment. Participation would be voluntary with, presumably, no negative consequences for non-participation. Widening the net is regarded as a non-issue because of the lack of negative consequences for non-participation and because no formal relationship with the criminal justice system exists.

VORP as a *diversion model* is different in that it depends largely on the criminal justice system for referrals either at the point of arrest or pre-trial. Practitioners are interested in working with 'pre-delinquents' and misdemeanants as a way of getting to them in order to forestall delinquent and criminal careers. This model requires a close working relationship with criminal justice officials. Funding would be accepted from private and government sources. Like their community conflict resolution counterparts, these practitioners do not view their programmes as punishment, and are not particularly concerned about questions of widening the net.

VORP as an *alternative to incarceration* takes yet another shape. Proponents of this model are very wary of the type of offender referred to the programme. Ideally they want to work only with jail or prison-bound offenders. They are particularly concerned about widening the net, even if doing so would assist more victims. They view VORP as an alternative sanction or punishment which could be used by judges as part of sentencing packages resulting in a de-emphasis on incarceration. Their relationship with criminal justice officials is close but characterized by tension as practitioners seek to screen for appropriate referrals. Offenders are accepted post-conviction and preferably prior to sentencing.

Others view VORP as essentially a *justice model*. Advocates of this model consider VORP a viable approach to enhance offender accountability to the victim – it is reasonable and just for an offender to make restitution to the victim. This model places greatest emphasis on the victim or the community as victim. Any offender is eligible. The model could be implemented within institutional settings, as well as in community settings, with prisoners meeting their own victims or surrogate victims. Proponents of this approach view VORP as an alternative or additional sanction or punishment. There is little concern for the issue of widening the net because it is just and right for the offender to be confronted with the personal impact of his or her crime. The formal justice system relationship is close, with little tension. Funding would come primarily from governmental sources.

Clearly, while the victim/offender reconciliation ultimate goal can permeate each of these models, the differences between the models can be quite significant philosophically and in practice. Each model is open to critique by proponents of the others.

Our data do not inform us as to whether one model is better than another. It may be the case that further research on programmes designed on these approaches will help to clarify the appropriateness of each VORP model.

Conclusion

This study suffers from the constraints of the demography of the programme sites. In particular, we continue to have questions about how VORP is received and functions in larger metropolitan areas with more diverse populations. To this end, this study will be replicated, in part, in the VORP in Minneapolis/St Paul, Minnesota.

Our data also suggest that VORP has considerable potential as an alternative sanction. Judges frequently use VORP along with other sanctions including jail. For this sample, a substantial number of incarceration days appear to have been displaced by use of VORP. However, it also appears that VORP is used to widen the net of social control. The balance between using VORP as a partial alternative to incarceration and using it to broaden social control efforts will no doubt be one of the points of contention in VORP's further development.

Notes

This research was supported by a grant from the Florence V. Burden Foundation. We would like to thank Lloyd E. Ohlin, Margaret K. Rosenheim, Burt Galaway and Mark Fraser for their helpful assistance with this project.

1 No adult offender who had been convicted of a prior felony is included in the matched sample, as they would have been mandated by Indiana state law to serve time in a state institution and would not, therefore, be eligible for VORP. Offenders in both the VORP and non-VORP samples could be sentenced to a state institution at the discretion of the sentencing judge.

2 When offenders had completed serving their sentence, actual time is recorded. In Indiana, juveniles are committed until the age of majority. Most, however, do not remain that long. Our estimate of time served is the average length of stay, 365 days, compiled by the Indiana Department of Corrections. For adults, we divided sentences in half, reflecting policies providing one day of good time (remission) for each day served without major violation of institutional rules.

References

Austin, James and Barry Krisberg (1982) 'The unmet promise of alternatives to incarceration', *Crime and Delinquency,* 28 (3): 374–408.

Coates, Robert B. (1977) 'Community-based corrections: concept, impact, dangers', in L.E. Ohlin, A.D. Miller and R.B. Coates (eds), *Juvenile Correctional Reform in Massachusetts.* Washington DC: US Government Printing Office. pp. 23–34.

Dittenhoffer, Tony and Richard V. Ericson (1983) 'The victim/offender reconciliation program: a message to correctional reformers', *University of Toronto Law Journal,* 33: 315–47.

18

What the Public Wants

Martin Wright

It is fairly widely understood that sending people to prison, particularly those who are a nuisance rather than a danger to the public, solves nothing and is likely to make matters worse; but courts continue to do so on an unprecedented scale. One of the main reasons for this appears to be a belief that the public requires it; but evidence is accumulating that the reality is otherwise. People want an adequate response, but not necessarily a punitive one (Wright, 1977).

In the first British Crime Survey (BCS), victims were asked an open-ended question about what their offenders deserved. Only half wanted the offender even brought to court, and 10 per cent wanted a custodial sentence; 15 per cent spontaneously mentioned reparation. ('Reparation' will be used here in its proper sense of a sanction in which the offender does something to make good the harm caused by his or her act; it does not necessarily imply victim/offender mediation, as some recent Home Office statements have misleadingly implied. In American writings the term 'restitution' is used.) But more victims of burglary and car theft were punitive: 38 and 31 per cent respectively wanted a prison sentence (Hough and Mayhew, 1983: 28; Hough and Moxon, 1985: 168).

The second BCS offered respondents a list of options on a show card. The proportion of victims wanting a prison sentence went down (to 33 per cent for burglaries involving loss, and 17 per cent for car thefts), and a substantial proportion specified community service (15 and 25 per cent respectively). A smaller proportion, 7 and 4 per cent, wanted 'just compensation' ('just' in the sense of 'only', presumably). In the case of burglary, one may surmise that the low figure was partly because half the victims were insured, and a quarter of the items taken were of largely sentimental rather than monetary value. For cars it may be relevant that 70 per cent of vehicles had been recovered and most of the remainder were insured.

Victims were not more punitive than others; what they do want is that offenders should make some redress (Hough, 1985; Hough and

Moxon, 1985: 169, 170). Of the total sample in the second BCS, victims and non-victims, a quarter would like to see burglars and car thieves pay compensation to victims, perform community service, or both (in most cases in addition to another penalty); and both community service and compensation were favoured instead of prison for 'some non-violent offenders' by over 80 per cent (Hough and Mayhew, 1983: 44–5).

In a survey of victims of violence, 28 per cent of those questioned in a final interview spontaneously commented that they would have liked compensation from the offender (Shapland et al. 1985: 136), and those who were awarded compensation orders were significantly more satisfied with the way the court had dealt with their case (p. 139). This response has been confirmed in a succession of research projects and public opinion surveys. The general message of burglary victims studied by Maguire (1982) was that the offender should repay his or her 'debt' in a useful way, either by straightforward restitution or by working for the community; and if he or she could be reformed other households would be spared the same experience. Purely retributive feelings were rare, and remarks like 'Prison does no good to anyone' were common (p. 139). It was found that more victims expressed punitive feelings about burglars in general than about their own offenders. Even among victims 'seriously affected' by the burglary, only 21 per cent wanted personal revenge, and among the remainder only 8 per cent felt that way.

Nor are these reactions confined to the United Kingdom. Compensation of the victim by the offender is regarded by 89 per cent of the Dutch public as a suitable method to address the crime problem, according to the 1982 National Crime Survey (Van Dijk, 1984). In America, strong support for the concept of 'creative restitution' (described as amends by offenders to their victims or the community in the form of goods, services, or money) was found by Gandy (1975: 141–61) among social work students, members of a women's community service organization, probation and parole officers, and (a slightly lower proportion of) police. Among probation officers there was less support from Catholics; among police, from those of a lower educational level. Gandy's questions were oriented towards restitution as an approach to rehabilitating offenders, rather than to benefiting victims (e.g. 1975: 273–6). Among the legal community (judges and attorneys) Gandy (1978) found that 82 per cent favoured the idea; and among a random sample of the general population in South Carolina, 80 per cent liked the idea of monetary restitution, 75 per cent community service, and 65 per cent personal service (Gandy and Galaway,

1980: 90, 92). (In fact, however, projects which offer the option of personal service have generally found few takers.)

As for the views of victims, two court consultants reviewed 100 cases in which they had interviewed victims on behalf of defendants. They state, in a somewhat impressionistic report, that at that time victims generally were unaware of community service or the availability of restitution, but when informed, almost all voluntarily agreed to a non-custodial and often a restitutive sentence. Those who were interviewed some time after the crime were inclined to be less punitive, and some even offered to testify on behalf of the offender at a sentencing hearing in order to prevent a prison sentence (Henderson and Gitchoff, 1981).

In a survey of 19 projects using reparation, community service, or both, Hudson et al. (1980: 182–9) asked samples of victims and offenders about their views. To the question 'Given only one choice, which punishment would be the fairest?', 37 per cent of offenders opted for community service, 29 per cent for monetary reparation, and 28 per cent for probation; among victims, 61 per cent preferred monetary reparation, 23 per cent jail or prison, and 9 per cent community service. When invited to choose a combination of measures, 21 per cent of victims wanted jail or prison to be combined with monetary reparation, and 38 per cent chose reparation – either alone, or combined with community service, probation, or both.

Several studies reaching similar conclusions are cited by Galaway (1983), whose own research was carried out in New Zealand. He asked two random samples of 1,200 people to decide sentences for six offenders whose offences were briefly described. For the experimental group, reparation was among the non-custodial sanctions which could be selected, but for the control group this option was omitted. For five of the six cases the experimental group chose imprisonment significantly less often. In all six cases at least 65 per cent of them wanted reparation, and Galaway concludes that the study supports the view that the public will accept a reduction in the use of imprisonment for serious property offenders if there is a concomitant increase in requiring these offenders to restore their victims' losses. For most offences, incidentally, victims were slightly less likely to want imprisonment than non-victims, whichever group they were in (Galaway, 1983: Table 7).

A somewhat similar survey had been carried out in Canada, on attitudes to sentencing. A sample was asked to choose a sentence for a first offender convicted of a burglary involving $250, from the options: probation, a fine, a fine and probation, or prison. Whichever reply they gave, they were then asked whether they would prefer instead reparation to the victim or the community; 30 per cent replied 'Yes, in all cases', 31 per cent 'in most cases' and 27 per cent 'in some cases'. Only 4 per cent said 'Never' (Doob and Roberts, 1983: 16).

As for those sentences which arouse resentment for being too lenient, the same researchers showed that when members of the public are given the facts of the case, they are capable of making a considered judgement. Half their sample was asked a question such as 'How would you evaluate a sentence of 18 months' imprisonment for someone who was charged with second degree murder and found guilty of manslaughter?' In this example, 80 per cent said it was too lenient, and no one said too harsh. The other group were given a 500-word summary of the case. Only 14.8 per cent of these thought the sentence was too lenient, and 44 per cent though it too harsh. The other case produced similar, though less striking, results. Yet 90 per cent of the total sample had said, before the questions were put, that in general courts were too lenient. Another study was based on actual newspaper coverage of a case, and on the court transcript. Of those who saw the newspaper account, 63 per cent thought the sentence too lenient; but 52 per cent of those who saw the transcript thought it was too harsh. It was also found in a nationwide survey that 74 per cent seriously overestimated the proportion of crimes that involved violence.

Finally, three public opinion polls in Britain reflect similar views. The first was carried out by National Opinion Polls for the *Observer* newspaper, in conjunction with the Prison Reform Trust. It found that 85 per cent of a sample of 988 thought it was a good idea to make some offenders do community service instead of going to prison, and 66 per cent wanted to make them pay compensation to their victims (Shaw, 1982: 20). A year later, MARPLAN found in a survey of 718 people for BBC Broadcasting Research Department that 93 per cent thought offenders should have to 'make good the consequences of their crime wherever possible', and 63 per cent thought that the money from fines should go to victims. Less than half thought it a good idea for offenders to meet the victim of their crime, but the question was apparently asked very baldly, and the concept was at that time little known in Britain, so perhaps it is surprising that as many as 40 per cent supported the idea. It is noteworthy that 83 per cent thought that the present system is not 'perfectly fair to victims', although only 55 per cent favoured spending ratepayers' money on schemes to help victims (BBC, 1983). Similarly, the London Weekend Television series 'Once a thief . . .?' commissioned an NOP poll which found that three-quarters of those questioned thought that more convicted adult offenders should be made to take part in community service instead of being sent to prison (Morgan, 1986).

This review has not addressed itself to a fundamental question: *should* public opinion in general, or the views of victims in particular, affect sentencing? In individual cases, most people in this country who stopped to think for a moment (how many respondents to opinion polls fall into that category?) would probably agree that it should not. Sentencing is already inconsistent enough, despite the efforts of the courts. The general level of sentencing is another matter. If it were possible to say that certain sentences were more likely to be effective, whether for deterrence or rehabilitation, that might serve as a basis; but it isn't. We are left with the courts' attempt to make sentences consistent with each other, which they can do to some extent, although they exclude from their minds the fact that the scale of penalties could be halved, or for that matter doubled, and still retain its internal consistency. There is no 'right' punitive sentence for any offence, except in relation to other sentences.

What these surveys show, however, is that many members of the public, including victims, are ready to shift the whole basis of the debate. Instead of debating, as judges and magistrates do, whether to use harsh or lenient punishment, a substantial number of people are beginning to say 'use reparative sanctions *instead of* punishment'. (Admittedly some suggest using both, but this is difficult to enforce in practice.) The Criminal Justice Act 1972 was in tune with this when it introduced community service orders (except that it did not specify that they should be regarded as reparative rather than punitive, with confusing results). The Act of 1982 took it a stage further by authorizing courts to impose compensation orders as a sole sanction. Perhaps it is time for courts to move towards a restorative sentencing philosophy.

Note

This chapter is reprinted by permission from *Justice of the Peace*, 151 (7), 14 February 1987: 105–7. Some further references are given by Immarigeon (1986).

References

BBC Broadcasting Research Department (1983) 'Results of a [*sic*] opinion poll carried out . . . by MARPLAN'. Unpublished report.
Doob, Anthony N. and Julian V. Roberts (1983) *Sentencing: An Analysis of the Public's View of Sentencing*. Ottawa: Department of Justice.
Galaway, Burt (1983) 'A survey of public acceptance of restitution as an alternative

to imprisonment for property offenders'. Unpublished paper. Wellington, New Zealand, Justice Department.

Gandy, John Thomas (1975) 'Community attitudes towards creative restitution and punishment'. Unpublished dissertation, University of Denver.

Gandy, John Thomas (1978) 'Attitudes towards the use of restitution', in J. Hudson and B. Galaway (eds), *Offender Restitution in Theory and Action*. Lexington, Mass.: Lexington Books. pp. 119–29. (Quoted by Shapland et al., 1985.)

Gandy, John Thomas and Burt Galaway (1980) 'Restitution as a sanction for offenders: a public's view', in J. Hudson and B. Galaway (eds), *Victims, Offenders and Alternative Sanctions*. Lexington, Mass.: Lexington Books. pp. 89–100.

Henderson, Joel H. and G. Thomas Gitchoff (1981) 'Victim perceptions of alternatives to incarceration: an exploratory study'. Unpublished paper, San Diego State University, Criminal Justice Administration.

Hough, Mike (1985) 'The impact of victimization: findings from the 1984 British Crime Survey', *Victimology* 10 (1–4): 488–97.

Hough, Mike and Pat Mayhew (1983) *The British Crime Survey: First Report*, Home Office Research Study 76. London: HMSO.

Hough, Mike and David Moxon (1985) 'Dealing with offenders: popular opinion and the views of victims. Findings from the British Crime Survey', *Howard Journal*, 24 (3): 160–75.

Hudson, Joe et al. (1980) *National Assessment of Adult Restitution Programs: Final Report*. University of Minnesota, School of Social Development.

Immarigeon, Russ (1986) 'Surveys reveal broad support for alternative sentencing', *National Prison Project Journal*, 9 (Fall): 1–4.

Maguire, Mike (1982) *Burglary in a Dwelling*. London: Heinemann.

Morgan, Jeff (1986) *Once a thief . . .?* London: London Weekend Television, Community Unit.

Shapland, Joanna et al. (1985) *Victims in the Criminal Justice System*. Aldershot: Gower.

Shaw, Stephen (1982) *The People's Justice: A Major Poll of Public Attitudes on Crime and Punishment*. London: Prison Reform Trust.

Van Dijk, J.J.M. (1984) 'Public perceptions and concerns: on the pragmatic and ideological aspects of public attitudes towards crime control', conference paper, later published in Dutch in *Justitiële Verkenningen*, 1985 (1).

Wright, Martin (1977) 'Nobody came: criminal justice and the needs of victims', *Howard Journal* 16 (1): 22–31.

Prospects

Burt Galaway

This volume reports on a wide range of conceptional and theoretical issues and programme developments regarding the use of mediation in relation to criminal and juvenile justice matters. The essays present theoretical concerns and practical experience from around the world and illustrate the use of mediation in such diverse countries as Japan, Finland, France, the Federal Republic of Germany, the United Kingdom, Canada, and the United States. Issues have emerged on which the authors take varying positions; but these issues must be addressed and resolved, in one way or another, to provide direction for the further development of mediation as a strategy for resolving criminal and juvenile justice matters. The emerging issues relate to the fit between mediation and the purposes of criminal law as well as the structures for the administration of criminal law.

The authors express two recurring differences. Should mediation programmes be administered by agencies outside the criminal and juvenile justice system or by staff of criminal justice agencies? Should mediation be an alternative to criminal and juvenile justice processing, or incorporated within juvenile and criminal justice systems to be used as a part of the programmes required of offenders, or can both approaches develop side by side? Margaret Shaw describes a mediation programme in New York which operates, in conjunction with social services, to divert juvenile status offenders and their parents from the juvenile justice system. Jean-Pierre Bonafé-Schmitt analyses mediation in France as a diversion from the justice system (both civil and criminal) and as a reaction to the bureaucratization of justice: 'the judicial machinery . . . is no longer adapted to the evolution of society towards greater decentralization, demands for more active participation by citizens, and the search for greater autonomy in relation to state structures.'

Mark Chupp believes that victim/offender reconciliation (VORP) should operate outside formal juvenile or adult justice systems. In contrast with this is Dean Peachey's description of the development of the original Victim/Offender Reconciliation Program in Kitchener, Ontario. The programme started with a probation officer who worked with a local church organization to develop and administer the VORP concept; after a Supreme Court decision that courts had been delegating too much discretion to probation officers, he was forced to move organizationally further away from the justice system and, consequently, the VORP has had difficulty sustaining the needed flow of referrals.

The Exeter scheme (Veevers), Coventry programme (Ruddick), and the programme at Rochester Youth Custody Centre (Launay and Murray) are mediation programmes working within the criminal justice system. The Exeter programme operates as an alternative to other types of juvenile justice system processing, but with close administrative ties to the juvenile justice system, including staffing by system staff, suggesting that it is an extension of the juvenile justice system. The Coventry programme receives referrals after adjudication for victim/offender mediation prior to sentencing. The programme has attempted to distance itself administratively from the justice system, expects participation to be voluntary on the part of both offenders and victims, stresses therapeutic and educational goods, places relatively little emphasis on monetary restitution, and does not perceive victim/offender agreements as being incorporated into the sentence. Reports, however, are made to the courts and the programme operates in close cooperation with courts, suggesting that it may be an extension rather than replacement for the justice process. The Dünkel and Rössner review of legal provision and programme developments in Germany, Austria, and Switzerland indicates that interest in mediation is a recognition of victim needs through development of a more victim-oriented and less punitive criminal and juvenile justice process; existing legal provision can be used to 'steer criminal law in the direction of reconciliatory conflict resolution . . . for which the aim might be the restoration of peace'. Martti Grönfors raises concern that mediation in Finland has shifted from a community-based alternative to one of justice system-influenced programming further serving as an extension to the justice system.

John Harding, from observation of the British experience, concludes that: 'the lessons of mediation, of a more reconciliative approach to justice issues, have to be absorbed by mainstream staff, if programmes are not to be written off as marginal, irrelevant and elitist.'

The administrative relationship of mediation programmes to the criminal or juvenile justice system may be dependent on the purpose of mediation. Is mediation appropriate to the purposes of

the criminal justice system? Or, do mediation programmes fulfil
other purposes which may not be compatible with juvenile and
criminal justice? Mediation was perceived as contributing to either
retributive or utilitarian goals of justice systems. Watson, Boucherat,
and Davis perceive restitution, which may be arrived at through a
process in mediation, as contributing to the retributive goals of
justice systems; they conceptualize the possibility of both coerced
and noncoerced (such as apology) restitution and, while the latter
cannot be ordered, its presence or absence is an appropriate consideration at sentencing. Mediation has also been advanced as useful for accomplishing utilitarian goals of criminal justice. Launay
and Murray believe that meetings between groups of offenders and
groups of victims perform an educational function for both victims
and offenders and may contribute to the rehabilitation of the
offenders. Ruddick stresses the therapeutic goals of mediation in
the Coventry programme; Veevers sees mediation as a rehabilitation tool for juvenile offenders; and Shaw identifies mediation
between juvenile status offenders and their parents as supportive of
other types of rehabilitative treatment. Umbreit and Chupp
emphasize the healing, reconciling nature of the mediation experience for both victims and offenders. John Haley, in his analysis of
Japanese criminal procedures and crime statistics, argues that the
emphasis on confession, repentance, and forgiveness in Japanese
criminal procedure contributes to the low Japanese crime rate. A
third, more practical, purpose for mediation might be to reduce
overload on the justice system by providing an alternative mechanism for dealing with less serious offences so that system resources
can be concentrated on the relatively more serious offences. Volpe
discusses the prospects as well as problems of mediation for police;
police officers may serve as mediators, or mediation programmes
may provide an alternative referral resource for police. In either
situation mediation may become a mechanism for police to dispose
of a matter rather than activate the criminal justice system.

An additional purpose, not typically associated with the juvenile
and criminal justice system, is put forth by the proponents of victim/
offender reconciliation programmes. Chupp, who describes the
mediation procedures in these programmes, is clear that the
primary, and perhaps only, purpose is to effect a reconciliation
between offender and victim. Umbreit takes a similar position in his
analysis of several cases in which VORP procedures were used with
victims of violent crime and their offenders; he emphasizes the
healing nature which the mediation process may have for the victim
and argues that this may be due to a sense of reconciliation. If one
accepts strengthening or maintaining social cohesion as a legitimate

goal of juvenile and criminal justice, then the goal of reconciliation may find a fit with juvenile and criminal justice goals.

Despite differing positions on the relation to juvenile and criminal justice system administration and the purposes of these programmes, mediation, as represented by the thrust of the chapters in this volume, clearly represents a significant departure from traditional and current ideas about the purpose and administration of juvenile and criminal justice. These chapters and programmes emphasize the role and opportunities of the victim, and focus on resolving the dispute between the victim and the offender in an orderly manner. Reeves expresses concern, however, that interest in mediation should not detract from provision of other victim services such as victims support schemes, and urges careful thought on the rationale for inviting victim participation. She argues that neither repayment of losses nor retaining ownership of conflict by individuals rather than having it stolen away by professionals will provide solid ground for victim participation; but the opportunity to put negative experience to a positive use and to receive an apology may be appealing to some victims and may provide a rationale for victim participation in mediation with offenders. She cautions that victim attitude and state of mind are to be the basis for inviting victims to meet their offenders. This process may contribute to other public purposes, and suggestions are made that the public may be better served through mediation processes than by the traditional juvenile and criminal justice procedures. Martin Wright, in a review of a series of international surveys of the public and of crime victims, finds evidence to support the proposition that both crime victims and the general public will be supportive of the use of restitution as a strategy for use with offenders and their victims. He interprets the evidence as suggesting that citizens want to change the focus of the debate, from whether the system is being too harsh or too lenient, to whether the current system should be replaced with procedures designed to bring about settlement by permitting victims and offenders to participate in the solution to the problem created by the offence. Mediation holds promise as a set of procedures for achieving settlement; programme experiences are that the majority of victims will participate in mediation if offered the opportunity.

One of the troubling issues is that of extending further social control over the offender. Chupp and Veevers deal with this by insisting that offender participation be voluntary. But, as Sally Merry points out, voluntariness is difficult to determine for programmes which operate in close cooperation with justice system officials, resulting in the possibility that offenders may be subject to sanctions for failure to participate. The Coates and Gehm research indicates that, even in programmes in which staff consider offender participation to be voluntary, offenders do not see it that way, and, contrary to the views of programme staff, perceive their participation as part of the punishment for their offences. Sally Merry raises a more fundamental question derived from her study of mediation in status offender cases. She suggests that mediation may be a mechanism by which middle- and upper-class professionals impose their particular dispute settlement procedures – negotiations involving verbal activity – on the lower classes. While her findings suggest that the young people and parents involved in the mediation programme were satisfied and found it helpful, she raises a fundamental question as to whether attempts to shift the dispute settlement mechanisms used by lower classes away from a more confrontational style (such as traditionally used by trade unions and civil rights movements) to a style involving more emphasis on negotiation and compromise will effectively serve the long-term interests of these classes who enter into negotiations from a position of power disadvantage. Conversely, mediation programmes, especially if introduced in schools, might offer opportunities for the less articulate to learn the combination of assertiveness and negotiating skills which the middle classes find so much to their advantage.

Where does this leave us in terms of the future for victim/offender mediation of disputes which might become juvenile or criminal justice matters? Is victim/offender mediation a passing fad? Will it take its place alongside more formal systems of justice and lead to the judicial pluralism suggested by Bonafé-Schmitt? Will mediation come to replace much of the work of the juvenile and criminal justice system, or can the juvenile and criminal justice systems be transformed, with victim/offender mediation becoming an integral part of the systems? The answer to these questions must, of course, await the future. But we see developments in society which suggest that victim/offender mediation may expand from the current pilot efforts and play a more significant role, either within the criminal and juvenile justice systems or as alternatives to these systems. There are four developments which may come together to result in either the replacement or the transformation of adult and juvenile justice. First is the cancerous growth of the prison industry, which is devouring huge amounts of public money at a time when public budgets are severely stressed and major domestic needs are being underfunded. The willingness of taxpayers to continue such a wasteful expenditure may be diminishing to the point that serious consideration can be given to other approaches to dealing with offenders. Second, the continuing renewal of interest in crime victims and interest in providing victims with an opportunity for meaningful participation in dispute resolution may contribute to strengthening the use of mediation. Third, there may be growing disenchantment with present systems for the administration of adult and juvenile justice, which appear to be relatively ineffective in responding to the crime problem, and which, in their largely de-humanizing approach to responding to offenders, be criminogenic. Finally, as Martin Wright has pointed out in his review of the research, there is strong public support for replacing traditional concepts of punishment, at least with property offenders, with notions of reparation and mediation. At the end of the eighteenth and early nineteenth centuries, we replaced corporal and capital punishment and transportation with prisons and jails as the pre-ferred form of penalty for offenders. But the basic principle remains retributive, although some countries cling to the vain hope that prisons rehabilitate people. Perhaps the late twentieth and early twenty-first centuries will mark the replacement of prisons and jails with the restorative principle of mediation and reparation.

Index

COOKING WITH YOUR INSTANT POT